John Newton, Josiah Bull

Letters by the Rev. John Newton of Olney and St. Mary Woolnoth

John Newton, Josiah Bull

Letters by the Rev. John Newton of Olney and St. Mary Woolnoth

ISBN/EAN: 9783744687362

Printed in Europe, USA, Canada, Australia, Japan

Cover: Foto ©Thomas Meinert / pixelio.de

More available books at **www.hansebooks.com**

Bequeathed

to

The University of Toronto Library

by

The late Maurice Hutton,
M.A., LL.D.
Principal of University College
1901=1928

Letters

BY THE

REV. JOHN NEWTON.

Uniform with the present Volume.

JOHN NEWTON OF OLNEY
AND ST. MARY WOOLNOTH.

AN AUTOBIOGRAPHY AND NARRATIVE,

COMPILED CHIEFLY FROM HIS DIARY AND OTHER UNPUBLISHED DOCUMENTS.

BY

THE REV. JOSIAH BULL, M.A.

8vo. 5s., *cloth boards.*

"John Newton was a man so good and useful, and in his early life, as contrasted with his subsequent career, was so romantic, that a complete narrative is, on every account, desirable. . . . . We very heartily commend this work, which will now be the standard memoir of a good and holy man."—*British Quarterly Review.*

"The book is replete with interesting details. It contains so much that is fresh in the Diary and Letters which Mr. Bull has supplied, that it is entitled to be spoken of as a distinct book from former biographies of this good man."—*Christian Observer.*

Letters

BY THE

REV. JOHN NEWTON

OF OLNEY AND ST. MARY WOOLNOTH.

Including several never before Published.

WITH

BIOGRAPHICAL SKETCHES

and Illustrative Notes.

BY THE

REV. JOSIAH BULL, M.A.,

Author of "John Newton; an Autobiography and Narrative."

LONDON:
THE RELIGIOUS TRACT SOCIETY,
56, PATERNOSTER ROW; 65, ST. PAUL'S CHURCHYARD;
AND 164, PICCADILLY.

LONDON: PRINTED BY WILLIAM CLOWES AND SONS, STAMFORD STREET
AND CHARING CROSS.

PREFACE.

If John Newton is not "facile princeps" of the writers of religious letters he certainly occupies a most distinguished place among them; and if the age of such letter-writing is now very much a thing of the past, there is yet a permanent value and interest in these productions of Newton. We have abundant evidence in the life of this good man that his letters were perused "with avidity and delight" wherever they were known, and that they were to a singular extent instrumental of good. Such testimonies came to him from all quarters. Mr. Newton's conviction of a special call to this service is evident from his reply, addressed, at the close of his life, to a friend who was speaking to him of the benefit he had derived from his letters, "Yes," he said, "the Lord saw I should be most useful by *them*." Hence his extraordinary diligence in this work. Not only were *Omicron, Cardiphonia,* and *Letters to a Wife,* published by himself, but there are also his *Posthumous Letters,* and several separate volumes published by his friends, together with very many more which have never seen the light.

Cardiphonia was the happy title which the poet Cowper suggested to Mr. Newton for the principal volumes of his letters, and they are truly *the voice of the heart*. It is an apt and beautiful description of them; for it must be remembered that, with the exception of *Omicron's Letters*, none of these productions were originally intended for publication. Written by a man of large Christian experience, of clear and discriminating views of truth, and of deep sympathy with those he addresses, these letters are, according to the various circumstances of his correspondents, designed to guide and direct, to comfort, or, if need be, with all tenderness to reprove, while they often become the ardent effusions of Christian love towards those who formed the inner circle of his friends. They are full of wisdom and piety, rich in kindly feeling, written in easy flowing language, with many happy turns of expression, and often made striking by their simple yet ingenious illustrations.

Notwithstanding all this, the letters of Mr. Newton are now little known. *Cardiphonia* has become a scarce book; other published series have had but a limited circulation, while the posthumous letters are well nigh buried in the six-volume edition of our Author's works. It is believed that the recent publication of *Newton's Life* has awakened a fresh interest in his memory; and it has been suggested to the Editor to prepare a Selection of his letters as a companion volume to that work. From the space to which he is limited their number is few, as compared with the many Mr. Newton wrote. He has been kindly furnished with some letters never before published; and for this and other help, he would here return his grateful thanks. To A. C. Hobart Seymour, Esq., he is under special obligation for the interest he has taken in this work, and the valuable assistance he has afforded.

There are one or two features in this volume it may be well to notice. It has been thought desirable to introduce each series of letters with a slight biographical sketch of the correspondent to whom such letters are addressed. The wish on the part of the reader for such information is natural and justifiable, as greatly enhancing his interest in their perusal. The remote period at which these letters were written renders it possible, without any impropriety, to gratify this feeling. Such an arrangement has another advantage. It is a pleasant relief to the attention which, otherwise, is apt to become wearied in the continuous perusal of a series of letters, especially of this class, however excellent in themselves, where there is otherwise no natural break nor pause. Wherever it has been necessary for explanation, notes have been added to throw light on the subject to which reference is made.

One other remark may be added. A tone of panegyric it may be thought, runs through most of the biographical sketches, bringing all their subjects up to the same high level of Christian experience and practice. The explanation is simple. The time when Mr. Newton wrote was a season of great spiritual revival in the Church. The godly people of that day were far more separate from the world than now, and exhibited, we venture to think, a higher type of the religious life. At all events, Mr. Newton's circle of friends was certainly amongst the best men and women of the day. Towards such, his affections were especially drawn out, and with them he came chiefly into contact and most entirely sympathized.

J. B.

South Norwood, Surrey:
November, 1869.

OLNEY CHURCH.

Contents.

	PAGE
THE REV. FRANCIS OKELEY	17
Sympathy with the spirit of his friend—Christian correspondence—Union in essential truths	18

MR. JOHN CATLETT	22
I. Danger of sceptical opinions—True idea of faith—His own experience—Liberty of conscience	22
II. A sceptic's thoughts in affliction—Nothing too hard for the Lord—Folly and danger of infidelity	26
III. The coronation—Anxious desires for the conversion of his correspondent	29
IV. Expressions of affectionate regard—Playful allusion to his neglect in writing—Vanity of earthly good	30
V. Pleasures of the world and religion contrasted—Religion alone gives its true relish to earthly good, and is the only support in trial	32

THE REV. MR. WHITFORD	38
I. Duty of bearing opposition in a right spirit—On looking to God for the wisdom which is profitable to direct	39
II. On seeking after peace and holiness—Vanity of religious disputation	41
III. Evil of a quarrelsome spirit—Ministers to be an example to their flock	44

Contents.

	PAGE
Miss MEDHURST	46
I. Duty and happiness of looking to Jesus	46
II. Trials ought not to discourage us—Gracious promises of future blessedness—Necessity of humility and watchfulness	49
III. How the unspeakable mercy of God in Christ ought to affect us—Happiness of the saints in heaven—Heaven near to us—Personal experience	52

Captain ALEXANDER CLUNIE	57
I. State of religion in Yorkshire—The blessed future—We know not how soon it may be ours—Duty of diligence and watchfulness	58
II. Ministerial responsibility, but comfort in the promises and power of God	60
III. Expressions of desire for more grace and trust in God	62
IV. Satan as an angel of light	63
V. Prayer-meetings at the Great House—The times call for prayer—Looking at present things in the light of eternity	65

Mrs. WILBERFORCE	68
I. Scriptural views of sin—Looking to Jesus	69
II. The Christian warfare—Assurance—Love to Christ	72
III. Sensible comfort—Rejoicing in God alone—Loss of friends—Deprivation of ordinances	76
IV. The Christian mourning and rejoicing—First love	79
V. Benefits of affliction	81
VI. Trials unwelcome but beneficial—Vanity of the world—The Lord our Guide and Strength	84

The EARL OF DARTMOUTH	87
I. On not doing the things we would	88
II. On doing the evil we would not	92
III. The existence of indwelling sin overruled for good	96
IV. Testimony of dying Christians to the reality of Gospel truth	99
V. Our entire dependence upon God for all we do—Blessedness of such a condition	102
VI. Things lawful, but not expedient	106

Contents.

	PAGE
THE REV. THOMAS JONES	112
I. On correcting evil tempers	113
II. Calvinism—Preaching to sinners	115

THE REV. THOMAS BOWMAN	119
I. Divine help in the work of the ministry—Guarding against extremes —Christian prudence	120
II. Experimental knowledge—Owen—Leighton—Edwards—Spread of the truth	123

DANIEL WEST, Esq.	126
I. How to regard our earthly comforts	127
II. What Christ is to his people, and what unprofitable servants they are to him	129
III. Christ the Great Physician—Spiritual prosperity at Olney	131
IV. The Life of faith a happy life	134
V. A striking portrait	136
VI. A blessed habitation	137

CAPTAIN SCOTT	140
I. A letter of encouragement in circumstances of trial	142
II. The benefit of religious exercises	144
III. On his friend leaving the army—Similarity of the experience in believing	145

MISS THORPE	147
The theatre	147

WILLIAM COWPER, Esq.	150
I. Encouragement against doubts and fears	151
II. Engagements in London—Desire to return home—Messages of kindness to his people	154
III. Franks—An accident—The spring—Hope of his friend's restoration	155
IV. Beating the parish boundaries—Further reference to his friend's state of mind—Request for some sketches	157

V. Interruption in his work—Thelyphthora—Present of oysters—Congregation at St. Mary Woolnoth 161
VI. Disappointments of authors—The praise or blame of mortals of little account 164

The Rev. JOSHUA SYMONDS 167

I. Degrees of glory—Christians not to be measured by gifts or services 168
II. On evidences of our spiritual state 171
III. Regret at not speaking to edification—The Moravians . . 174
IV. Satan's opportunity—Our ingratitude—The divine patience . 175
V. Happiness of his situation in London—Sympathy with all true Christians, whatever their name 177

The Rev. MATTHEW POWLEY 179

I. Baxter—What a Christian ought to be 180
II. Dependence on God—Personal experience . . . 183
III. Christian prudence 185

Miss DELAFIELD (afterwards Mrs. Cardale) . 187

I. Blessing of God's presence—Frames and faith 187
II. Christian intercourse—Disadvantages of being from home—The path of duty the right path 189

The Rev. WILLIAM HOWELL 192

I. Depression arising from affliction—Christ our Helper—The imperfections of our services no reason for despair 193
II. Christ saves to the uttermost—Sin of unbelief—True grace . 196
III. The only true satisfaction in religion—Humility learned by suffering—Hutchinsonianism 201

The Rev. JOHN RYLAND, Jun. 204

I. The church safe in the keeping of Christ—Falls of professors . 205
II. A sight of the Heavenly King 206
III. Following Christ—The soul a besieged city 207

Contents.

	PAGE
JOSEPH FOSTER BARHAM, Esq.	209
I. How trials are to be estimated	210
II. The lessons of Christian experience	211
III. Self-complaints	213
IV. Divine sovereignty in the sufferings of believers—Christian friendship	214
Miss MARY BARHAM	217
I. On Christ carrying on his work in the hearts of his people	217
II. Christian growth gradual—Special manifestations	219
Mrs. TALBOT	223
I. Consolation in affliction	224
II. On a true estimate of ourselves—Communion of saints	227
III. Our imperfect state here not a ground of distrust—Holiness of sinners and angels—Views of death	230
Mrs. PLACE	234
I. Prayer in perilous times—The changes and disappointments of the present state contrasted with the glories of the future	234
II. Danger of London professors—What Jesus is to his people	237
The Rev. THOMAS SCOTT	240
I. Athanasian creed—Subscription—Religious knowledge gradual	243
II. Sincere inquirers after truth—The Trinity—The way of salvation not a matter of doubt	248
III. The New Birth—Its fruits—The Gospel designed for man as a sinner—Human depravity—Error respecting the apostle Paul	253
IV. Predestination—Divine sovereignty—Man made willing by the power of God	260
V. Reason and Scripture—Faith and works—God not the author of sin—Fruits of faith	266
Mrs. THORNTON	272
I. On maintaining a right spirit towards those who differ from us—Fault of some evangelical preachers—Divinity of Christ	273
II. Sympathy of Jesus	277
III. How to bear afflictions	279

	PAGE
Mrs. GARDINER	282
I. Deprivation of Gospel ordinances—Simplicity of Gospel truth—Doubts and fears	282
II. Satan's assaults, and how to meet them	286

The Rev. WILLIAM ROSE	289
I. On being kept by the power of God	289
II. Congratulation—Danger of prosperity—World at its best estate vanity	291
III. Growing old—Gratitude for mercies—Looking to the future	295

The Rev. WILLIAM BULL	298
I. Presence of the Lord, its blessed effects—His own state of mind—Occupations	300
II. Duty and benefit of exercising charity and patience—Expressions of regard—A speckled bird	303
III. Forgetfulness — A pleasant visit — Requests his friend's prayers	305
IV. An invitation	306
V. A troublesome lodger	307
VI. An accident at Norwich—Providence of God	308
VII. Comfort in the loss of friends—Special reference to the death of Mrs. Newton	310
VIII. His friendship unbroken — Requests his friend's prayers in his old age	312
IX. Still able to preach—Miss Catlett's illness	315

The Rev. W. BARLASS	317
I. Satan's temptations — Humiliating thoughts from his former condition	318
II. His own experience—False zeal—Uncertainty of earthly good	322

Miss FLOWER (afterwards Mrs. Dawson)	326
I. How to overcome the snares of the world	326
II. King Alphonso's folly—Happiness of the married state—Sketch of sermon—A believer's complaints—How to meet them	329

III. Regret at their separation	334
IV. Desire for her spiritual welfare—Lot's wife—Renewed expressions of friendship	336
V. On compliance with the practices of the world	339
VI. Knowledge of our hearts—What may be learnt from children—Deprivation of ordinances	341

Mrs. HANNAH MORE ... 346

I. Loss of rural scenery, but other sights more attractive—Spiritual blessings to be obtained only from Christ, to whom we must come as sinners—The perception of spiritual things gradual	347
II. Idolatrous love of his wife—Creature love and divine love	351
III. Case of the poet Cowper—Lessons to be learnt from it—Reference to his own circumstances	355
IV. Suffering for righteousness' sake—The providence of God in the events of the times	358

The Rev. JOHN CAMPBELL ... 362

I. Intellect and heart—Fuller on the Calvinistic and Socinian systems	363
II. Interest in the work of God—Our sufficiency of Him—Dreams—Holiness of men and angels—Dying experiences	365
III. Special manifestations of God to the soul—Toleration and Romanism	369
IV. Calvinism and Arminianism—Secret prayer	372
V. Itinerant labours in Scotland—Prosperity at St. Mary's—Personal experience	374
VI. Evil of pride—Religion and politics	377

The Rev. JAMES COFFIN and Mrs. COFFIN ... 379

I. False humility—Flight of time	379
II. Simple faith	381
III. Advice about accepting another living	383
IV. Strong and weak faith—Witness of the Spirit	386
V. Benefits of change—Earthly blessings God's gifts—Arguments against discouragement	389
VI. On serving God in the ordinary duties of life—Doing what we can	392
VII. Illness of Miss Catlett—Desire to glorify God by submission to his will	395

Contents.

	PAGE
THOMAS RING, Esq., M.D., AND Mrs. RING	399
I. Recollections of the past—Sympathy with his friends in their devotedness to God, and in their religious advantages	400
II. A tour—God's providence—Preparation for the future—Mr. Simeon—True use of life	404
III. On the death of Mr. Cadogan	407
THE HON. AND REV. W. B. CADOGAN	410
I. Desire to visit him—God's wondrous grace in calling men to his service, and keeping them faithful in it	411
II. Value of afflictions to a minister	414

LETTERS OF NEWTON.

The Rev. Francis Okeley.

MR. OKELEY was born in Bedford in the year 1719, was educated at the Charterhouse school, and afterwards at St. John's College, Cambridge, where he took his Bachelor's degree. It does not appear under what circumstances he became decided for God; but that decision was real, and led to an entire change in Mr. Okeley's future course. With an earnest desire to preach the gospel to his fellow men, he became impatient of his college life, and supposing that he should be under considerable restraint if he entered the ministry in the church of England, he determined to sacrifice his prospect of a fellowship with his Charterhouse exhibition, and to join the United Brethren, with whose church order and doctrine he became acquainted, and whose zeal and devotedness had, probably, won his regard. He accordingly left the university, and subsequently received ordination in the Brethren's church. Whether before or after this we do not know, but about the time of Mr. Newton's acquaintance with him, Mr. Okeley seems to have been associated with the well-known Rev. B. Ingham, in preaching in Yorkshire, and subsequently we find, according to a statement in the *Life and Times of the Countess of Huntingdon*, that in connection with the Rev. Jacob Rogers, he was labouring with great success in the promotion of the truth in Bedfordshire.

Mr. Okeley was at one time desirous to re-enter the Church of England that so he might have a more settled sphere of labour, but he could not bring himself to submit to re-ordination. He fixed his abode, as a Moravian minister, at Northampton, where he continued for twenty years, labouring also, with much success, among the members of the Society in some of the neighbouring villages. Mr. Okeley's last days were spent in his native town, where he occasionally ministered in the Moravian chapel. He died at Bedford in the year 1794, greatly beloved and honoured.

In addition to these statements, kindly given us by a surviving representative of Mr. Okeley, we have Mr. Newton's testimony to the spirit of meekness and love so manifest in this good man; and the Editor is able to speak, from the evidence of several letters in his possession addressed by Mr. Okeley to the Rev. W. Bull, both to his piety and learning.

It will be seen that, in arranging the letters of this volume, we have followed the order of their dates at the commencement of each series. The following letter to Mr. Okeley is not, however, actually the earliest in point of time, but it is placed at the beginning of the volume, because it seemed from the nature of its contents to form an appropriate introduction to it.

To the REV. FRANCIS OKELEY.

Sympathy with the spirit of his friend—Christian correspondence—Union in essential truths.

April 3, 1759.

DEAR SIR,—You see I have prevented you in your promise of writing first; and, having found a pretext for troubling Mr. ———, I was willing to venture upon you without any, unless you will let me plead a desire of showing you how welcome your correspondence would be to me. I know not if my heart was ever more united to any person, in so short a space of time, than to you; and what engaged me so much was, the spirit of meekness and of love (that peculiar and inimitable mark of true Christianity) which I observed in you. I mean it not to your praise. May all the praise be to Him, from whom every good and perfect gift cometh, who alone maketh the best to differ from the worst. But I think I may well mention, to your encouragement, that all who conversed with you greatly regret your speedy departure; and I am persuaded, the same temper, the same candour, will make you acceptable, honourable, and useful, wherever you go. Blessed are the poor in spirit, the meek, the merciful, and the peace-makers; they shall obtain the mercy they want, and possess the peace they love. They shall inherit the earth. The earth, sinful and miserable as it is, shall be worthy to be called an inheritance to them, for they shall enjoy a comparative heaven in it. They shall be called the children of God, though dignified with no title among men. Alas! how much are these things overlooked, even by many who, I would hope, are real believers! Methinks a very different spirit from that of the church of Laodicea is to be seen amongst us, though perhaps it is not easy to say which is the best of the two. That was neither cold nor hot, this *(mirabile dictu)* is both cold and hot at once, and both to the extreme. Hot, hasty, and arbitrary in those few things where mediocrity is a virtue; but cool and remiss in those great points, where the application of the whole heart and soul and mind and strength is so absolutely necessary, and so positively enjoined. Surely there is too much room for this observation, and I perhaps stand self-condemned in making it. . . .

I hope to hear soon and often from you. I number my Christian correspondents among my principal blessings,—a few judicious, pious friends, to whom, when I can get leisure to write, I send my heart by turns. I can trust them with my inmost sentiments, and can write with no more disguise than I think. I shall rejoice to add you to the number, if you can agree to take me as I am, (as I think you will,) and suffer me to commit my whole self to paper, without respect to names, parties, and sentiments. I endeavour to observe my Lord's command, to call no man master upon earth; yet I desire to own and honour the image of God wherever I find it. I dare not say I have no bigotry, for I know not myself, and remember to my shame that formerly, when I ignorantly professed myself free from it, I was indeed overrun with it; but this I can say, I allow it not; I strive and pray against it; and thus far by the grace of God I have attained, that I find my heart as much united to many who differ from me in some points, as to any who agree with me in all. I set no value upon any doctrinal truth, further than it has a tendency to promote practical holiness. If others should think those things hindrances, which I judge to be helps in this respect, I am content they should go on in their own way, according to the light God has given them, provided they will agree with me εν τω Επαναγκες.* If it should be asked, Which are the necessary things? I answer, Those in which the spiritual worshippers of all ages and countries have been agreed. Those, on the contrary, are mere subordinate matters, in which the best of men, those who have been the most eminent for faith, prayer, humility, and nearness to God, always have been, and still are, divided in their judgments. Upon this plan, I should think it no hard matter to draw up a form of sound words, (whether dignified with the name of a creed or no, I care not,) to which true believers of all sorts and sizes would unanimously subscribe. Suppose it ran something in the

* In things necessary.

following manner: I believe that sin is the most hateful thing in the world; that I and all men are by nature in a state of wrath and depravity, utterly unable to sustain the penalty, or to fulfil the commands of God's holy law; and that we have no sufficiency of ourselves to think a good thought. I believe that Jesus Christ is the chief among ten thousands; that He came into the world to save the chief of sinners, by making a propitiation for sin by his death, by paying a perfect obedience to the law, in our behalf; and that He is now exalted on high, to give repentance and remission of sins to all that believe; and that He ever liveth to make intercession for us. I believe that the Holy Spirit (the gift of God, through Jesus Christ) is the sure and only guide into all truth, and the common privilege of all believers; and under his influence, I believe the Holy Scriptures are able to make us wise unto salvation, and to furnish us thoroughly for every good work. I believe that love to God, and to man for God's sake, is the essence of religion, and the fulfilling of the law; that without holiness no man shall see the Lord: that those who, by a patient course in well doing, seek glory, honour, and immortality, shall receive eternal life; and I believe that this reward is not of debt but of grace, even to the praise and glory of that grace, whereby He has made us accepted in the Beloved. Amen.

I pretend not to accuracy in this hasty draught; they are only outlines, which if you please to retouch, and fill up at your leisure, I hope you will favour me with a sight of it. I fear I have tired you. I shall only add my prayers, that the Lord may be with you, and crown your labours of love with success, that you may hereafter shine among those who have been instrumental in turning many to righteousness. I am, etc.

Mr. John Catlett.

MR. CATLETT, one of Mrs. Newton's brothers, was by profession a solicitor. He was a man of the world, and had imbibed infidel notions. It was Mr. Newton's great anxiety when he himself became acquainted with the truth to be the instrument of reclaiming one so nearly connected with him from these fatal errors. It is evident that they were held with great tenacity, and advocated with all the skill which a man of ability could employ in their defence.

The perusal of Mr. Newton's letters, in which he attempts to persuade his brother-in-law to a better mind, will show the wisdom, force, and Christian temper in which they are written.

Mr. Catlett died, after a short illness, at a comparatively early age, in December of the year 1764, and it may be hoped with some better ground of future happiness than infidelity could afford him. The reference to his death in Mr. Newton's *Diary* is very brief, but we have found the following passage in a letter addressed to Mrs. Wilberforce some time after Mr. Catlett's death. Mr. Newton says, "My other brother was an infidel till about the last year of his life, but there is reason to believe that he was savingly changed before he died." There is little doubt that the allusion is to Mr. John Catlett; and if so, Mr. Newton must have been truly thankful to God in the reflection that his earnest and prayerful efforts had not been made in vain.

To Mr. John Catlett.

LETTER I.—Danger of sceptical opinions—True idea of faith—His own experience—Liberty of conscience.

DEAR BROTHER, . . . I know not what to say to the bulk of your letter. A continuation of those prayers and good wishes, which you allow to be so charitable, is the best I can offer. Nothing but the real regard I have for you would make me so often resume an argument I have so little success in enforcing. In this case I know that none but He who made the heart can have access to it; yet, as He is often pleased to make use of mean and unlikely instruments that the glory of his own work may more fully appear, I am not willing to desist.

It was formerly my unhappy folly to busy myself in perverting others to as great a degree of infidelity as my own. I am now desirous to repair the mischief I have done as far as I am able; and how ought I to strive when duty and friendship engage me! I must use plain terms with you. I look upon your opinions as dangerous to profess, and destruction to persist in. My own experiences are as good as mathematical demonstrations to me. I beg you would reflect on my case. I was one of the loudest in the free-thinking strain. Do you think I changed in a whim or a frolic? You are pleased to express a good opinion of my understanding. Why then will you suppose that a change was effected in my whole conduct and behaviour, so that in one day I became diametrically opposite to what I was the day before, and continued so without an hour's alteration to this instant (I mean as to principle, though I continually fall short in my practice). Why, I say, must this proceed from caprice, and without a cause suitable to the effect, which is not a jot less surprising than for a man born blind to obtain his sight?

As to what you say of the impossibility of forcing ourselves to believe, I must call it downright sophistry. I acknowledge that belief is not immediately in our power, but the means are. If I should undertake to move a body of a thousand pounds weight, you ought not thence to infer that I pretended to lift it. It is sufficient if I can contrive a purchase (as we call it) upon mathematical principles, that shall enable me to do it, without requiring any person to help me. The allusion will hold in our argument. Faith is the gift of God, but then He is always ready to bestow it. When I was first brought to consider the evil of my life, and to endeavour at amendment, the same difficulty lay in my way. I could not pretend to say in my prayers that I believed the gospel. Alas! I did not at that time believe a word of it. I was confounded, but not convinced. However, it pleased God (as I am firmly persuaded) to lead me to the following resolution: Though I am not assured of the truth of the New Testament, yet I cannot be certain that it is false, I will endeavour therefore, if I mistake, that it shall be on the safe side. I will take its truth for granted. I will study the promises and comply with the commands I find there, and if it did indeed proceed from God, He who revealed it, and sees my sincerity in trying to quit my prejudices may, nay, if that is his word indeed, He undoubtedly will, assist me and enable me to understand it by degrees, till at length I believe it from the bottom of my heart.

This way of reasoning I dare recommend to any one; and in this view I will not come behind you in extolling the Divine mercy and goodness. It is not reasoning but neglecting to reason, and to extend conclusions to their just consequences, that I condemn as the vice of the age. What you call liberty of conscience is nothing but carelessness and inconsideration in matters of the highest importance, which the All-just Being (a term which you seem fond of) will never allow in rational creatures, whom He has endowed with a capacity of distinguishing right from wrong. I would wish you to consider that the fitness of things is fixed invariably. Our debates will make no alterations in them; and notwithstanding you suppose we agree in essentials, I fear, shall I say, or I hope, that we differ extremely. I would not subscribe to the best system I could pick out of your letters for a thousand such toys as made the great Alexander weep.

I must say that you gentlemen professors are very arrogant in your decisions. You modestly comprise at least ninety-nine parts in a hundred of our own and every civilized nation under the rank of weak enthusiastic creatures, and every two or three lines deny to others the liberty you claim for yourselves, and this is the general strain. I am not angry at being included with so much good company, and could glory in the reproach, but that I consider it proceeds from you. But I must leave off for want of room. Lodge some sort of an answer for me at Liverpool, for which place I hope to set out in about three weeks.

I am, with true affection,
    Your most affectionate friend and
        Humble servant,
            JOHN NEWTON.

ST. KITT'S: *June* 28, 1753.

To Mr. John Catlett.

Letter II.—A sceptic's thoughts in affliction—Nothing too hard for the Lord—Folly and danger of infidelity.

1755.

Dear Brother,—I suppose you will receive many congratulations on your recovery from your late dangerous illness; most of them perhaps more sprightly and better turned, but none, I persuade myself, more sincere and affectionate than mine. I beg you would prepare yourself by this good opinion of me before you read further; and let the reality of my regard excuse what you may dislike in my manner of expressing it.

When a person is returned from a doubtful distant voyage, we are naturally led to inquire into the incidents he has met with, and the discoveries he has made. Indulge me in a curiosity of this kind, especially as my affection gives me an interest and concern in the event. You have been, my dear friend, upon the brink, the very edge of an eternal state; but God has restored you back to the world again. Did you meet with, or have you brought back nothing *new?* Did nothing occur to stop or turn your usual train of thought? Were your apprehensions of invisible things exactly the same in the height of your disorder, when you were cut off from the world and all its engagements, as when you were in perfect health, and in the highest enjoyment of your own inclinations? If you answer me, "Yes, all things are just the same as formerly, the difference between sickness and health only excepted," I am at a loss how to reply. I can only sigh and wonder;—*sigh*, that it should be thus with any, that it should be thus with you, whom I dearly love;—and *wonder*, since this unhappy case, strange as it seems in one view, is yet so frequent; why it was not always thus with myself, for long and often it was just so. . . . And though my case was in some respects uncommon, yet something like it is known by one and another every day; and I have myself conversed with many who, after a course of years spent in defending deistical principles, or indulging libertine practices, when they have thought themselves confirmed in their schemes, by the cool assent of what they then deemed impartial reason, have been, like me, brought to glory in the cross of Christ, and to live by that faith which they had before slighted and opposed. By these instances, I know that nothing is too hard for the Almighty. The same power which humbled me can undoubtedly bring down the most haughty infidel upon earth. . . .

I shall not at present trouble you in an argumentative way. If, by dint of reasoning, I could effect some change in your notions, my arguments, unless applied by a superior power, would still leave your heart unchanged and untouched. A man may give his assent to the gospel and be able to defend it against others, and yet not have his own spirit truly influenced by it. This thought I shall leave with you, that if your scheme be not true to a demonstration it must necessarily be false; for the issue is too important to make a doubt on the dangerous side tolerable. If the Christian could possibly be mistaken, he is still upon equal terms with those who pronounce him to be so; but if the deist be wrong (that is, if we are in the right), the consequence to him must be unavoidable and intolerable. This, you will say, is a trite argument. I own it; but, beaten as it is, it will never be worn out or answered. . . .

Remember that we must all, each one for himself, experience on which side the truth lies. I used a wrong word when I spoke of your *recovery*. Dear brother, look upon it as no more than a REPRIEVE; for you carry the sentence of death about with you still; and unless you should be cut off (which God of his infinite mercy prevent) by a sudden stroke, you will as surely lie on a dying bed as you have now got up from a bed of sickness. And remember, too (I can hardly bear to write it), that should you neglect my admonitions, they will all tend to render you more inexcusable. I have delivered my own soul by faithfully warning you. But if you will not examine the matter with that seriousness which it deserves,—if you will not look up to God, the former of your body and the preserver of your spirit, for direction and assistance how to please Him,—if you will have your reading and your conversation only on one side of the question,—if you will suffer mercies and providences, afflictions and deliverances, to pass unimproved and unacknowledged, and live in the world as though you were created only to eat, sleep, and play, and after a course of years to be extinguished like the snuff of a candle,—why, then, you must abide by the consequences. But, assuredly, sooner or later, God will meet you. My hearty, daily, constant prayer is, that it may be in a way of mercy, and that you may be added to the number of the trophies of rich, free, and sovereign grace. Amen. Your sister sends her love.

I am, yours, sincerely,

J. NEWTON.

CHATHAM: *July* 15, 1755.

To Mr. John Catlett.

LETTER III.—The Coronation—Anxious desires for the conversion of his Correspondent.

DEAR BROTHER, . . . You were at the coronation, no doubt. We shall be glad of a letter in your own way upon the subject. You know I am not very keen myself after these things; but your sister, grave as you think her, has still a laugh in reserve at your wit's service. Upon that happy occasion I laid aside one half of my recluseness, mixed with public company, waited upon the mayor at his house, and had the honour to stand as a kind of cypher in three long rows of a procession to the Exchange. Then the company were halved, quartered, and disjointed to all the inns and taverns in town; but none of them were good enough for me to solemnize such an evening. Therefore I deserted, went to Edmund-street,* drank tea, and spent the evening with an acquaintance of yours. In such a situation I envied neither the honours nor the pleasures of kings, queens, lords, or commons.

If any thing occurs before to-morrow's post worth your reading it shall be inserted. At present I am as unfurnished as Dr. Ratcliffe's library. Polly is in tolerable health, and I as usual. We live in peace, and want for nothing but a more grateful sense of our innumerable obligations to the God of our lives. I would ask you to pray for us, if I were sure you prayed for yourself; but whether you will thank me for it or not I must tell you that I pray often for you. Oh! how should I rejoice to see my wise brother begin to be suspected for

* Where he resided.

a fool. This must be before you will be truly wise in the best sense. And though there are comparatively but few persons of fine parts and great accomplishments, humbled by the plain and artless power of the gospel, yet it is my encouragement that some are. We have some scholars, some wits; nay, what is more, some attorneys and lawyers amongst us, and therefore I must not quite despair of you. Judge how dear you would be to me then, when even at present, *inter tot discrepantia*,* I can, with the greatest sincerity, subscribe myself,

Your most affectionate brother,
J. NEWTON.

Oct. 5, 1761.

To MR. JOHN CATLETT.

LETTER IV.—Expressions of affectionate regard—Playful allusion to his neglect in writing—Vanity of earthly good.

DEAR BROTHER, . . . You are, I suppose, pushing on to be a great man, and I wish you all reasonable success; but consider, what good will your money and offices and titles do you, if they will not suffer you to remember what you owe to yourself and to your friends. I tell you all your thousands (when you get them) will not purchase you such cordial well-wishers as two old-fashioned acquaintances (not to say a sister and a brother) who lie by neglected at Liverpool. Surely you could rise one quarter-of-an-hour sooner, once in six months, to retrieve an opportunity of favouring us with a letter.

However, to encourage you, I send you herewith a free and absolute pardon for all that is past, and exempt you from the trouble of apologies of every kind, real or

* When in so many things we differ.

imaginary, provided that, before you go down to Chatham this Christmas, you testify your repentance by your amendment. Otherwise, expect a letter upon coarse paper, in a coarse style, as tart as vinegar, as bitter as wormwood, as angry as my Lord B——p of G——.

We go on in the usual way. Polly has often slight complaints, but is seldom very ill. Her constitution is tender and feeble; but many stronger have gone before her, and at present she eats and sleeps, and looks as well as she did seven years ago. Our wealth is like our health, in a mediocrity. The God whom we serve does not see it good for us to be rich, but I trust He will give us what is needful and best, and I hope we do not envy those who ride in coaches.

My friend Mr. Haweis has lately published a volume of sermons. Can I persuade you to read them? Methinks they contain a plain appeal to a man of sense. I should wonder that any could deny the premises he lays down, or be indifferent to the consequences he draws, if I did not remember how it once was with myself. . . .

As I said before, I wish you success in your business. I would propose nothing inconsistent with a due regard to it. But can I bound my desires for you within such narrow limits? Allow me to wish you more lasting riches, greater honours, and better pleasures than this world can afford. Alas! what a poor acquisition to be what is usually called a thriving man for a few years, and then to drop unawares into an unknown eternity. How often do we see that when a man has just compassed his point, made his fortune, and is about to sit down to enjoy all his heart can wish, he is hastily called away! What a contrast between living to-day in affluence and pleasure, regardless of that great God who has made us, and to-morrow perhaps to be summoned away to appear, naked and alone, before his tribunal, to give an account what use we have made of the talents so long entrusted to us! I pray God to impress the thought upon your heart before it is too late. I cannot but think there will be something within you suggesting while you read, that what I hint may possibly be true.

I have tried both ways, and find that religion, I mean the true inward religion which is so generally scorned and opposed, does not destroy but greatly heightens the relish of temporal things. It teaches me to live comfortably here, as well as enables me to look with comfort beyond the grave. In this way I possess peace which in every other way I sought in vain.

I heartily commend you to the protection and teaching of God. We join in assuring you of our cordial love and esteem, and are, yours,

J. and M. NEWTON.

Dec. 17, 1762.

To MR. JOHN CATLETT.

LETTER V.—Pleasures of the world and of religion contrasted—Religion alone gives its true relish to earthly good, and is the only support in trial.

Feb. 8, 1763.

DEAR BROTHER,—Though I truly love you, and have no reason to doubt of the reality of your friendship to me; yet I cannot but apprehend that, notwithstanding our mutual regard, and my frequent attempts to be witty (if I could) for your diversion, there is something in most of my letters (which I cannot, dare not, wholly suppress) that disgusts and wearies you, and makes you less inclined to keep up a frequent intercourse than you would otherwise be. Rather than lose you quite, I will in general spare you as much as I can; but at present you must bear with me, and allow me full scope. You have given me a challenge, which I know not how to pass over; and since you so far justify my preaching, as to condescend to preach (in your way) yourself, permit me for this time to preach again, and to take some passages in your letter for my text.

In the present debate I will accept your compliment, and suppose myself to be, as you say, a man of sense. You allow, then, that *all* the sense is not on your side. This indeed you cannot deny; for whatever becomes of me, it is needless to tell you, that Hale, Boyle, and other great names I could mention, were men of as great penetration and judgment, had as good opportunities, and took as much pains to be informed of the truth, as any of the advocates for infidelity can pretend to. And you cannot, with any modesty or consistence, absolutely determine, that they had not as good grounds for thinking themselves right as you can have for concluding they were wrong.

But declining the advantage of human authority, I am content the point shall rest between you and me. And here I beg you to observe, that I have one evident advantage over you in judging, namely, that I have experienced the good and evil on *both* sides, and you only on *one*. If you were to send me an inventory of your pleasures, how charmingly your time runs on, and how dexterously it is divided between the coffee-houses, play-house, the card-table, and tavern, with intervals of balls, concerts, etc., I could answer that most of these I have tried and tried again, and know the utmost they can yield, and have seen enough of the rest most heartily to despise them all. Setting religion entirely out of the question, I profess I had rather be a worm to crawl upon the ground, than to bear the name of MAN upon the poor terms of whiling away my life in an insipid round of such insignificant and unmanly trifles. I will return your own expression. I believe you to be a person of sense; but, alas! how do you prostitute your talents and capacity, how far do you act below yourself, if you know no higher purpose of life than these childish dissipations, together with the more serious business of rising early and sitting up late, to amass money, that you may be able to enlarge your expenses! I am sure while I lived in these things I found them unsatisfying and empty to the last degree; and the only advantage they afforded (miserable are they who are forced to *deem* it an advantage) was, that they often relieved me from the trouble and burden of thinking. If you have any other pleasures than these, they are such as must be evil and inconvenient even upon your own plan; and therefore my friendship will not allow me to bring them into the account. I am willing to hope you do not stoop still lower in pursuit of satisfaction. Thus far we stand upon even ground. You know all that a life of pleasure can give, and I know it likewise.

On the other hand, if I should attempt to explain to you the source and streams of *my* best pleasures, such as a comfortable assurance of the pardon of my sins, and habitual communion with the God who made heaven and earth, a calm reliance on the Divine Providence, the cheering prospect of a better life in a better world, with the pleasing foretastes of heaven in my own soul; should I, or could I, tell you the pleasure I often find in reading the Scripture, in the exercise of prayer, and in that sort of preaching and conversation which you despise, I doubt not but you would think as meanly of my happiness as I do of yours. But here lies the difference, my dear friend, you condemn that which you have never tried. You know no more of these things than a blind man does of colours; and notwithstanding all your flourishes, I defy you to be at all times able to satisfy yourself, that things may not possibly be as I have represented them.

Besides, what do I lose, upon my plan, that should make me so worthy of your pity? Have you a quicker relish in the prudent use of temporal comforts? Do you think I do not eat my food with as much pleasure as you can do, though perhaps with less cost and variety? Is your sleep sounder than mine? Have not I as much satisfaction in social life? It is true, to join much with the gay fluttering tribe, who spend their days in laugh and sing-song, is equally contrary to my duty and inclination. But I have friends and acquaintance as well as you. Among the many who favour me with their esteem and friendship, there are some who are persons of sense, learning, wit, and (what perhaps may weigh as much with you) of fortune and distinction. And if you should say, "Ay, but they are all enthusiasts like yourself," you would say nothing to the purpose, since upon your maxim, that "happiness is according to opinion," it cannot be an objection, but the contrary, to have my acquaintance to my own taste. Thus much for the brighter side of your situation; or let me add one thing more. I know you have thoughts of marriage: do you think, if you should enter into this relation, your principles are calculated to make you more happy in it than I am? You are well acquainted with our family life: do you propose to know more of the peace and heart-felt joy of domestic union than I have known, and continue to know to this hour? I wish you may equal us; and if you do, we shall still be, as before, but upon even ground. I need not turn deist, to enjoy the best and the most that this life can afford.

But I need not tell you, that the present life is not made up of pleasurable incidents only. Pain, sickness, losses, disappointments, injuries, and affronts, will more or less, at one time or other, be our lot. And can you bear these trials better than I? You will not pretend to it. Let me appeal to yourself: how often do you toss and disquiet yourself, like a wild bull in a net, when things cross your expectations? As your thoughts are more engrossed by what you see, you must be more keenly sensible of what you feel. You cannot view these trials as appointed by a wise and heavenly Father, in subservience to your good; you cannot taste the sweetness of his promises, nor feel the secret supports of his strength, in an hour of affliction; you cannot so cast your burden and care upon him, as to find a sensible relief to your spirit thereby, nor can you see his hand engaged and employed in effecting your deliverance. Of these things you know no more than of the art of flying; but I seriously assure you, and I believe my testimony will go further with you than my judgment, that they are realities, and that I have found them to be so. When my worldly concerns have been most thorny and discouraging, I have once and again felt the most of that peace which the world can neither give nor take away. However, I may state the case still lower. You do pretty well among your friends; but how do you like being alone? Would you not give something for that happy secret, which could enable you to pass a rainy day pleasantly without the assistance of business, company, or amusement? Would it not mortify you greatly to travel for a week in an unfrequented road, where you should meet with no lively incidents to recruit and raise your spirits? Alas! what a poor scheme of pleasure is yours, that will not support an interval of reflection!

What you have heard is true; I have a few friends who meet at my house once a fortnight, and we spend an hour or two in worshipping the God who made us. And can this move your indignation, or your compassion? Does it show a much nobler spirit, a more refined way of thinking, to live altogether without God in the world? If I kept a card-assembly at those times, it would not displease you. How can you, as a person of sense, avoid being shocked at your own unhappy prejudice? But I remember how it was once with myself, and forbear to wonder. May He who has opened my eyes, open yours. He only can do it. I do not expect to convince you by any thing I can say as of myself; but if He be pleased to make use of me as his instrument, then you will be convinced. How should I then rejoice! I should rejoice to be useful to any one; but especially to you, whom I dearly love. May God show you your true self, and your true state; then you will attentively listen to what you now disdain to hear of, his goodness in providing redemption and pardon for the chief of sinners, through him who died upon the cross for sins not his own. Keep this letter by you at my request; and when you write, tell me that you receive it in good part, and that you still believe me to be

Your affectionate brother,
JOHN NEWTON.

The Rev. Mr. Whitford.

OUR information of Mr. Whitford is very scanty. He was an early correspondent of Mr. Newton, and seems to have been on very intimate terms with him during his residence at Liverpool. Mr. Whitford was originally connected with the Methodists, but afterwards became a minister of the Independent communion. During Mr. Newton's residence at Olney he received a visit from his old friend. It was in the year 1775. "The sight of him," says Mr. Newton, "revived the remembrance of many incidents long since passed." It is a somewhat singular fact that not long after this Mr. Drake, the Independent minister at Olney, being removed by death, Mr. Whitford became his successor, and as long as Mr. Newton remained in the country the intimacy of former years continued unimpaired.

It was a common practice in those days to preach sermons to the young at the beginning of the year, and at Olney Mr. Newton and his dissenting brethren did so on successive evenings, ministers and people attending each others' services. They were occasions of much interest; and Mr. Newton often speaks of them in his *Diary*. We introduce the following extract, both as referring to the subject of this notice, and as illustrating the truly Christian spirit of Mr. Newton: "In the evening heard Mr. Whitford's sermon to the young people. He was very faithful and earnest. May Thy blessing crown this threefold service. Help me to entreat Thy presence with the other ministers equally with myself. I beg that good may be done, and to be well pleased that all who serve Thee in the gospel may have a share in it, as instruments in Thy hands, without limiting my regard to names, parties, or persons. Such a spirit would be the best token for comfort and success to myself."

To the REV. MR. WHITFORD.

LETTER I.—Duty of bearing opposition in a right spirit—On looking to God for the wisdom which is profitable to direct.

August 31, 1757.

DEAR SIR,—I wish you much of that spirit which was in the apostle, which made him content to become all things to all men, that he might gain some. I am persuaded that love and humility are the highest attainments in the school of Christ, and the brightest evidences that He is indeed our Master. If any should seem inclined to treat you with less regard, because you are, or have been a Methodist teacher, you will find forbearance, meekness, and long-suffering, the most prevailing means to conquer their prejudices. Our Lord has not only taught us to expect persecution from the world, though this alone is a trial too hard for flesh and blood; but we must look for what is much more grievous to a renewed mind, to be in some respects slighted, censured, and misunderstood, even by our Christian brethren, and that, perhaps, in cases where we are really striving to promote the glory of God and the good of souls, and cannot, without the reproach of our consciences, alter our conduct, however glad we should be to have their approbation. Therefore we are required, not only to resist the world, the flesh, and the devil, but likewise to bear one another's burdens: which plainly intimates there will be something to be borne with on all hands; and happy indeed is he that is not offended. You may observe what unjust reports and surmises were received, even at Jerusalem, concerning the apostle Paul; and it seems he was condemned unheard, and that by many thousands too, Acts xxi. 20, 21 ; but we do not find he was at all ruffled, or that he sought to retort any thing upon them, though doubtless, had he been so disposed, he might have found something to have charged them with in his turn ; but he calmly and willingly complied with everything in his power to soften and convince them. Let us be followers of this pattern, so far as he was a follower of Christ; for even Christ pleased not himself. How did He bear with the mistakes, weakness, intemperate zeal, and imprudent proposals, of his disciples while on earth ; and how does He bear with the same things from you and me, and every one of his followers now? and do we, can we, think much to bear with each other for his sake? Have we all a full remission of ten thousand talents, which we owed him, and were utterly unable to pay, and do we wrangle amongst ourselves for a few pence ? God forbid!

If you should be numbered among the regular Independents, I advise you not to offend any of them by unnecessary singularities. I wish you not to part with any truth, or with any thing really expedient; but if the omitting any thing of an indifferent nature will obviate prejudices, and increase a mutual confidence, why should not so easy a sacrifice be made? Above all, my dear friend, let us keep close to the Lord in a way of prayer: He giveth wisdom that is profitable to direct; He is the Wonderful Counsellor; there is no teacher like him. Why do the living seek to the dead ? why do we weary our friends and ourselves, in running up and down, and turning over books for advice? If we shut our eyes upon the world and worldly things, and raise our thoughts upwards in humility and silence, should we not often hear the secret voice of the Spirit of God whispering to our hearts, and pointing out to us the way of truth and peace? Have we not often gone astray, and hurt either ourselves or our brethren, for want of attending to this divine instruction? Have we not sometimes mocked God, by pretending to ask direction from him, when we had fixed our determination beforehand? It is a great blessing to know that we are sincere; and next to this, to be convinced of our insincerity, and to pray against it.

I am, etc.

To the REV. MR. WHITFORD.

LETTER II.—On seeking after peace and holiness—Vanity of religious disputation.

November 21, 1757.

DEAR SIR,—Can you forgive so negligent a correspondent? I am indeed ashamed; but (if that is any good excuse) I use you no worse than my other friends. Whenever I write, I am obliged to begin with an apology; for, what with business and the incidental duties of every day, my time is always mortgaged before it comes into my hands, especially as I have so little skill in redeeming and improving it. I long to hear from you, and I long to see you; and indeed, from the terms of yours, I expected you here before this; which has been partly a cause of my delay. I have mislaid your letter, and cannot remember the particulars; in general, I remember you were well, and going on comfortably in your work; which was matter of joy to me; and my poor prayers are for you, that the Lord may own and prosper you more and more. The two great points we are called to pursue in this sinful divided world, are peace and holiness: I hope you are much in the study of them. These are the peculiar characteristics of a disciple of Jesus; they are the richest parts of the enjoyments of heaven; and so far as they are received into the heart, they bring down heaven upon earth; and they are more inseparably connected between themselves than some of us are aware of. The longer I live, the more I see of the vanity and the sinfulness of our unchristian disputes: they eat up the very vitals of religion. I grieve to think how often I have lost my time and my temper that way, in presuming to regulate the vineyards of others, when I have neglected my own; when the beam in my own eye has so contracted my sight, that I could discern nothing but the mote in my neighbour's. I am now desirous to choose a better part. Could I speak the publican's words with a proper feeling I wish not for the tongue of men or angels to fight about notions or sentiments. I allow that every branch of gospel truth is precious, that errors are abounding, and that it is our duty to bear an honest testimony to what the Lord has enabled us to find comfort in, and to instruct with meekness such as are willing to be instructed; but I cannot see it my duty, nay, I believe it would be my sin, to attempt to beat my notions into other people's heads. Too often I have attempted it in times past; but now I judge, that both my zeal and my weapons were carnal. When our dear Lord questioned Peter, after his fall and recovery, he said not, Art thou wise, learned, and eloquent? nay, he said not, Art thou clear and sound, and orthodox? But this only, "Lovest thou me?" An answer to this was sufficient then, why not now? Any other answer, we may believe, would have been insufficient then. If Peter had made the most pompous confession of his faith and sentiments, still the first question would have recurred, "Lovest thou me?" This is a Scripture precedent. Happy the preacher, whoever he be my heart and my prayers are with him, who can honestly and steadily appropriate Peter's answer. Such a man, I say, I am ready to hear, though he should be as much mistaken in some points as Peter afterwards appears to have been in others. What a 'pity it is, that Christians in succeeding ages should think the constraining force of the love of Christ too weak, and suppose the end better answered by forms, subscriptions, and questions of their own devising. I cannot acquit even those churches who judge themselves nearest the primitive rule in this respect: alas! will-worship and presumption may creep into the best external forms. But the misfortune both in churches and private Christians is, that we are too prone rather to compare ourselves with others, than to judge by the Scriptures; and while each can see that they give not into the errors and mistakes of the opposite party, both are ready to conclude that they are right; and thus it happens, that an attachment to a supposed gospel order will recommend a man sooner and further to some churches, than an eminency of gospel practice. . . . Let us endeavour to keep close to God, to be much in prayer, to watch carefully over our hearts, and leave the busy warm spirits to make the best of their work. The secret of the Lord is with them that fear him, and that wait on him continually; to these He will show his covenant, not notionally, but experimentally. A few minutes of the Spirit's teaching will furnish us with more real useful knowledge, than toiling through whole folios of commentators and expositors: they are useful in their places, and are not to be undervalued by those who can perhaps in general do better without them; but it will be our wisdom to deal less with the streams, and be more close in applying to the fountain-head. The Scripture itself, and the Spirit of God, are the best and the only sufficient expositors of Scripture. Whatever men have valuable in their writings, they got it hence; and the way is as open to us as to any of them. There is nothing required but a teachable, humble spirit; and learning, as it is commonly called, is not necessary in order to this. I commend you to the grace of God, and remain,

Yours, etc.

To the REV. MR. WHITFORD.

LETTER III.—Evil of a quarrelsome spirit—Ministers to be an example to their flock.

July 29, 1761.

DEAR SIR,—Are the quarrels made up? Tell those who know what communion with Jesus is worth, that they will never be able to maintain it, if they give way to the workings of pride, jealousy, and anger. This will provoke the Lord to leave them dry, to command the clouds of his grace that they rain no rain upon them. These things are sure signs of a low frame, and a sure way to keep it so. Could they be prevailed upon, from a sense of the pardoning love of God to their own souls, to forgive each other as the Lord forgives us, freely, fully, without condition and without reserve, they would find this like breaking down a stone wall, which has hitherto shut up their prayers from the Lord's ears, and shut out his blessing from filling their hearts. Tell them I hope to hear that all animosities, little and big, are buried by mutual consent in the Redeemer's grave. Alas! the people of God have enemies enough: why, then, will they weaken their own hands? Why will they help their enemies to pull down the Lord's work? Why will they grieve those who wish them well, cause the weak to stumble, the wicked to rejoice, and bring a reproach upon their holy profession. Indeed this is no light matter: I wish it may not lead them to something worse: I wish they may be wise in time, lest Satan gain further advantage over them, and draw them to something that shall make them (as David did) roar under the pains of broken bones. But I must break off. May God give you wisdom, faithfulness, and patience; take care that you do not catch an angry spirit yourself, while you aim to suppress it in others: this will spoil all, and you will exhort, advise, and weep in vain. May you rather be an example and pattern to the flock; and in this view, be not surprised if you yourself meet some hard usage; rather rejoice, that you will thereby have an opportunity to exemplify your own rules, and to convince your people, that what you recommend to them you do not speak by *rote*, but from the experience of your heart. One end why our Lord was tempted, was for the encouragement of his poor followers, that they might know him to be a High Priest suited to them, having had a fellow-feeling in their distresses. For the like reason He appoints his ministers to be sorely exercised, both from without and within, that they may sympathize with their flock, and know in their own hearts the deceitfulness of sin, the infirmities of the flesh, and the way in which the Lord supports and bears with all that trust him. Therefore be not discouraged: usefulness and trials, comforts and crosses, strength and exercise go together. But remember He has said, "I will never leave thee, nor forsake thee: be thou faithful unto death, and I will give thee a crown of life." When you get to heaven, you will not complain of the way by which the Lord brought you. Farewell. Pray for us.

Yours, etc.

Miss Medhurst.

THE following letters are taken from Mr. Newton's sequel to *Cardiphonia*, published after his death. They are headed "Eighteen Letters addressed to several Ladies," principally however to Miss Medhurst. These ladies lived in Yorkshire, and were frequently visited by Mr. Newton in the several tours he made in that district, at the time of his residence in Liverpool. It is presumed that these friends lived near together, and sought each other's society that by religious intercourse they might promote their own spiritual life and devise plans of usefulness for the good of others. The strain of Mr. Newton's letters shows them to have been eminently devout women. Miss Medhurst was related to the Countess of Huntingdon.

To Miss Medhurst.

LETTER I.—Duty and happiness of looking to Jesus.

September 10, 1760.

DEAR MADAM,—I address my letter to you, but consider myself as writing to the whole of the little society I had the pleasure of meeting at your house, and at Miss K.'s. I still reflect with pleasure on the opportunities I was favoured with among you; and if, as I hope, my little visits were not unacceptable to each or any of you, let us not lose a moment in apologies or compliments to each other, but refer the whole praise to where it is wholly due. . . . . Though we can but lisp a little word about the Lord's goodness, yet when He is pleased to be near us, his presence and blessing can work by the meanest instrument, and cause our hearts to burn within us. . . .

The best advice I can send, or the best wish I can form

for you, is, that you may have an abiding and experimental sense of those words of the apostle which are just now upon my mind—"*Looking unto Jesus.*" The duty, the privilege, the safety, the unspeakable happiness, of a believer, are all comprised in that one sentence. Let us first pray that the eyes of our faith and understanding may be opened and strengthened; and then let us fix our whole regard upon him. But how are we to behold him? I answer, in the glass of his written word: there He is represented to us in a variety of views. The wicked world can see no form nor comeliness in the portraiture He has given of himself; yet blessed be God, there are those who can "behold his glory as the glory of the only begotten Son of God, full of grace and truth;" and while they behold it, they find themselves, "changed into the same image, from glory to glory," by the transforming influence of the Spirit. In vain we oppose reasonings and arguments, and resolutions, to beat down our corruptions, and to silence our fears; but a believing view of Jesus does the business. When heavy trials in life are appointed to us, and we are called to give up, or perhaps to pluck out, a right eye, it is an easy matter for a stander-by to say "Be comforted;" and it is as useless as easy; but a view of Jesus by faith comes home to the point. When we can fix our thoughts upon him, as laying aside all his honours, and submitting for our sakes to drink off the bitter cup of the wrath of God to the very dregs; and when we further consider, that He who thus suffered in our nature, who knows and sympathizes with all our weakness, is now the Supreme Disposer of all that concerns us, that He numbers the very hairs of our heads, appoints every trial we meet with in number, weight, and measure, and will suffer nothing to befall us but what shall contribute to our good, this view, I say, is a medicine suited to the disease, and powerfully reconciles us to every cross. So when a sense of sin prevails, and the tempter is permitted to assault us with dark and dreadful suggestions, it is easy for us to say, "Be not afraid;" but those who have tried well know, that looking to Jesus is the only and sure remedy in this case. If we can get a sight of him by faith, as He once hung between the two thieves, and as He now pleads within the vail, then we can defy sin and Satan, and give our challenge in the apostle's words, "Who is he that condemneth? It is Christ that died, yea rather that is risen again, who also maketh intercession for us." (Rom. viii. 34.) Again, are we almost afraid of being swallowed up by our many restless enemies? or, are we almost weary of our long pilgrimage through such a thorny, tedious, barren wilderness? A sight of Jesus, as Stephen saw him, crowned with glory, yet noticing all the sufferings of his poor servants, and just ready to receive them to himself, and make them partakers of his everlasting joy, this will raise the spirits and restore strength; this will animate us to hold on, and to hold out; this will do it and nothing but this can. So, if obedience be the thing in question, looking unto Jesus is the object that melts the soul into love and gratitude; and those who greatly love, and are greatly obliged find obedience easy. When Jesus is upon our thoughts, either in his humbled or his exalted state, either as bleeding on the cross, or as worshipped in our nature by all the host of heaven, then we can ask the apostle's question with a becoming disdain, "Shall we continue in sin that grace may abound? God forbid. What! shall I sin against my Lord, my Love, my Friend, who once died for my sins, and now lives and reigns on my behalf; who supports, and leads, and guides, and feeds me every day? God forbid. No; rather I would wish for a thousand hands and eyes, and feet, and tongues for ten thousand lives, that I might devote them all to his service. He should have all then; and surely He shall have all now. Alas, that in spite of myself there still remains something that resists his will! but I long and pray for its destruction; and I see a day coming when my wish shall be accomplished, and I shall be wholly and for ever the Lord's.

I am your affectionate servant.

To Miss Medhurst and her Friends.

LETTER II.—Trials ought not to discourage us—Gracious promises of future blessedness—Necessity of humility and watchfulness.

November 2, 1761.

MY DEAR SISTERS,—Your letter was welcome and comfortable. I praise the Lord on your behalf. . . You have reason, indeed, to praise the Lord, and so have I. Oh, what a wonder of grace, that He should say to those who were children of wrath, "Behold I go to my Father and to your Father, to my God and to your God!" "Henceforth I call you not servants but friends," and as a proof of it, "Ask what ye will, and it shall be done unto you." Here are words sufficient either to raise our souls up to heaven, or to bring heaven down to our souls, according to that glorious promise which to many is fulfilled even in our day. (Rev. xxi. 3.)

Let us not be greatly discouraged at the many tribulations, difficulties, and disappointments which lie in the path that leads to glory, seeing our Lord has told us before, has made a suitable provision for every case we can meet with, and is himself always near to those that call upon him, a sure refuge and almighty strength, a neverfailing ever-present help in every time of trouble; seeing likewise that He himself was a man of sorrows, and acquainted with grief for our sakes. He drank off the full cup of unmixed wrath for us; shall we then refuse to taste of the cup of affliction at his appointment, especially when his wisdom and love prepare it for us, and proportion every circumstance to our strength; when He put it into our hands, not in anger but in tender mercy, to do us good, to bring us near to himself; and when He sweetens every bitter draught with those comforts which none but He can give? Let us rather say, None of these things move us, neither do we count anything on this side eternity dear, so that we may finish our course with joy, and run with patience the race which is set before us.

The time is short, the world is passing away, all its cares and all its vanities will soon be at an end. Yet a little while, and "we shall see him as He is." Every vail shall be taken away, every seeming frown be removed from his face, and every tear wiped away from ours. We shall also be like him. Even now, when we contemplate his glory as shining in the glass of the Gospel, we feel ourselves, in some measure, transformed into the same image: what a sudden, wonderful, and abiding change shall we then experience, when He shall shine directly, immediately, and eternally upon our souls without one interposing cloud between! Because He lives, we shall live also; because He shines, we likewise shall shine forth as the sun, in our Saviour's brightness: then shall we sing with understanding those glorious songs, Isaiah xii. lxi. 10; Rev. v. 9, and vii. 10, without one jarring note, or one wandering thought for ever.

"Having therefore these promises, dearly beloved, let

us cleanse ourselves from all filthiness of flesh and spirit, perfecting holiness in the fear of the Lord." "Let us lay aside every weight;" "Let us not be slothful," but followers of that cloud of witnesses who in every age have set their word to the truth and power of God. They were once as poor as we are now; they had their complaints and their fears, their enemies, and temptations; they were exercised with a wicked heart, and a wicked world; and I doubt not but many of them, in a fit of unbelief, have been ready to conclude, "I shall one day perish by the hand of Saul;" but at length the "blood of Jesus, and the word of his testimony," made them more than conquerors; and now their warfare is finished, they are "before the throne of God and the Lamb, and shall go no more out." While we are sighing, they are singing; while we are fighting they are triumphing; but their song, their triumph, their joy, will not be complete till we are called up to join them. The Lord prepare us for, and hasten, the happy hour.

The strain of your present experience requires you, above all others, to be humble and watchful; and I trust you are so. However, it is our duty to exhort one another daily. One of the greatest contradictions in human nature, and the very strongest proof of our depravity is, that the communication of extraordinary measures of divine comforts, which in their own nature have a direct tendency to humble, has, through our corruptions, sometimes a contrary effect; not in the present moment, indeed that is impossible, but afterwards. Paul himself was liable to danger in this matter: see 2 Cor. xii. 7. You will do well, therefore, to entreat the Lord to give you a double guard on this side, to keep you in continual remembrance what you were by nature, and what you still are in yourselves. We are often forced to buy this recollection by bitter experience.

Again, be watchful. Many eyes are upon you. Satan envies you. Oh! he hates to see any persons, especially young persons, walking very closely with God. So far as he is permitted, he will spread snares for your feet every hour. He desires to have you, "that he may sift you as wheat." Further, the world observes you: many would rejoice at your halting; and a little thing in you would give them more pleasure and advantage in opposing the truth, than a greater slip in others who are content to plod on in the common way. . . . I do not mention these things to discourage you. No, were every leaf upon the trees, and every blade of grass a sworn enemy to our souls, we are safe under the shadow of our great Rock; the blessing is his and He will not withhold it; but the appointed means are our part, and it is our wisdom and happiness to be found waiting on him in the use of them.

Yours, etc.

To Miss Medhurst.

LETTER III.—How the unspeakable mercy of God in Christ ought to affect us—Happiness of the saints in heaven—Heaven near to us—Personal experience.

May 25, 1762.

MY DEAR MADAM,—How can I begin better than with the apostle's words,—"Blessed be the God and Father of our Lord Jesus Christ, the Father of mercies and God of all consolation, who, according to His abundant mercy, hath begotten us again to a lively hope by the resurrection of Jesus Christ from the dead?" What a fountain of life and joy and praise is here! that the God and Father of our Lord Jesus Christ should vouchsafe to be our Father, our God; that He who is the source of all mercy and consolation, should direct the stream of his fulness to flow into our souls; that when we are dead in sins, He should look upon us and bid us live; that when we were sunk into the depths of despair, He should send his word and raise us to a lively hope; that He should give us such a bright prospect, and such a sweet foretaste of the exceeding riches of his glory! Oh! who can say which is the most wonderful part of this wonderful subject? that He should provide such a happiness for such hell-deserving wretches, and that He should commend his great and undeserved love to us in such a wonderful way, as to give his own and his only Son to be born, to be buffeted, to be crucified for us? Alas! alas! for our stupidity, that we can write, or hear, or speak of these things, with so little feeling, affection, and fruitfulness. Oh! that the power of God would set my heart and pen at liberty while writing, and fill your heart while reading, that we may rejoice with joy unspeakable and full of glory! Oh this unbelief! Why can we not pierce through the vail of flesh and blood, and by faith behold the humble worship of heaven? What countless multitudes have gone before us in the path that leads to that kingdom! They were, in their time, followers of an unseen Saviour, as we are now; but now they see him as He is, face to face in all his glory, and in all his love. With them are joined the innumerable hosts of angels. Angels and saints however distinguished, are joined in one happiness and one employment. Even now, while I write, and while you read, they are praising the Lamb that was slain, and casting their crowns at his feet. And perhaps this scene is not so far distant as we imagine. Where is heaven? Is it some millions of leagues from us, far beyond the sun and the fixed stars? What have immortal spirits to do with space and place? Who knows, but a heaven-born soul, who is freed from the clog of this vile body, and filled with all the fulness of God, may pass as easily and quickly from one verge of the creation to the other, as our thoughts can change and fly from east to west, from the past to the future? Perhaps, even now, we live in the midst of this glorious assembly; heaven is there where our God and Saviour displays himself; and do not you feel him near you, nearer than any of his visible works? Perhaps there is nothing but this thin partition of flesh and blood between us and those blessed spirits that are before the throne. If our eyes were open, we should see the mountains around us covered with chariots and horses of fire; if our ears were unstopped we should hear the praises of our great Immanuel resounding in the air, as once the shepherds heard. What a comfortable meditation is this to strengthen our weak faith in such a dark declining day as this, when sense would almost persuade us that we are left to serve God alone! When we are wearied with looking on careless sinners and backsliding professors, let us remember that we have invisible friends present in our assemblies, our conferences, and our closets, who watch over us, and, in ways which we cannot possibly conceive, are helpers in our joy, and witnesses of our conflicts. They are with us now, and we shall soon be with them. Ah! how little does the vain world think of the privileges and the company in which a believer lives! and, what is worse, how faintly do we think of these things ourselves! and this is the reason we are so full of fears and complaints, so prone to distrust the Lord's methods of dealing with us, and so easily drawn aside to seek for something to rest upon in creatures like ourselves.

With respect to my own experience, I have little now to add, to what I have formerly offered, at least, little variety; for, in one sense, every new day is filled up with new things, new mercies on the Lord's part, new ingratitude on mine; instances of the vileness of my nature, and new proofs of the power of sovereign pardoning grace; new hills of difficulty, new valleys of humiliation; and now and then (though alas! very short and seldom), new glimpses of what I would be, and where I would be. The everlasting love of God, the unspeakable merits of Christ's righteousness, and the absolute freeness of the gospel promises, these form the threefold cord by which my soul maintains a hold of that which is within the vail. Sin, Satan, and unbelief, often attempt to make me let go, and cast away my confidence, but as yet they have not prevailed. No thanks to me who am weaker than water, but I am wonderfully kept by the mighty power of God, who is pleased to take my part, and therefore I trust in him that they never shall prevail against me. A vile sinner, indeed, I am; but since God, who alone has a right to judge, is pleased to justify the believer in Jesus, who is there that shall dare condemn? I bless the Lord for that comfortable portion of Scripture, Zech. iii. 1—5. When the Lord is pleased to pluck a brand out of the fire to save it from perishing, what power in heaven or earth, shall presume or prevail to put it in again? No, He has done it, and who can reverse it? He has said it, and his word shall stand. And I humbly believe (Lord help my unbelief) that not one good thing shall fail of all that the Lord my God has, in his word, spoken to me of.

Yet, alas! I must still charge myself with a great want

of watchfulness and diligence; the enemy cannot destroy my foundation, but he spreads many nets for my feet, to weaken me, and to interrupt my peace; and, to my shame I must confess, he too often prevails. The Lord in great mercy preserves me from such sins as would openly dishonour my profession; and a mercy I desire to esteem it, for I can infer from my heart what my life would be, if I were left to myself. I hate sin: I long to be delivered from it; but it is still in me, and works in me. "O wretched man that I am, who shall deliver me?" I bless God for Jesus Christ my Lord. To his grace I commend each of you.

I am yours.

Captain Alexander Clunie.

CAPT. CLUNIE was engaged in the West-Indian trade; and, as the readers of Mr. Newton's Life will remember, the latter became acquainted with him at St. Kitts on his homeward voyage from Africa in the year 1754. From the time of his conversion the peculiar circumstances of Mr. Newton had very much shut him out from all intercourse with professing Christians. The Lord was pleased to lead him, he tells us, for the space of about six years in a secret way, and his religious conceptions were in many respects confused. He proceeds to say that the conversation of Capt. Clunie, a man of experience in the things of God, was greatly helpful to him. Amongst other advices, his friend urged upon him the duty of a public profession, and directed him to some of his religious connections in London, and especially to his pastor, the Rev. Samuel Brewer of Stepney.* In a letter of Mr. Newton to Capt. Clunie, dated Liverpool, Feb. 1761, he further says: "I often think of you with peculiar pleasure and thankfulness, as by you the Lord was pleased to bring me to know his people. Your conversation was much blessed to me at St. Kitts; and the little knowledge I have of men and things took its first rise thence."

The connection thus formed became very close and

---

* Mr. Brewer was pastor of the Independent Church at Stepney, a position which he held for fifty years, from 1746 to 1796. He was a man of great worth, very successful in his ministry, and highly esteemed by all who knew him. Mr. Newton was introduced to Mr. Brewer, as stated above, by Captain Clunie, and speaks of the great pleasure and benefit he derived from his ministry and from intercourse with him. Some years afterwards, Mr. Newton writes of his kindness, saying that the intimacy between them had continued to that time, adding, "Of all my friends I am most deeply indebted to him." He speaks in the same strain of Mr. Brewer's visits to Olney at a subsequent period. Mr. Brewer's tenderness of spirit, his deep piety and sound judgment were bonds which united him very closely to Mr. Newton. See the Editor's Life of Newton, p. 58.

intimate. Mr. Newton always addressed Mr. Clunie as his "dear brother." In his letters to him, which are very frequent, Mr. Newton opens his whole heart to his friend, and is ever very solicitous for an interest in his prayers. Capt. Clunie was often at Olney and was sometimes accompanied by Mr. Brewer, whose friendship Mr. Newton greatly valued.

About the end of the year 1769 the health of Capt. Clunie began to fail; and, writing to him during his illness, Mr. Newton says, "You were remembered at our Bethel to-night. Our hearts, you may be assured, are much interested in your welfare. I hope to see the day when you will come to join us in praise to a prayer-hearing God." This however was not to be, for early in 1770 this truly excellent man, whose connection with Mr. Newton had proved so pleasant and so valuable, was removed to a better world.

To Captain Alexander Clunie.

Letter I.—State of religion in Yorkshire—The blessed Future—We know not how soon it may be ours—Duty of diligence and watchfulness.

LIVERPOOL: *May* 21, 1763.

DEAR BROTHER,—I have lately been a journey into Yorkshire, which is one reason why I have not written sooner. That is a flourishing country indeed, like Eden, the garden of the Lord, watered on every side by the streams of the Gospel. There the voice of the turtle is heard in all quarters, and multitudes rejoice in the light. I have a pretty large acquaintance there among various denominations, who, though they differ in some lesser things, are all agreed to exalt Jesus and his salvation. I do not mean that the truth is preached in every church and meeting through the county, but in many, perhaps in more proportionably than in any other part of the land,

and with greater effect both as to numbers, and as to the depth of the work in particular persons. It is very refreshing to go from place to place and find the same fruits of faith, love, joy and peace. What then shall it be ere long, when the Lord shall call us up to join with those who are now singing before the throne? What shall it be, when all the children of God, who in different ages and countries have been scattered abroad, shall be all gathered together, and enter into that glorious and eternal rest provided for them; when there shall not be one trace of sin or sorrow remaining, not one discordant note to be heard, nothing to disturb or defile, or alleviate the never-ceasing joy? Such is the hope to which God has called us: that day will as surely come, as the present day is already arrived; every moment brings on its approach. While I am writing and you are reading, we may say, "Now is our full salvation nearer." Many a weary step we have taken since the Lord first gave us to believe in his name; but we shall not have to tread the past way over again. Some difficulties may remain, but we know not how few: perhaps before we are aware, the Lord may cut short our conflict and say, Come up hither; or at the most it cannot be very long, and He who has been with us thus far, will be with us to the end. He knows how to manifest himself even here, to give more than He takes away, and to cause our consolations to exceed our greatest afflictions. And when we get safe home, we shall not complain that we have suffered too much in the way. We shall not say, Is this all I must expect after so much trouble? No, when we awake into that glorious world, we shall in an instant be satisfied with his likeness. One sight of Jesus as He is, will fill our hearts, and dry up all our tears. Let us then resign ourselves into his hands;

let us gird up the loins of our minds, be sober and hope to the end. Let us, like faithful servants, watch for our Lord's appearance, and pray earnestly that we may be found ready at his coming. We live in a trying time: how many erroneous principles and scandalous practices abound! how many fair professors miscarry! This should teach us to be jealous of ourselves. We may feel the same root of bitterness in our own hearts; and, if we stand when others fall, we have nothing of our own to boast. But neither need we be distressed and unbelieving: Jesus is able to keep us from falling. Let us be steady in the use of his instituted means, and sincerely desirous to abstain from all appearance of evil. The rest we may confidently leave to him, in whom whosoever trusts shall never be ashamed.

Mrs. Newton joins in respects to you and Mrs. Clunie. We beg a frequent remembrance in your prayers.

I am, etc.,

J. N.

To Captain Clunie.

Letter II.—Ministerial responsibility, but comfort in the promises and power of God.

Olney: *July* 26, 1766.

My dear Brother,—I seldom choose to let Semples go without a line; nor will I now, though I have little to offer. Indeed, we should never be weary of writing and reading about Jesus: if his name sounds warm in your heart, you may well call this a good letter, though I should not add a word more.

How fast the weeks return! We are again upon the eve of a sabbath. May the Lord give us much of his own Spirit on his own day. I trust I have a remembrance in your prayers. I need them much: my service is great. It is, indeed, no small thing to stand between God and the people, to divide the word of truth aright, to give every one their portion, to withstand the counter tides of opposition and popularity, and to press those truths upon others, the power of which, I, at times, feel so little of in my own soul. A cold, corrupt heart is uncomfortable company in the pulpit. Yet, in the midst of all my fears and unworthiness, I am enabled to cleave to the promise, and to rely on the power of the great Redeemer. I know I am engaged in the cause against which the gates of hell cannot prevail. If He died and rose again, if He ever lives to make intercession, there must be safety under the shadow of his wings: there would I lie. In his name I would lift up my banner; in his strength I would go forth, do what He enables me, then take shame to myself that I can do no better, and put my hand upon my mouth, confessing that I am dust and ashes,—less than the least of all his mercies.

I suppose you will get this before your next meeting at Mr. West's;* my heart will be with you there, and I and my dear friends attempting to pray for you all. May that little meeting be as a garden planted and watered by the Lord: may great grace be with your dear minister,† and with all the members; and may you and Mrs. Clunie grow up as plants of renown, and find every ordinance, opportunity, and providence sanctified to the good of your souls.

Yours, etc.,
J. N.

* The allusion is to a prayer meeting regularly held at the house of Mr. West.
† The Rev. S. Brewer of Stepney.

To Captain Clunie.

Letter III.—Expressions of desire for more grace and trust in God.

Olney: *Oct.* 12, 1766.

My dear Brother, . . . I have not written to you lately, because you had one with you who could tell you much of my mind. I have had my health perfectly, and all things have been well with us abroad and at home, only the common causes of complaint, arising from a depraved nature, and the workings of indwelling sin. I wish I was more humbled for them, and watchful against them. I trust I do, in some measure, know what manner of persons the Lord's redeemed ought to be; and I hope sincerely to be growing and pressing forward; but, indeed, I am not what I would be or should be. I would be thankful; few have more evident causes: I would be humble; none can have greater reason: I would be more spiritually-minded; for even *my* experience tells me all below is vanity; and surely my lot is peculiarly favoured, for the Lord has wonderfully prevented and exceeded my wishes on every hand; but without the light of his countenance all is faint and tasteless. Blessed be God for the news of a better world, where there will be no sin, change, nor defect for ever. And let us praise him, likewise, that He has appointed means of grace and seasons for refreshment here below, for a throne of grace, a precious Bible, and returning ordinances: these are valuable privileges; and so they appear to us when our hearts are in a lively frame. Then everything appears little and worthless, in comparison of communion with God. Oh, for a coal of fire from the heavenly altar to warm our frozen spirits! Oh, for a taste of love and a glimpse of glory, that we might mount up as with eagle's wings! Let us pray for each other.

Sunday morning.—I am unwilling to send the paper half empty, therefore would scribble something. Mrs. Newton came home well, but was yesterday morning seized with a complaint that has proved rather violent. . . . It is a comfort, under all changes, to be enabled to look to covenant love and special grace. The Lord has promised to direct, moderate, sanctify, and relieve every trial of every kind. I long to have a more entire submission to his will, and a more stedfast confidence in his word, to trust him and wait on him, to see his hand and praise his name in every circumstance of life great and small. The more of this spirit, the more heaven is begun upon earth. And why should we not trust him at all times? Which part of our past experience can charge him with unfaithfulness? Has He not done all things well? And is He not the same yesterday, to-day, and for ever? O my soul, wait thou only upon him. And may this be the desire and attainment of you and dear Mrs. Clunie.

The bells are just beginning to call me to church. Lord, meet me there, and pour forth thy good Spirit on all my fellow-labourers and fellow-worshippers. May you and yours taste to-day that He is gracious.

Our best love to you both. Remember us to all friends. Time presses.

I am, sincerely,

J. N.

To CAPTAIN CLUNIE.

LETTER IV.—Satan as an angel of light.

OLNEY: *Oct.* 19, 1766.

DEAR BROTHER,—I received your letter, and thank you for your intelligence. The Lord has brought us through another sabbath. I have been some time (in a morning) on Isaiah xlii.; to-day began the 5th verse. In the afternoon I spoke a little of Satan's trials, from 2 Cor. ii. 11. The good Lord keeps us from his delusions: he is always dangerous, but never more so than when he pleads for Gospel doctrines in order to abuse them, and when he tries to pass his counterfeit humility, zeal, and sanctity upon us for pure gold. No coiner can equal him for imitation. Where Christ has a church, he will have a synagogue; where the Spirit produces any graces, he, like the magicians of Egypt, will do something as like it, and yet as unlike it, as possible. He has a something that comes so near the Gospel, that it is called by St. Paul another gospel, and yet in reality it is no gospel at all. He deals much in half convictions, and almost Christians, but does not like thorough work. He will let people talk about grace as much as they please, and commend them for it, provided talking will satisfy them. They may be zealous either for the blood or the water or the Spirit, which they themselves choose, provided they will be content with one, to the neglect of the other two. He will preach free grace when he finds people willing to receive the notion, as an excuse and cloak for idleness. But, let him look and talk as he list, he is Satan still; and those who are experienced and watchful may discern his cloven foot hanging below his fine garment of light; and he is never more a devil than when he looks most like an angel. Let us beware of him; for many wise have been deceived, and many strong have been cast down by him. Let us continually apply to him who is able to keep us from falling, and to present us spotless in the end.

I remain, etc.,

J. N.

To Captain Clunie.

LETTER V.—Prayer meetings at the Great House—The times call for prayer—Looking at present things in the light of eternity.

OLNEY: *April* 1, 1769.

MY DEAR BROTHER, . . . On Thursday evening I preached a funeral sermon for Sally Perry, from Job xxxiii. 23, 24, which passage I hope and believe was remarkably verified in her case. I have been pretty full handed in preaching of late. I trust the Lord was graciously with us in most or all of the opportunities. We are going to remove our prayer meetings to the great room in the Great House,* which I do not know if you have seen. We proposed to open it next Tuesday evening; but if the present very sharp weather continues, we may perhaps defer it a week longer. It is a noble place, with a parlour behind it, and holds one hundred and thirty people conveniently. Pray for us that the Lord may be in the midst of us there; and that as He has now given us a Rehoboth, and has made room for us,

---

* The Great House, a mansion in Olney, commonly so designated, was the property of Lord Dartmouth. Being unoccupied, and Mr. Newton thinking its spacious rooms might be available for some of his religious services, he obtained the use of it in the first instance for the meetings of the children. He met them there once a week; but their numbers so increased that it was necessary to remove them to the chancel. Subsequently, as appears from this letter to Captain Clunie, the meetings for prayer and exhortation were held at the Great House. In Mr. Newton's Diary there are many interesting references to these gatherings. It was for this special occasion that two of the hymns in the Olney Collection were composed, the forty-third and forty-fourth of the second book—the first beginning, "O Lord, our languid frame inspire," by Mr. Newton, and the second, "Jesus, where'er thy people meet," by Mr. Cowper.

so that He may be pleased to add to our numbers, and make us fruitful in the land. Surely there is a need of prayer to disperse the clouds which seem to be gathering around us. Every newspaper brings us sad tidings from your great city, but I hope there will be mercy afforded for the sake of the Lord's remnant. Oh that all who know his name may be found crying day and night before him, that iniquity may not be our ruin! Then, at least, we shall have a mark set upon us, and find favour for ourselves if the sentence should be gone forth.

Saturday evening is returned again. How quick the time flies! Oh that we may have grace to number our days, and to begin to view the things of this world in that light which they will, doubtless, appear in when we are upon the point of leaving them. How many things, which are too apt to appear important now, and to engross too much of our time, and thoughts, and strength, will then be acknowledged as vain and trivial as the imperfect recollection of a morning dream! The Lord help us to judge now as we shall judge then, that all things on this side of the grave are of no real value further than they are improved in subservience to the will and glory of God; and that an hour's enjoyment of the light of his countenance is worth more than the wealth of the Indies and the power of kings. How often we are like Martha, cumbered about many things, though we say and (I hope) at the bottom believe, that one thing alone is needful. The Lord give us a believing, humble, spiritual frame of mind, and make it our earnest desire and prayer, that we may be more like the angels of God, who are always employed, and always happy, in doing his will and beholding his glory. The rest we may be content to leave to those who are strangers to the love of Jesus and the foretaste of heaven.

I have been attempting to pray that you and our friends in London may, together with us, behold the King in his beauty to-morrow; that we may, like David, be satisfied in our souls as with marrow and fatness, and feel something of what Thomas felt, when he put his finger upon the print of his nails and cried out with transport, My Lord and my God!

With our dear love to Mrs. Clunie and all friends,

I remain, etc.,

J. N.

Mrs. Wilberforce.

IN 1764 Mr. Newton went to London to receive ordination. He was compelled to stay several weeks, but that protracted stay, he says, gave him the opportunity of acquaintance with many whom, perhaps, he would otherwise have never known, and he adds: "I have cause for wonder, praise, and humiliation, when I think what favour the Lord gave me in the eyes of his people, some of rank and eminence." We think we are justified in the supposition that Mr. Newton, at that time, made the acquaintance of Mrs. Wilberforce, both from the circle to which he was then introduced, and from the fact that a few months afterwards his correspondence with her was commenced.

Mrs. Wilberforce was the wife of William Wilberforce, Esq., uncle to the celebrated statesman and philanthropist, William Wilberforce. With these relatives he spent some of his earlier years, and then, probably, received those religious impressions which were fully developed in after life. Mrs. Wilberforce was also sister to John Thornton, Esq. She was a remarkably godly woman, a lover of all true Christians, and ever anxious and ready with her influence and her wealth to promote the cause of Christ. Many of her letters to the Rev. William Bull are in the possession of the Editor, all of them breathing a most devout spirit.

Writing to Mrs. Wilberforce, in 1769, Mr. Newton says: "We are much obliged for your late visit, and I am glad to find that the Lord is pleased to give you some tokens of his presence, when you are with us, because I hope it will encourage you to come again." And speaking in another letter of praying specially on the Saturday evening for the Lord's ministers and people, Mr. Newton adds: "At such times I particularly remember those friends with whom I have gone to the house of God in company, consequently you are not forgotten. I can venture to assure you that if you have a value for our prayers you have a frequent share in them—yea, are loved and remembered by many here." Mrs. Wilberforce had visited Olney several times. When Mr. Newton went to reside in London, it was his practice to go regularly to the house of Mrs. Wilberforce, when she was in town, to conduct, what he terms, "parlour preaching." There at one time he expounded the Pilgrim's Progress.

Mrs. Wilberforce died at the close of the year 1788. From her dying bed she wrote a brief and touching letter to her friend, Mr. Bull. Referring to the decease of the Rev. J. Symonds of Bedford, a godly man, and much respected by Mrs. Wilberforce, "Happy," she says, "is the dear man who is gone to glory, now in the presence of Jesus, whom unseen he loved. My heart seemed to jump for joy. Things have an awful appearance, and such as you can be ill spared. Myself better and worse: Jesus as good as ever."

To Mrs. Wilberforce.

LETTER I.—Scriptural views of sin—Looking to Jesus.

July, 1764.

MY DEAR MADAM,—The complaints you make are inseparable from a spiritual acquaintance with our own hearts: I would not wish you to be less affected with a sense of indwelling sin. It becomes us to be humbled into the dust; yet our grief, though it cannot be too great, may be under a wrong direction; and if it leads us to impatience or distrust, it certainly is so.

Sin is the sickness of the soul, in itself mortal and incurable, as to any power in heaven or earth but that of the Lord Jesus only. But He is the great, the infallible Physician. Have we the privilege to know his name? Have we been enabled to put ourselves into his hand?

We have then no more to do but to attend his prescriptions, to be satisfied with his methods, and to wait his time. It is lawful to wish we were well; it is natural to groan, being burdened; but still He must and will take his own course with us; and however dissatisfied with ourselves, we ought still to be thankful that He has begun his work in us, and to believe that He will also make an end. Therefore, while we mourn, we should likewise rejoice; we should encourage ourselves to expect all that He has promised; and we should limit our expectations by his promises. We are sure, that when the Lord delivers us from the guilt and dominion of sin, He could with equal ease free us entirely from sin if He pleased. The doctrine of sinless perfection is not to be rejected, as though it were a thing simply impossible in itself, for nothing is too hard for the Lord, but because it is contrary to that method which He has chosen to proceed by. He has appointed that sanctification should be effected, and sin mortified, not at once completely, but by little and little; and doubtless He has wise reasons for it. Therefore, though we are to desire a growth in grace, we should at the same time acquiesce in his appointment, and not be discouraged nor despond, because we feel that conflict which his word informs us will only terminate with our lives.

Again, some of the first prayers which the Spirit of God teaches us to put up, are for a clearer sense of the sinfulness of sin, and our vileness on account of it. Now, if the Lord is pleased to answer your prayers in this respect, though it will afford you cause enough for humiliation, yet it should be received likewise with thankfulness, as a token for good. Your heart is not worse than it was formerly, only your spiritual knowledge is increased; and this is no small part of the growth in grace which you are thirsting after, to be truly humbled, and emptied, and made little in your own eyes.

Further, the examples of the saints recorded in Scripture prove (and indeed of the saints in general), that the greater measure any person has of the grace of God in truth, the more conscientious and lively they have been; and the more they have been favoured with assurances of the divine favour, so much the more deep and sensible their perception of indwelling sin and infirmity has always been: so it was with Job, Isaiah, Daniel, and Paul. It is likewise common to overcharge ourselves. Indeed, we cannot think ourselves worse than we really are; yet some things which abate the comfort and alacrity of our Christian profession are rather impediments than properly sinful, and will not be imputed to us by him who knows our frame, and remembers that we are but dust. Thus, to have an infirm memory, to be subject to disordered, irregular, or low spirits, are faults of the constitution, in which the will has no share, though they are all burdensome and oppressive, and sometimes needlessly so by our charging ourselves with guilt on their account. The same may be observed of the unspeakable and fierce suggestions of Satan, with which some persons are pestered, but which shall be laid to him from whom they proceed, and not to them who are troubled and terrified, because they are forced to feel them. Lastly, it is by the experience of these evils within ourselves, and by feeling our utter insufficiency, either to perform duty, or to withstand our enemies, that the Lord takes occasion to show us the suitableness, the sufficiency, the freeness, the unchangeableness of his power and grace. This is the inference St. Paul draws from his complaint, Rom. vii. 25, and he learnt it upon a trying occasion from the Lord's own mouth, 2 Cor. xii. 8, 9.

Let us, then, dear madam, be thankful and cheerful, and, while we take shame to ourselves, let us glorify God, by giving Jesus the honour due to his name. Though we are poor, He is rich; though we are weak, He is strong; though we have nothing, He possesses all things. He suffered for us; He calls us to be conformed to him in suffering. He conquered in his own person, and He will make each of his members more than conquerors in due season. It is good to have one eye upon ourselves, but the other should ever be fixed on him who stands in the relation of Saviour, Husband, Head, and Shepherd: in him we have righteousness, peace, and power. He can control all that we fear; so that, if our path should be through the fire or through the water, neither the flood shall drown us, nor the flame kindle upon us, and ere long He will cut short our conflicts, and say, Come up hither. "Then shall our grateful songs abound, and every tear be wiped away." Having such promises and assurances, let us lift up our banner in his name, and press on through every discouragement. . . .

I am, dear madam,

Your much obliged and affectionate servant,

JOHN NEWTON.

To MRS. WILBERFORCE.

LETTER II.—The Christian warfare—Assurance—Love to Christ.

September, 1764.

MY DEAR MADAM,—Your welfare I rejoice in; your warfare I understand something of. St. Paul describes his own case in a few words, "Without were fightings, within were fears." Does not this comprehend all you would say? And how are you to know experimentally either your own weakness or the power, wisdom, and grace of God, seasonably and sufficiently afforded, but by frequent and various trials? How are the graces of patience, resignation, meekness, and faith, to be discovered and increased, but by exercise? The Lord has chosen, called, and armed us for the fight; and shall we wish to be excused? Shall we not rather rejoice that we have the honour to appear in such a cause, under such a Captain, such a banner, and in such company? A complete suit of armour is provided, weapons not to be resisted, and precious balm to heal us if haply we receive a wound, and precious ointment to revive us when we are in danger of fainting. Further, we are assured of the victory beforehand; and oh what a crown is prepared for every conqueror, which Jesus, the righteous Judge, the gracious Saviour, shall place upon every faithful head with his own hand! Then let us not be weary and faint, for in due season we shall reap. The time is short; yet a little while, and the struggle of indwelling sin, and the contradiction of surrounding sinners, shall be known no more. You are blessed, because you hunger and thirst after righteousness. He whose name is Amen has said you shall be filled. To claim the promise is to make it our own; yet it is becoming us to practise submission and patience, not in temporals only, but also in spirituals. We should be ashamed and grieved at our slow progress, so far as it is properly chargeable to our remissness and miscarriage; yet we must not expect to receive every thing at once, but wait for a gradual increase; nor should we forget to be thankful for what we may account a little, in comparison of the much we suppose others have received. A little grace, a spark of true love to God, a grain of living faith, though small as mustard-seed, is worth a thousand worlds. One draught of the water of life gives interest in and earnest of the whole fountain. It becometh the Lord's people to be thankful; and to acknowledge his goodness in what we have received, is the surest as well as the pleasantest method of obtaining more. Nor should the grief, arising from what we know and feel of our own hearts, rob us of the honour, comfort and joy, which the word of God designs us, in what is there recorded of the person, offices, and grace of Jesus, and the relations He is pleased to stand in to his people. . . . Though the believer is nothing in himself, yet having all in Jesus, he may rejoice in his name all the day. The Lord enable us so to do. The joy of the Lord is the strength of his people: whereas unbelief makes our hands hang down, and our knees feeble, dispirits ourselves, and discourages others; and though it steals upon us under a semblance of humility, it is indeed the very essence of pride. By inward and outward exercises the Lord is promoting the best desire of your heart, and answering your daily prayers. Would you have assurance? The true solid assurance is to be obtained no other way. When young Christians are greatly comforted with the Lord's love and presence, their doubts and fears are for that season at an end. But this is not assurance; so soon as the Lord hides his face, they are troubled, and ready to question the very foundation of hope. Assurance grows by repeated conflict, by our repeated experimental proof of the Lord's power and goodness to save; when we have been brought very low and helped, sorely wounded and healed, cast down and raised again, have given up all hope, and been suddenly snatched from danger, and placed in safety; and when these things have been repeated to us and in us a thousand times over, we begin to learn to trust simply to the word and power of God, beyond and against appearances; and this trust, when habitual and strong, bears the name of assurance; for even assurance has degrees.

You have good reason, madam, to suppose that the love of the best Christians to an unseen Saviour is far short of what it ought to be. If your heart be like mine, and you examine your love to Christ by the warmth and frequency of your emotions towards him, you will often be in a sad suspense, whether or no you love him at all. The best mark to judge by, and which He has given us for that purpose, is to inquire if his word and will have a prevailing, governing influence upon our lives and temper. If we love him, we do endeavour to keep his commandments; and it will hold the other way; if we have a desire to please him, we undoubtedly love him. Obedience is the best test; and when, amidst all our imperfections, we can humbly appeal concerning the sincerity of our view, this is a mercy for which we ought to be greatly thankful. He that has brought us to will, will likewise enable us to do according to his good pleasure. I doubt not but the Lord whom you love, and on whom you depend, will lead you in a sure way, and establish, and strengthen, and settle you in his love and grace. Indeed He has done great things for you already. . . .

As to daily occurrences, it is best to believe that a daily portion of comforts and crosses, each one the most suitable to our case, is adjusted and appointed by the hand which was once nailed to the cross for us; that where the path of duty and prudence leads, there is the best situation we could possibly be in at that juncture. We are not required to afflict ourselves immoderately for what is not in our power to prevent, nor should anything that affords occasions for mortifying the spirit of self be accounted unnecessary.

    I am, my dear madam,
     Your obliged and affectionate servant,
         JOHN NEWTON.

To Mrs. Wilberforce.

LETTER III.—Sensible comfort—Rejoicing in God alone—Loss of friends —Deprivation of ordinances.

1769.

MY DEAR MADAM,—We are much obliged to you for your late visit; and I am glad to find that the Lord is pleased to give you some tokens of his presence when you are with us, because I hope it will encourage you to come again. I ought to be very thankful that our Christian friends in general are not wholly disappointed of a blessing when they visit us.

I hope the Lord will give me a humble sense of what I am, and that broken and contrite frame of heart in which He delights. This is to me the chief thing. I had rather have more of the mind that was in Christ, more of a meek, quiet, resigned, peaceful and loving disposition, than to enjoy the greatest measure of sensible comforts, if the consequence should be (as perhaps it would) spiritual pride, self-sufficiency, and a want of that tenderness to others which becomes one who has reason to style himself the chief of sinners. I know, indeed, that the *proper* tendency of sensible consolations is to humble; but I can see that, through the depravity of human nature, they have not always that effect. And I have been sometimes disgusted with an apparent want of humility, an air of self-will and self-importance, in persons of whose sincerity I could not at all doubt. It has kept me from envying them those pleasant frames with which they have sometimes been favoured; for I believe Satan is never nearer us than at some times when we think ourselves nearest the Lord.

What reason have we to charge our souls in David's words, "My soul, wait thou *only* upon God!" A great stress should be laid upon that word *only*. We dare not entirely shut him out of our regards, but we are too apt to suffer something to share with him. This evil disposition is deeply fixed in our hearts; and the Lord orders all his dispensations towards us with a view to rooting it out; that being wearied with repeated disappointments, we may at length be compelled to betake ourselves to him alone. Why else do we experience so many changes and crosses? why are we so often in heaviness? We know that He delights in the pleasure and prosperity of his servants; that He does not willingly afflict or grieve his children; but there is a necessity on our parts, in order to teach us that we have no stability in ourselves, and that no creature can do us good but by his appointment. . . . The Lord gives us a dear friend to our comfort; but ere long we forget that the friend is only the channel of conveyance, and that all the comfort is from himself. To remind us of this, the stream is dried up, the friend torn away by death, or removed far from us, or perhaps the friendship ceases, and a coolness insensibly takes place, we know not *how* or *why*: the true reason is, that when we rejoiced amiss in our gourd, the Lord, for our good, sent a worm to the root of it. Instances of this kind are innumerable; and the great inference from them all, cease from man, cease from creatures, for wherein are they to be accounted of? My soul, wait thou *only, only* upon the Lord, who is (according to the expressive phrase, Heb. iv. 13) He with whom we have to do for soul and body, for time and eternity. What thanks do we owe, that though we have not yet attained perfectly this great lesson, yet we are admitted into that school where alone it can be learnt; and though we are poor, slow scholars, the great and effectual teacher to whom we have been encouraged and enabled to apply, can and will bring us forward! . . . Though all are very dunces when He first receives them, not one was ever turned out as *incapable,* for He makes them what He would have them to be. Oh that we may set him always before us, and consider every dispensation, person, thing, we meet in the course of every day, as messengers from him, each bringing us some *line of instruction* for us to copy into that day's experience! Whatever passes within us or around us may be improved (when He teaches us how) as a perpetual commentary upon his good word. If we converse and observe with this view, we may learn something every moment, wherever the path of duty leads us, in the streets as well as in the closet, and from the conversation of those who know not God, (when we cannot avoid being present at it,) as well as from those who do.

Separation of our dear friends is, as you observed, hard to flesh and blood; but grace can make it tolerable. I have an abiding persuasion, that the Lord can easily give more than ever He will take away. . . . A time of weeping must come, but the morning of joy will make amends for all. Who can expound the meaning of that one expression, "an exceeding and eternal weight of glory?" The case of unconverted friends is still more burdensome to think of; but we have encouragement and warrant to pray and to hope. He who called *us* can easily call others; and He seldom lays a desire of this sort very closely and warmly upon the hearts of his people, but when it is his gracious design sooner or later to give an answer of peace. However, it becomes us to be thankful for ourselves, and to bow our anxieties and reasoning before his sovereign will, who doth as He pleases with his own. . . .

When we have opportunity of enjoying many ordinances, it is a mercy to be able to prize and improve them: but when He cuts us short for a season, if we wait upon him, we shall do well without them. Secret prayer, and the good word, are the chief *wells* from whence we draw the water of salvation. These will keep the soul alive when creature streams are cut off; but the richest variety of public means, and the closest attendance upon them, will leave us lean and pining in the midst of plenty, if we are remiss and formal in the other two. I think David never appears in a more lively frame of mind than when he wrote the 42nd, 63rd, and 84th Psalms, which were all penned in a dry land, and at a distance from the public ordinances.

I am, with the greatest regard, dear madam,

Your most obedient and obliged servant,

JOHN NEWTON.

To Mrs. WILBERFORCE.

LETTER IV.—The Christian mourning and rejoicing—First love.

MY DEAR MADAM,—I did not hear of your late illness till I was informed you were much better. I praise the Lord for your recovery, and hope you will have reason to praise him for all his chastisements, for surely they are sent in love, for the sake of the supports with which they are accompanied, and the fruits which (by his blessing) they produce; they deserve a place in the list of our peculiar and covenant mercies. Of Mr. Thornton's recovery I had the pleasure to be informed by himself. May the Lord long preserve him and you for many years, for the comfort of your friends and the glory of his name.

Your letter was truly welcome. All yours are so, and therefore I do not choose to remain longer in your debt than I can avoid, that I may have hope of hearing from you again.

I observe your experience is a mixture of joy and complaint, and thus it must be till the Lord shall be pleased to put an end to our conflict with indwelling sin. Both are right. We have reason to mourn that there is such an opposition within us to all that is good; and we have reason to rejoice, for Jesus is all-sufficient, and we are complete in him. We cannot but mourn to find that our passage lies through fire and water; we ought to rejoice that this difficult way will lead us to a wealthy place, where joy will be unspeakable, glorious and endless. We may well mourn that our love to the Lord is so faint and wavering; but oh! what a cause of joy to know that his love to us is infinite and unchangeable. Our attainment in sanctification is weak and our progress slow; but our justification is perfect, and our hope sure. May we so look to the bright side of our case as not to be cast down and discouraged, and may we maintain such a sense of the dark side as may keep us from being exalted above measure.

You say you are not as you once were. It is generally true that the time of espousals, the beginning of our profession, is attended with sensible sweetnesses and a liveliness of spirit which we afterwards look back upon with regret when we are led into a different dispensation. The young believer is like a tree in blossom. But I have a good hope that if you seem to have lost in point of sensible affections you have proportionally gained in knowledge, judgment, and an establishment in the faith. You see more of your own heart than you did or could in those early days; and you have a clearer view of the wisdom, glory, and faithfulness of God, as manifested in the person of Christ. Though the blossoms have gone off the fruit is found, and, I trust, ripening for glory. The Lord deals with us as children. Children, when they are young, have many little indulgences. As they grow up, they are subject to discipline and must learn obedience. So when faith and knowledge are in their infancy, the Lord helps this weakness by cordials and sensible comforts; but when they are advanced in growth He exercises and proves them by many changes and trials, and calls us to live more directly upon his power and promises in the face of all discouragements, to hope even against hope, and at times seems to deprive us of every subsidiary support, that we may lean only and entirely upon our beloved. . . . .

I am sincerely, dearest madam,
Your most affectionate and obliged servant,
JOHN NEWTON.

OLNEY: *January* 18, 1770.

To MRS. WILBERFORCE.

LETTER V.—Benefits of affliction.

MY DEAR MADAM, . . . Though afflictions in themselves are not joyous, but grievous, yet in due season they yield the peaceful fruits of righteousness. Various and blessed are the fruits they produce. By affliction prayer is quickened, for our prayers are very apt to grow languid and formal in a time of ease. Affliction greatly helps us to understand the Scriptures, especially the promises, most of which being made to times of trouble, we cannot so well know their fulness, sweetness, and certainty, as when we have been in the situation to which they are suited, have been enabled to trust and plead them, and found them fulfilled in our own case. We are usually indebted to affliction as the means or occasion of the most signal discoveries we are favoured with of the wisdom, power, and faithfulness of the Lord. These are best observed by the evident proofs we have that He is near to support us under trouble, and that He can and does deliver us out of it. Israel would not have seen so much of the Lord's arm outstretched in their behalf, had not Pharaoh oppressed, opposed, and pursued them. Afflictions are designed likewise for the manifestation of our sincerity to ourselves and to others. When faith endures the fire, we know it to be of the right kind; and others, who see we are brought safe out, and lose nothing but the dross, will confess that God is with us of a truth. Dan. iii. 27, 28. Surely this thought should reconcile us to suffer, not only with patience, but with cheerfulness, if God may be glorified in us. This made the apostle rejoice in tribulation, that the power of Christ might be noticed, as resting upon him, and working mightily in him. Many of our graces, likewise, cannot thrive or show themselves to advantage without trials, such as resignation, patience, meekness, long-suffering. I observe some of the London porters do not appear to be very strong men; yet they will trudge along under a burthen which some stouter people could not carry so well; the reason is, they are accustomed to carry burdens, and by continual exercise their shoulders acquire a strength suited to their work. It is so in the Christian life; activity and strength of grace is not ordinarily acquired by those who sit still and live at ease, but by those who frequently meet with something which requires a full exertion of what power the Lord has given them. So again, it is by our own sufferings we learn to pity and sympathise with others in their sufferings; such a compassionate disposition, which excites our feelings for the afflicted, is an eminent branch of the mind which was in Christ. But these feelings would be very faint, if we did not in our own experience know what sorrows and temptations mean. Afflictions do us good likewise, as they make us more acquainted with what is in our own hearts, and thereby promote humiliation and self-abasement. There are abominations which, like nests of vipers, lie so quietly within, that we hardly suspect they are there till the rod of affliction rouses them; then they hiss and show their venom. This discovery is indeed very distressing; yet, till it is made, we are prone to think ourselves much less vile than we really are, and cannot so heartily abhor ourselves, and repent in dust and ashes.

But I must write a sermon rather than a letter, if I would enumerate all the good fruits which, by the power of sanctifying grace, are produced from this bitter tree. May we, under our several trials, find them all revealed in ourselves, that we may not complain of having suffered in vain. While we have such a depraved nature, and live in such a polluted world; while the roots of pride, vanity, self-dependence, self-seeking, are so strong within us, we need a variety of sharp dispensations to keep us from forgetting ourselves, and from cleaving to the dust.

I am, dearest madam,
Your much obliged and affectionate servant,
JOHN NEWTON.

To Mrs. Wilberforce.

LETTER VI.—Trials unwelcome but beneficial—Vanity of the world—
The Lord our guide and strength.

MY DEAR MADAM,—(After referring to the fact of domestic affliction in his own family and in Mrs. Wilberforce's, Mr. Newton thus continues),—What a mercy it is to know that all is in safe hands; that sickness and health, comfort or affliction, life or death, are all equally in the inventory of a believer's privileges,—all equally blessings, though some in one view are more apparently so, and some are sent more under a disguise to do us good; so that, perhaps, we are afraid of them, and would willingly, if we could, prevent them from coming; but they are the Lord's messengers, they have a gracious errand to deliver, and therefore they must have admittance; and though at first we do not like their looks or their language, yet afterwards, when we have received the benefits, the peaceable fruits of righteousness they were commissioned to bestow, we are not sorry they were sent, or that we were not able to shut them out.

The hour is coming when we shall be astonished to think what mere trifles were once capable of discouraging us; for though many things we now meet with have a kind of importance respecting the present life and our natural feelings, yet when we come to see things *as they are*, and get a clearer view of the difference between temporary and eternal,—of the lightness of the one and the weight of the other,—we shall be satisfied there is a greater disproportion between them than between molehills and mountains; and that when the Lord has put us in possession of the pearl of great price, the gain or loss of a pebble was hardly worth a serious thought. It appears so to us in some measure now, when we are first seeking the Lord's peace. How common is it, then, to think,—Oh! if my sins were but pardoned, and I had reason to hope that I was one of his children other things would not greatly move me. There are times, too, afterwards, when for a season we form the like judgment, as when we are favoured with a golden hour of the light of his countenance, how little does the world and its concerns appear! So, likewise, if we stand by the bed of a dying believer, just ripe for glory, upon the point of entering, we see then how light such a one makes both of the trials he has passed through, and of the world he is about to leave; we feel something of the same spirit, and could wish, if it were the Lord's pleasure, to go along with him. When Peter was upon the Mount, he was so filled with the glory which he beheld, he was for remaining there, and could have bid farewell to all his connections he had left below. Had we in a lively degree that faith in exercise which is the evidence of things not seen, we should live at another rate than we often do. But it is a mercy to be aiming aright, though we have not as yet attained.

. . . It is a comfort to think that in our several changes and movements, the same Lord is present with us all. If we are in the path of duty and follow as He leads, we may depend on him to do us good. Every good is connected with his favour. He will withhold nothing from us but what he sees we had better be without; and we shall meet with nothing but what He will overrule for our benefit. Oh, how pleasant to lean upon an almighty arm, and to commit ourselves without anxiety to the guidance of infinite wisdom and love! Hitherto the Lord has helped us. The enemy has often thrust sore at us that we might fall; but the Lord has been our stay. And as mercy and goodness have followed us all our days, each Ebenezer we have already set up is an encouraging monument to engage us to trust him to the end. For this God is our God for ever and ever! He will be our guide even unto death; and beyond death, to the land of life and joy, where we shall hear the voice of war no more. I commend you and your family and friends to his gracious care. . . .

I am, my dear madam,

Your obliged and affectionate servant,

JOHN NEWTON.

HOXTON: *June* 11, 1783.

The Earl of Dartmouth.

WILLIAM LEGGE, second Earl of Dartmouth, was born in 1731. Early in life he was deprived of his father, and his education devolved on his surviving parent. Upon the death of his grandfather, in 1750, he succeeded to the earldom. Soon after his marriage with the daughter and heiress of Sir Charles G. Nicholl, he was introduced to Lady Huntingdon. At her house he made the acquaintance of Mr. Whitefield, Mr. Romaine, the Wesleys, and other good men of the same class. Indeed, Lord and Lady Dartmouth very soon attracted general attention for the profession of religion they made, and the countenance they afforded to faithful ministers of Christ, suspected of what was called "Methodism." As early as 1757, Mr. Hervey wrote to Lady Fanny Shirley,—"I have not the honour of Lord Dartmouth's acquaintance; but I hear he is full of grace, and valiant for the truth,—a lover of Christ, and an ornament to his gospel."

Exalted as was the social position of Lord Dartmouth, he did not escape the misrepresentations and even the ridicule of some of his friends, who regarded his opinions and practices as fanatical and absurd. They, however, afterwards saw cause entirely to change their views.

Lord Dartmouth befriended the college for the American Indians, and contributed largely towards the Orphan House in Georgia. He was also, with Baron Smyth (Lord Chief Baron of the Exchequer), one of the principal supporters of evangelical preaching at the Lock Chapel. It was through Dr. Haweis that Mr. Newton was introduced to Lord Dartmouth as a person well qualified to take the vacant curacy at Olney. His lordship prevailed on the Bishop of Lincoln to ordain Mr. Newton; and, ever afterwards, in various ways, showed a true friendship for him. The twenty-six first letters in Cardiphonia are addressed to Lord Dartmouth.

It may be added that the Earl of Dartmouth was highly

esteemed by George III. He appointed him principal Secretary of State for the American department, which office his lordship afterwards exchanged for the place of Lord Keeper of the Privy Seal; and some years after he was constituted Lord Steward of his Majesty's household. "They call my Lord Dartmouth an enthusiast," said the king, in an interview with Dr. Beattie, "but surely he says nothing on the subject of religion but what any Christian may and ought to say."

Lord Dartmouth died in 1801. It is to him that the poet Cowper refers in the following lines:—

> "We boast some rich ones whom the gospel sways,
> And one who wears a coronet and prays;
> Like gleanings of an olive tree they show
> Here and there one upon the topmost bough."*

To Lord Dartmouth.

LETTER I.—On not doing the things we would.

February, 1772.

My Lord,—I have been sitting, perhaps a quarter of an hour, with my pen in my hand, and my finger upon my upper lip, contriving how I should begin my letter. . . . At length my suspense reminded me of the apostle's words, Gal. v. 17, "Ye cannot do the things that ye would." This is a humbling but a just account of a Christian's attainments in the present life, and is equally applicable to the strongest and to the weakest. The weakest need not say *less*, the strongest will hardly venture to say *more*. The Lord has given his people a desire and will aiming at great things; without this they would be unworthy the name of Christians; but they cannot do as they would. Their best desires are weak and ineffectual, not absolutely so (for He who works in them to will, enables them in a

* Poem on Truth.

measure to do likewise), but in comparison with the mark at which they aim. So that while they have great cause to be thankful for the desire He has given them, and for the degree in which it is answered, they have equal reason to be ashamed and abased under a sense of their continual defects, and the evil mixtures which taint and debase their best endeavours. It would be easy to make out a a long list of particulars, which a believer would do if he could, but in which, from first to last, he finds a mortifying inability. Permit me to mention a few, which I need not transcribe from books, for they are always present to my mind.

He would willingly enjoy God in prayer. He knows that prayer is his duty; but, in his judgment, he considers it likewise as his greatest honour and privilege. In this light he can recommend it to others, and can tell them of the wonderful condescension of the great God, who humbles himself to behold the things that are in heaven, that He should stoop so much lower, to afford his gracious ear to the supplications of sinful worms upon earth. He can bid them expect a pleasure in waiting upon the Lord, different in kind and greater in degree than all that the world can afford. By prayer he can say, You have liberty to cast all your cares upon him that careth for you. By one hour's intimate access to the throne of grace, where the Lord causes his glory to pass before the soul that seeks him, you may acquire more true spiritual knowledge and comfort, than by a day or a week's converse with the best of men, or the most studious perusal of many folios. And in this light he would consider it and improve it for himself. But, alas; how seldom can he do as he would! How often does he find this privilege a mere task, which he would be glad of a just excuse to omit! and the chief pleasure he derives from the performance, is to think that his task is finished: he has been drawing near to God with his lips, while his heart was far from him. Surely this is not doing as he would, when (to borrow the expression of an old woman here,) he is dragged before God like a slave, and comes away like a thief.

The like may be said of reading the Scripture. He believes it to be the word of God: he admires the wisdom and grace of the doctrines, the beauty of the precepts, the richness and suitableness of the promises; and therefore, with David, he accounts it preferable to thousands of gold and silver, and sweeter than honey or the honeycomb. Yet, while he thus thinks of it, and desires that it may dwell in him richly, and be his meditation night and day, he cannot do as he would. It will require some resolution to persist in reading a portion of it every day; and even then his heart is often less engaged than when reading a pamphlet. Here again his privilege frequently dwindles into a task. His appetite is vitiated, so that he has but little relish for the food of his soul.

He would willingly have abiding, admiring thoughts of the person and love of the Lord Jesus Christ. Glad he is, indeed, of those occasions which recall the Saviour to his mind; and with this view, notwithstanding all discouragements, he perseveres in attempting to pray and read, and waits upon the ordinances. Yet he cannot do as he would. Whatever claims he may have to the exercise of gratitude and sensibility towards his fellow-creatures, he must confess himself mournfully ungrateful and insensible towards his best Friend and Benefactor. Ah! what trifles are capable of shutting *Him* out of our thoughts, of whom we say, He is the Beloved of our souls, who loved us, and gave himself for us, and whom we have deliberately chosen as our chief good and portion! What can make us amends for the loss we suffer here? Yet surely if we *could*, we *would* set him always before us; his love should be the delightful theme of our hearts

From morn to noon, from noon to dewy eve.

But though we aim at this good, evil is present with us: we find we are renewed but in part, and have still cause to plead the Lord's promise, to take away the heart of stone, and give us a heart of flesh.

He would willingly acquiesce in all the dispensations of divine Providence. He believes that all events are under the direction of infinite wisdom and goodness, and shall surely issue in the glory of God, and the good of those who fear him. He doubts not but the hairs of his head are all numbered, that the blessings of every kind which he possesses were bestowed upon him, and are preserved to him, by the bounty and special favour of the Lord whom he serves; that afflictions spring not out of the ground, but are fruits and tokens of Divine love, no less than his comforts; that there is a need-be, whenever for a season he is in heaviness. Of these principles he can no more doubt, than of what he sees with his eyes; and there are seasons when he thinks they will prove sufficient to reconcile him to the sharpest trials. But often when he aims to apply them in an hour of *present* distress, he cannot do what he would. He feels a law in his members warring against the law in his mind; so that, in defiance of the clearest convictions, seeing as though he perceived not, he is ready to complain, murmur, and despond. Alas! how vain is man in his best estate! How much weakness and inconsistency, even in those whose hearts are right with the Lord! and what reason have we to confess that we are unworthy, unprofitable servants!

It were easy to enlarge in this way, would paper and time permit. But, blessed be God, we are not under the law, but under grace. And even these distressing effects of the remnants of indwelling sin are overruled for good. By these experiences the believer is weaned more from self, and taught more highly to prize and more absolutely to rely on him, who is appointed to us of God, Wisdom, Righteousness, Sanctification, and Redemption. The more vile we are in our own eyes, the more precious He will be to us; and a deep repeated sense of the evil of our hearts is necessary to preclude all boasting, and to make us willing to give the whole glory of our salvation where it is due. Again, a sense of these evils will (when hardly anything else can do it) reconcile us to the thoughts of death; yea, make us desirous to depart that we may sin no more, since we find depravity so deep-rooted in our nature, that, like the leprous house, the whole fabric must be taken down before we can be freed from its defilement. Then, and not till then, we shall be able to do the thing that we would: when we see Jesus, we shall be transformed into his image, and have done with sin and sorrow for ever.

I am, with great deference, etc.

To Lord Dartmouth.

Letter II.—On doing the evil we would not.

March, 1772.

My Lord,—I think my last letter turned upon the apostle's thought, Gal. v. 17, "Ye cannot do the things that ye would." In the parallel place, Rom. vii. 19, there is another clause subjoined, "The evil which I would not, that I do." This, added to the former, would complete the dark side of my experience. Permit me to tell your lordship a little part, (for some things must not, cannot be told,) not of what I have read, but of what I have felt, in illustration of this passage.

I *would not* be the sport and prey of wild, vain, foolish, and worse imaginations; but this evil is present with me: my heart is like a highway, like a city without walls or gates. Nothing so false, so frivolous, so absurd, so impossible, or so horrid, but it can obtain access, and that at any time, or in any place: neither the study, the pulpit, nor even the Lord's table, exempt me from their intrusion. I sometimes compare my *words* to the treble of an instrument, which my *thoughts* accompany with a kind of bass, or rather anti-bass, in which every rule of harmony is broken, every possible combination of discord and confusion is introduced, utterly inconsistent with, and contradictory to the intended melody. Ah! what music would my praying and preaching often make in the ears of the Lord of Hosts, if He listened to them as they are *mine* only! By men, the upper part only (if I may so speak) is heard; and small cause there is for self-gratulation, if *they* should happen to commend, when conscience tells me they would be struck with astonishment and abhorrence could they hear the whole.

But if this awful effect of heart-depravity cannot be wholly avoided in the present state of human nature, yet, at least, I would not allow and indulge it; yet this I find I do. In defiance of my best judgment and best wishes, I find something within me, which cherishes and cleaves to those evils, from which I ought to start and flee, as I should if a toad or a serpent was put in my food or in my bed. Ah! how vile must the heart (at least my heart) be, that can hold a parley with such abominations, when I so well know their nature and their tendency. Surely he who finds himself capable of this, may, without the least affectation of humility (however fair his outward conduct appears), subscribe himself less than the least of all saints, and of sinners the very chief.

I would not be influenced by a principle of self on any occasion; yet this evil I often do. I see the baseness and absurdity of such a conduct as clearly as I see the light of the day. I do not affect to be thought ten feet high, and I know that a desire of being thought wise or good, is equally contrary to reason and truth. I should be grieved or angry if my fellow-creatures supposed I had such a desire; and therefore, I fear the very principle of self, of which I complain, has a considerable share in prompting my desires to conceal it. The pride of others often offends me, and makes me studious to hide my own; because their good opinion of me depends much upon their not perceiving it. But the Lord knows how this dead fly taints and spoils my best services, and makes them no better than specious sins.

I would not indulge vain reasonings concerning the counsels, ways, and providences of God; yet I am prone to do it. That the Judge of all the earth will do right, is to me as evident and necessary as that two and two make four. I believe that He has a sovereign right to do what He will with his own, and that this sovereignty is but another name for the unlimited exercise of wisdom and goodness. But my reasonings are often such, as if I had never heard of these principles, or had formally renounced them. I feel the workings of a presumptuous spirit, that would account for every thing, and venture to dispute whatever it cannot comprehend. What an evil is this, for a potsherd of the earth to contend with its Maker! I do not act thus towards my fellow-creatures; I do not find fault with the decisions of a judge, or the dispositions of a general, because, though I know they are fallible, yet I suppose they are wiser in their respective departments than myself. But I am often ready to take this liberty when it is most unreasonable and inexcusable.

I would not cleave to a covenant of works: it should seem from the foregoing particulars, and many others which I could mention, that I have reasons enough to deter me from this. Yet even this I do. Not but that I say, and I hope from my heart, "Enter not into judgment with thy servant, O Lord;" I embrace it as a faithful saying, and worthy of all acceptation, that Jesus Christ came into the world to save sinners; and it is the main pleasure and business of my life, to set forth the necessity and all-sufficiency of the Mediator between God and Man, and to make mention of his righteousness, even of his only. But here, as in every thing else, I find a vast difference between my judgment and my experience. I am invited to take the water of life *freely*, yet often discouraged, because I have nothing wherewith to pay for it. If I am at times favoured with some liberty from the above-mentioned evils, it rather gives me a more favourable opinion of myself, than increases my admiration of the Lord's goodness to so unworthy a creature; and when the returning tide of my corruptions convinces me that *I am still the same*, an unbelieving legal spirit would urge me to conclude that the Lord is changed: at least I feel a weariness of being beholden to him for such continued multiplied forgiveness; and I fear that some part of my striving against sin, and my desires after an increase of sanctification, arise from a secret wish that I might not be so absolutely and entirely indebted to him.

This, my lord, is only a faint sketch of my heart; but it is taken from the life: it would require a volume rather than a letter to fill up the outlines. But I believe you will not regret that I choose to say no more upon such a subject. But though my disease is grievous, it is not desperate; I have a gracious and infallible Physician. I shall not die, but live, and declare the works of the Lord.

I remain, my lord, etc.

To Lord Dartmouth.

Letter III.—The existence of indwelling sin overruled for good.

April, 1772.

My Lord,—My two last letters turned upon a mournful subject—the depravity of the heart, which impedes us when we would do good, and pollutes our best intended services with evil. We have cause, upon this account, to go softly all our days; yet we need not sorrow as they who have no hope. The Lord has provided his people relief under those complaints, and teaches us to draw improvement from them. If the evils we feel were not capable of being overruled for good, He would not permit them to remain in us. This we may infer from his hatred to sin, and the love which He bears to his people.

As to the remedy, neither our state nor his honour are affected by the workings of indwelling sin, in the hearts of those whom He has taught to wrestle, strive, and mourn, on account of what they feel. Though sin wars, it shall not reign; and though it breaks our peace, it cannot separate from his love. Nor is it inconsistent with his holiness and perfection to manifest his favour to such poor defiled creatures, or to admit them to communion with himself; for they are not considered as in themselves, but as one with Jesus, to whom they have fled for refuge, and by whom they live a life of faith. They are accepted in the Beloved. . . . They act from a principle of love, they aim at no less than his glory, and their habitual desires are supremely fixed upon himself. There is a difference in kind between the feeblest efforts of faith in a real believer, while he is covered with shame at the thoughts of his miscarriages, and the highest and most specious attainments of those who are wise in their own eyes and prudent in their own sight. Nor shall this conflict remain long, or the enemy finally prevail over them. They are supported by almighty power, and led on to certain victory. They shall not always be as they are now; yet a little while, and they shall be freed from this vile body, which, like the leprous house, is incurably contaminated, and must be entirely taken down. Then they shall see Jesus as He is, and be like him, and with him for ever.

The gracious purposes to which the Lord makes the sense and feeling of our depravity subservient, are manifold. Hereby his own power, wisdom, faithfulness, and love, are more signally displayed; his power, in maintaining his own work in the midst of so much opposition, like a spark burning in the water, or a bush unconsumed in the flames; his wisdom in defeating and controlling all the devices which Satan, from his knowledge of the evil of our nature, is encouraged to practise against us. He has overthrown many a fair professor, and, like Goliath, he challenges the whole army of Israel; yet he finds there are some against whom, though he thrusts sorely, he cannot prevail; notwithstanding any seeming advantage he gains at some seasons, they are still delivered, for the Lord is on their side. The unchangeableness of the Lord's love, and the riches of his mercy, are likewise more illustrated by the multiplied pardons He bestows upon his people, than if they needed no forgiveness at all.

Hereby the Lord Jesus Christ is more endeared to the soul; all boasting is effectually excluded, and the glory of a full and free salvation is ascribed to him alone. . . . The righteous are said to be scarcely saved, not with respect to the certainty of the event, for the purpose of God in their favour cannot be disappointed, but in respect of their own apprehensions, and the great difficulties they are brought through. But when, after a long experience of their own deceitful hearts, after repeated proofs of their weakness, wilfulness, ingratitude, and insensibility, they find that none of these things can separate them from the love of God in Christ, Jesus becomes more and more precious to their souls. They love much, because much has been forgiven them. They dare not, they will not ascribe anything to themselves, but are glad to acknowledge, that they must have perished (if possible) a thousand times over, if Jesus had not been their Saviour, their Shepherd, and their Shield. When they were wandering He brought them back, when fallen He raised them, when wounded He healed them, when fainting He revived them. By him out of weakness they have been made strong; He has taught their hands to war, and covered their heads in the day of battle. In a word, some of the clearest proofs they have had of his excellence have been occasioned by the mortifying proofs they have had of their own vileness. They would not have known so much of him if they had not known so much of themselves.

Further, a spirit of humiliation, which is both the *decus et tutamen*, the strength and beauty of our profession, is greatly promoted by our feeling, as well as reading, that when we would do good evil is present with us. A broken and contrite spirit is pleasing to the Lord. He has promised to dwell with those who have it; and experience shows, that the exercise of all our graces is in proportion to the humbling sense we have of the depravity of our nature. . . . Whoever is truly humbled will not be easily angry, will not be positive and rash, will be compassionate and tender to the infirmities of his fellow-sinners, knowing that if there be a difference it is grace that has made it, and that he has the seeds of every evil in his own heart. And under all trials and afflictions, he will look to the hand of the Lord, and lay his mouth in the dust, acknowledging that he suffers much less than his iniquities have deserved. These are some of the advantages and good fruits which the Lord enables us to obtain from that bitter root, indwelling sin.

I am, with great deference, etc.

To Lord Dartmouth.

LETTER IV.—Testimony of dying Christians to the reality of gospel truth.

March 10, 1771.

My Lord,—For about six weeks past I have had occasion to spend several hours of almost every day with the sick and the dying. These scenes are to a minister like walking the hospitals to a young surgeon. The various cases which occur, exemplify, illustrate, and explain, with a commanding energy, many truths, which may be learned indeed at home, but cannot be so well understood, or their force so sensibly felt, without the advantage of experience and observation. . . .

Though the grand evidence of those truths upon which our hopes are built arises from the authority of God speaking them in his word, and revealing them by his Spirit, to the awakened heart, (for till the heart is awakened it is incapable of receiving this evidence,) yet some of these truths are so mysterious, so utterly repugnant to the judgment of depraved nature, that, through the remaining influence of unbelief and vain reasoning, the temptations of Satan, and the subtle arguments with which some men reputed wise attack the foundations of our faith, the minds even of believers are sometimes capable of being shaken. I know no better corroborating evidence for the relief of the mind under such assaults than the testimony of dying persons, especially of such as have lived out of the noise of controversy, and who perhaps never heard a syllable of what has been started in these evil days, against the deity of Christ, his atonement, and other important articles. Permit me, my lord, to relate, upon this occasion, some things which exceedingly struck me in the conversation I had with a young woman whom I visited in her last illness about two years ago. She was a sober, prudent person, of plain sense, could read her Bible, but had read little besides. Her knowledge of the world was nearly confined to the parish: for I suppose she was seldom, if ever, twelve miles from home in her life. She had known the gospel about seven years before the Lord visited her with a lingering consumption, which at length removed her to a better world. A few days before her death, I had been praying by her bed-side, and in my prayer I thanked the Lord that he gave her now to see that she had not followed cunningly-devised fables. When I had finished, she repeated that word, "No," she said, "not cunningly-devised fables; these are realities indeed; I feel their truth, I feel their comfort. Oh! tell my friends, tell my acquaintance, tell inquiring souls, tell poor sinners, tell all the daughters of Jerusalem, (alluding to Solomon's Song, v. 16, from which she had just before desired me to preach at her funeral,) what Jesus has done for my soul. Tell them, that now in the time of need I find him my beloved and my friend, and as such I commend him to them." She then fixed her eyes stedfastly upon me, and proceeded, as well as I can recollect, as follows: "Sir, you are highly favoured in being called to preach the gospel. I have often heard you with pleasure; but give me leave to tell you, that I now see all you have said, or can say, is comparatively but little. Nor, till you come into my situation, and have death and eternity full in your view, will it be possible for you to conceive the vast weight and importance of the truths you declare. Oh! Sir, it is a serious thing to die; no words can express what is needful to support the soul in the solemnity of a dying hour."

I believe it was the next day when I visited her again. After some discourse as usual, she said, with a remarkable vehemence of speech, "Are you sure I cannot be mistaken?" I answered without hesitation, "Yes, I am sure; I am not afraid to say, my soul for yours, that you are right." She paused a little, and then replied, "You say true; I know I am right. I feel that my hope is fixed upon the Rock of ages; I know whom I have believed. Yet if you could see with my eyes you would not wonder at my question. But the approach of death presents a prospect, which is till then hidden from us, and which cannot be described." She said much more to the same purpose; and in all she spoke there was a dignity, weight, and evidence, which I suppose few professors of divinity, when lecturing from the chair, have at any time equalled. We may well say with Elihu, Who teacheth like him? Many instances of the like kind I have met with here. I have a poor girl near me who looks like an idiot, and her natural capacity is indeed very small; but the Lord has been pleased to make her acquainted alternately with great temptations, and proportionably great discoveries of his love and truth. Sometimes, when her heart is enlarged, I listen to her with astonishment. I think no books, nor ministers I ever met with have given me such an impression and understanding of what the apostle styles τα βαθη του Θεου,* as I have upon some occasions received from her conversation. . . .

I am, etc.

To Lord Dartmouth.

Letter V.—*Our entire dependence upon God in all we do—Blessedness of such a condition.*

February 23, 1775.

My Lord,—I assent to our Lord's declaration, "Without me ye can do nothing;" not only upon the authority of the speaker, but from the same irresistible and experimental evidence, as if He had told me, that I cannot make the sun to shine, or change the course of the seasons. Though my pen and my tongue sometimes move freely, yet the total incapacity and stagnation of thought I labour under at other times, convince me, that in myself I have not sufficiency to think a good thought; and I believe the case would be the same if that little measure of knowledge and abilities, which I am too prone to look upon as my own, were a thousand times greater than it is. For every new

---

* The deep things of God. 1 Cor. ii. 10.

service I stand in need of a new supply, and can bring forth nothing of my supposed store into actual exercise, but by his immediate assistance. His gracious influence is that to those who are best furnished with gifts, which the water is to the mill, or the wind to the ship, without which the whole apparatus is motionless and useless. I apprehend that we lose much of the comfort which might arise from a sense of our continual dependence upon him, and of course fall short of acknowledging, as we ought, what we receive from him, by mistaking the manner of his operation. Perhaps we take it too much for granted, that communications from himself must bear some kind of sensible impression that they are *his*, and therefore are ready to give our own industry or ingenuity credit for those performances in which we can perceive no such impression: yet it is very possible that we may be under his influence when we are least aware: and though what we say, or write, or do, may seem no way extraordinary, yet that we should be led to such a particular turn of thought at one time rather than at another, has, in my own concerns, often appeared to me remarkable, from the circumstances which have attended, or the consequences which have followed. How often in the choice of a text, or in the course of a sermon, or in a letter to a friend, have I been led to speak a word in season! and what I have expressed at large, and in general, has been so exactly suited to some case which I was utterly unacquainted with, that I could hardly have hit it so well, had I been previously informed of it. Some instances of this kind have been so striking, as hardly to admit a doubt of superior agency. And indeed, if believers in Jesus, however unworthy in themselves, are the temples of the Holy Ghost; if the Lord lives, dwells, and walks in them; if He is their life and their light; if He has promised to guide them with his eye, and to work in them to will and to do of his own good pleasure; methinks what I have mentioned, and more, may be reasonably expected. That line in the hymn,

> Help I every moment need,

is not a hyperbolical expression, but strictly and literally true, not only in great emergencies, but in our smoother hours, and most familiar paths. This gracious assistance is afforded in a way imperceptible to ourselves, to hide pride from us, and to prevent us from being indolent and careless with respect to the use of appointed means; and it would be likewise more abundantly, and perhaps more sensibly afforded, were our spirits more simple in waiting upon the Lord. But, alas! a divided heart, an undue attachment to some temporal object, sadly deadens *our* spirits, (I speak for myself,) and grieves the Lord's Spirit; so that we walk in darkness, and at a distance, and though called to great privileges, live far below them. But methinks the thought of him who is always near, and upon whom we do and must incessantly depend, should suggest a powerful motive for the closest attention to his revealed will, and the most punctual compliance with it; for so far as the Lord withdraws we become as blind men, and with the clearest light, and upon the plainest ground, we are liable, or rather sure, to stumble at every step.

Though there is a principle of consciousness, and a determination of the will sufficient to denominate our thoughts and performances our own, yet I believe mankind in general are more under an invisible agency than they apprehend. . . .

How great and honourable is the privilege of a true believer! That he has neither wisdom nor strength in himself is no disadvantage; for he is connected with infinite wisdom and almighty power. Though weak as a worm, his arms are strengthened by the mighty God of Jacob, and all things become possible, yea easy to him, that occur within the compass of his proper duty and calling. The Lord, whom he serves, engages to proportion his strength to his day, whether it be a day of service or of suffering; and though he be fallible and short-sighted, exceeding liable to mistake and imposition, yet, while he retains a sense that he is so, and with the simplicity of a child asks counsel and direction of the Lord, he seldom takes a wrong step, at least not in matters of consequence; and even his inadvertencies are overruled for good. If he forgets his true state, and thinks himself to be something, he presently finds he is indeed nothing; but if he is content to be nothing, and to have nothing, he is sure to find a seasonable and abundant communication of all that he wants. Thus he lives, like Israel in the wilderness, upon mere bounty; but then it is a bounty unchangeable, unwearied, inexhaustible, and all-sufficient. Moses, when speaking of the methods the Lord took to humble Israel, mentions his feeding them with manna, as one method. I could not understand this for a time. I thought they were rather in danger of being proud, when they saw themselves provided for in such an extraordinary way. But the manna would not keep, they could not hoard it up; and were therefore in a state of absolute dependence from day to day: this appointment was well suited to humble them. Thus it is with us in spirituals. We should be better pleased, perhaps, to be set up with a stock or sufficiency at once, such an inherent portion of wisdom and power, as we might depend upon, at least for common occasions, without being constrained by a sense of indigence, to have continual recourse to the Lord for every thing we want. But his way is best. His own glory is most displayed, and our safety best secured, by keeping us quite poor and empty in ourselves, and supplying us from one minute to another, according to our need. This, if any thing, will prevent boasting, and keep a sense of gratitude awake in our hearts. This is well adapted to quicken us to prayer, and furnishes us with a thousand occasions for praise, which would otherwise escape our notice.

But who or what are we, that the Most High should thus notice us; should visit us every morning, and water us every moment? It is an astonishing thought, that God should thus dwell with men; that He, before whom the mightiest earthly potentates are less than nothing and vanity, should thus stoop and accommodate himself to the situation, wants, and capacities of the weakest, meanest, and poorest of his children. But so it hath pleased him. He seeth not as man seeth.

I am, etc.

To Lord Dartmouth.

Letter VI.—Things lawful, but not expedient.

November, 1776.

My Lord,—My London journey, which prevented my writing in October, made me amends by an opportunity of waiting upon your lordship in person. Such seasons are not only pleasant at the time, but afford me pleasure in the review. I could have wished the half hour we were together by ourselves prolonged to half a day. The subject your lordship was pleased to suggest has been often upon my mind; and glad should I be, were I able to offer you any thing satisfactory upon it. There is no doubt but first religious impressions are usually mingled with much of a legal spirit, and that conscience at such a time is not only tender, but misinformed and scrupulous; and I believe, as your lordship intimated, that when the mind is more enlightened, and we feel a liberty from many fetters we had imposed upon ourselves, we are in danger of verging too far towards the other extreme. It seems to me that no one person can adjust the medium, and draw the line exactly for another. There are so many particulars in every situation, of which a stranger cannot be a competent judge, and the best human advices and models are mixed with such defects, that it is not *right* to expect others to be absolutely guided by our rules, nor is it *safe* for us implicitly to adopt the decisions or practices of others. But the Scripture undoubtedly furnishes sufficient and infallible rules for every person, however circumstanced; and the throne of grace is appointed for us to wait upon the Lord for the best exposition of his precepts. Thus David often prays to be led in the right way, in the path of judgment. By frequent prayer, and close acquaintance with the Scripture, and a habitual attention to the frame of our hearts, there is a certain delicacy of spiritual taste and discernment to be acquired, which renders a nice disquisition concerning the nature and limits of the Adiaphthora,* as they are called, or how near we may go the utmost bounds of what is right, without being wrong, quite unnecessary. Love is the clearest and most persuasive casuist: and when our love to the Lord is in lively exercise, and the rule of his word is in our eye, we seldom make great mistakes. . . .

From the time we know the Lord, and are bound to him by the cords of love and gratitude, the two chief points we should have in our view, I apprehend, are, to maintain

* Titus ii. 7.

communion with him in our own souls, and to glorify him in the sight of men. Agreeably to these views, though the Scripture does not enumerate or decide, *totidem verbis**, for or against many things which some plead for, and others condemn, yet it furnishes us with some general canons, which, if rightly applied, will perhaps go a good way towards settling the debate, at least to the satisfaction of those who would rather please God than man. Some of these canons I will just remark to your lordship; Rom. xii. 1, 2; 1 Cor. viii. 13, and x. 31; 2 Cor. vi. 17; Eph. iv. 30, and v. 11, 15, 16; 1 Thess. v. 22; Eph. vi. 18; to which I may add, as suitable to the present times, Isa. xxii. 12; Luke xxi. 34. I apprehend the spirit of these and similar passages of Scripture (for it would be easy to adduce a larger number,) will bring a Christian under such restrictions as follow.

To avoid and forbear, for his own sake, from whatever has a tendency to damp and indispose his spirit in attendance upon the means of grace; for such things, if they be not condemned as sinful *per se*, if they be not absolutely unlawful, yea though they be, when duly regulated, lawful and right, (for often our chief snares are entwined with our blessings,) yet if they have a repeated and evident tendency to deaden our hearts to divine things, of which each person's experience must determine, there must be something in them, either in season, measure, or circumstance, wrong to us; and let them promise what they will, they do but rob us of our gold to pay us with counters. For the light of God's countenance, and an open cheerfulness of spirit in walking with him in private, is our chief joy; and we must be already greatly hurt, if any thing can be pursued, allowed, or rested in, as a tolerable substitute for it.

For the sake of the church, and the influence example

* In so many words.

may have upon his fellow Christians, the law of charity and prudence will often require a believer to abstain from some things, not because they are unlawful, but inexpedient. Thus the apostle, though strenuous for the *right* of his Christian liberty, would have abridged himself of the *use*, so as to eat no meat, rather than offend a weak brother, rather than mislead him to act against the present light of his conscience. Upon this principle, if I could, without hurt to myself, attend some public amusements, as a concert or oratorio, and return thence with a warm heart to my closet, (the possibility of which in my own case I greatly question,) yet I should think it my duty to forbear, lest some weaker than myself should be encouraged by me to make the like experiment, though in their own minds they might fear it was wrong, and have no other reason to think it lawful but because I did it; in which case I should suspect, that though I received no harm, they would. And I have known and conversed with some who, I fear, have made shipwreck of their profession, who have dated their first decline from imitating others, whom they thought wiser and better than themselves, in such kind of compliances. And it seems that an obligation to this sort of self-denial rises and is strengthened and proportioned to the weight and influence of our characters. Were I in private life, I do not know that I should think it sinful to kill a partridge or a hare; but, as a minister, I no more dare do it than I dare join in a drunken frolic, because I know it would give offence to some, and be pleaded for as a license by others.

There is a duty and a charity likewise, which we owe to the world at large, as well as a faithfulness to God and his grace, in our necessary converse among them. This seems to require, that though we should not be needlessly singular, yet, for their instruction, and for the honour of our

Lord and Master, we should keep up a certain kind of singularity, and show ourselves called to be a separated people; that, though the providence of God has given us callings and relations to fill up, (in which we cannot be too exact,) yet we are not of the world, but belong to another community, and act from other principles, by other rules, and to other ends, than the generality of those about us. I have observed, that the world will often leave professors in quiet possession of their notions and sentiments, and places of worship, provided they will not be too stiff in the matter of conformity with their more general customs and amusements. But I fear many of them have had their prejudices strengthened against our holy religion by such compliances, and have thought, that if there were such joy and comfort to be found in the ways of God as they hear from our pulpits, professors would not, in such numbers, and so often run amongst them, to beg a relief, from the burden of time hanging upon their hands. . . . .

Providential and necessary calls of duty, that lead us into the world, will not hurt us, if we find the spirit of the world unpleasant, and are glad to retire from it, and keep out of it as much as our relative duties will permit. That which is our cross is not so likely to be our snare; but if that spirit, which we should always watch and pray against, infects and assimilates our minds to itself, then we are sure to suffer loss, and act below the dignity of our profession. . . .

Upon the whole, it appears to me, that it is more honourable, comfortable, and safe, (if we cannot exactly hit the golden mean,) to be thought by some too scrupulous and precise, than actually to be found too compliant with those things which, if not absolutely contrary to a divine commandment, are hardly compatible with the genius of the gospel, or conformable to the mind that was in Christ Jesus, which ought also to be in his people. The places and amusements which the world frequent and admire, where occasions and temptations to sin are cultivated, where the law of what is called good-breeding is the only law which may not be violated with impunity, where sinful passions are provoked and indulged, where the fear of God is so little known or regarded, that those who do fear him must hold their tongues though they should hear his name blasphemed, can hardly be a Christian's voluntary chosen ground. Yet I fear these characters will apply to every kind of polite amusement or assembly in the kingdom.

As to family connexions, I cannot think we are bound to break or slight them. But as believers and their friends often live as it were in two elements, there is a mutual awkwardness, which makes their interviews rather dry and tedious. But upon that account they are less frequent than they would otherwise be, which seems an advantage. Both sides keep up returns of civility and affection; but as they cannot unite in sentiment and leading inclination, they will not contrive to be very often together, except there is something considerable given up by one or the other; and I think Christians ought to be very cautious what concessions they make upon this account. But, as I said at the beginning, no general positive rules can be laid down.

I have simply given your lordship such thoughts as have occurred to me while writing, without study, and without coherence. I dare not be dogmatical; but I think what I have written is agreeable both to particular texts and to the general tenor of Scripture. I submit it to your judgment.

I am, etc.

The Rev. Thomas Jones.

MR. JONES was one of the six students who, in 1768, were expelled from St. Edmund's Hall, Oxford, for holding "Methodistical tenets." It may not be uninteresting, before proceeding with this brief account of Mr. Jones, to quote the following relation of this act of bigotry and injustice, as it appeared in the *St. James's Chronicle* for that date. "On Friday last (March 11, 1768), six students belonging to Edmund Hall, were expelled the university, after a hearing of several hours before the vice-chancellor, and some of the heads of houses, *for holding Methodistical tenets, and taking upon them to pray, read and expound the Scriptures, and singing hymns in private houses.* The principal of the college (Dr. Dixon), defended their doctrines from the thirty-nine articles of the Established Church, and spoke in the highest terms of the piety and exemplariness of their lives; but his motion was overruled, and sentence pronounced against them. One of the heads of houses present observed, that as these six gentlemen were expelled for having too much religion, it would be very proper to inquire into the conduct of some who had too little. Yet Mr. Vice-Chancellor Durrell was heard to tell the chief accuser that the university was much obliged to him for his good work."

To proceed with the account of Mr. Jones. He was originally in business as a hair-dresser, a circumstance which is mentioned here because it was matter of accusation against these students that they had all been tradesmen. Indeed, a letter was produced in evidence on the above occasion, in which the writer stated that Mr. Jones had made a very good periwig for him only two years before. The real fact, however, was that Mr. Jones had left the business four years before he went to college. Previous to this he resided for some time with Mr. Newton, and under his instruction made considerable progress in the study of the Greek and Hebrew Scriptures. After his expulsion from Oxford, he was much noticed by Lady Huntingdon, by whom he, with the other students referred to, had been recommended to Dr. Dixon. He was ordained, and became curate of Clifton, a village very near Olney. Mr. Jones married the sister of Lady Austin, the relative of Mr. Cowper.

To the REV. THOMAS JONES.

LETTER I.—On correcting evil tempers.

January 7, 1767.

DEAR SIR, . . . You seem sensible where your most observable failing lies, and to take reproof and admonition concerning it in good part; I therefore hope and believe the Lord will give you a growing victory over it. You must not expect habits and tempers will be eradicated instantaneously; but by perseverance in prayer, and observation upon the experiences of every day, much may be done in time. Now and then you will (as is usual in the course of war) lose a battle; but be not discouraged, but rally your forces, and return to the fight. There is a comfortable word, a leaf of the tree of life, for healing the wounds we receive, in 1 John ii. 1. If the enemy surprises you, and your heart smites you, do not stand astonished as if there were no help, nor give way to sorrow, as if there were no hope, nor attempt to heal yourself; but away immediately to the throne of grace, to the great Physician, to the compassionate High Priest, and tell him all. Satan knows, that if he can keep us from confession, our wounds will rankle; but do you profit by David's experience, Psal. xxxii. 3—5. When we are simple and open-hearted in abasing ourselves before the Lord, though we have acted foolishly and

I

ungratefully, he will seldom let us remain long without affording us a sense of his compassion; for He is gracious; He knows our frame, and how to bear with us, though we can hardly bear with ourselves, or with one another.

The main thing is to have *the heart right with God:* this will bring us in the end safely through many mistakes and blunders; but a double mind, a selfish spirit, that would halve things between God and the world, the Lord abhors. Though I have not yet had many opportunities of commending your *prudence,* I have always had a good opinion of your *sincerity* and *integrity:* if I am not mistaken in this, I make no doubt of your doing well. If the Lord is pleased to bless you, He will undoubtedly make you humble; for you cannot be either happy or safe, or have any probable hope of abiding usefulness, without it. I do not know that I have had any thing so much at heart in my connexions with you, as to impress you with a sense of the necessity and advantages of a humble frame of spirit; I hope it has not been in vain. Oh! to be little in our own eyes! This is the ground-work of every grace; this leads to a continual dependence upon the Lord Jesus; this is the spirit which He has promised to bless; this conciliates us good-will and acceptance amongst men; for he that abaseth himself is sure to be honoured. And that this temper is so hard to attain and preserve, is a striking proof of our depravity—For are we not sinners? Were we not rebels and enemies before we knew the gospel; and have we not been unfaithful, backsliding, and unprofitable ever since? Are we not redeemed by the blood of Jesus? and can we stand a single moment except He upholds us? Have we any thing which we have not received? or have we received any thing which we have not abused? Why then is dust and ashes proud?

I am glad you have found some spiritual acquaintance in your barren land. I hope you will be helpful to them, and they to you. You do well to guard against every appearance of evil. If you are heartily for Jesus, Satan owes you a grudge. One way or other he will try to cut you out work, and the Lord may suffer him to go to the length of his chain. But though you are to keep your eye upon him, and expect to hear from him at every step, you need not be slavishly afraid of him; for Jesus is stronger and wiser than he, and there is a complete suit of armour provided for all who are engaged on the Lord's side.

I am, etc.

To the REV. THOMAS JONES.

LETTER II.—Calvinism—Preaching to sinners.

October 20, 1767.

DEAR SIR,—A concern for the perplexity you have met with, from objections which have been made against some expressions in my printed sermons, and in general against exhorting sinners to believe in Jesus, engages me to write immediately; otherwise I should have waited a little longer; for we are now upon the point of removing to the vicarage, and I believe this will be the last letter I shall write from the old house. I shall chiefly confine myself at present to the subject you propose.

In the first place, I beg you to be upon your guard against a reasoning spirit. Search the Scriptures; and where you can find a plain rule or warrant for any practice, go boldly on; and be not discouraged because you may not be clearly able to answer or reconcile every difficulty that may either occur to your own mind, or be put in your way by others. Our hearts are very dark and narrow, and the very root of all apostacy is a proud disposition to question the necessity or propriety of divine appointments. But the child-like simplicity of faith is to follow God without reasoning; taking it for granted a thing must be right if He directs it, and charging all seeming inconsistencies to the account of our own ignorance.

I suppose the people that trouble you upon this head are of two sorts: 1st, those who preach upon Arminian principles, and suppose a free will in man, in a greater or less degree, to turn to God when the gospel is proposed. These, if you speak to sinners at large, though they will approve of your doing so, will take occasion, perhaps, to charge you with acting in contradiction to your own principles. . . . If I had a proper call, I would undertake to prove, that to exhort and deal plainly with sinners, to stir them up to flee from the wrath to come, and to lay hold of eternal life, is an attempt not reconcilable to sober reason upon any other grounds than those doctrines which we are called Calvinists for holding; and that all the absurdities which are charged upon us, as consequences of what we teach, are indeed truly chargeable upon those who differ from us in these points. . . . As to myself, if I was not a Calvinist, I think I should have no more hope of success in preaching to men, than to horses or cows.

But these objections are more frequently urged by Calvinists themselves; many of them, I doubt not, good men, but betrayed into a curiosity of spirit, which often makes their ministry (if ministers) dry and inefficacious, and their conversation sour and unsavoury. . . .

I advise you to keep close to the Bible and prayer; bring your difficulties to the Lord, and intreat him to give you, and maintain in you, a simple spirit. Search the

Scripture. How did Peter deal with Simon Magus? We have no right to think worse of any who can hear us, than the apostle did of him. He seemed almost to think his case desperate, and yet he advised him to repentance and prayer. Examine the same apostle's discourse, Acts iii. and the close of St. Paul's sermon, Acts xiii. The power is all of God; the means are likewise of his appointment; and He always is pleased to work by such means as may show that the power is his. What was Moses's rod in itself, or the trumpets that threw down Jericho? What influence could the pool of Siloam have, that the eyes of the blind man, by washing in it, should be opened? or what could Ezekiel's feeble breath contribute to the making dry bones live? All these means were exceedingly disproportionate to the effect; but He who ordered them to be used accompanied them with his power. Yet if Moses had gone without his rod, if Joshua had slighted the rams' horns, if the prophet had thought it foolishness to speak to dry bones, or the blind man refused to wash his eyes, nothing could have been done. The same holds good in the present subject: I do not reason, expostulate, and persuade sinners, because I think I can prevail with them, but because the Lord has commanded it. He directs me to address them as reasonable creatures: to take them by every handle: to speak to their consciences; to tell them of the terrors of the Lord, and of his tender mercies; to argue with them what good they find in sin; whether they do not need a Saviour; to put them in mind of death, judgment, and eternity, etc. When I have done all, I know it is to little purpose, except the Lord speaks to their hearts; and this to his own, and at his own time, I am sure He will, because he has promised it. See Isaiah lv. 10, 11; Matt. xxviii. 20. Indeed I have heard expressions in the warmth of delivery, which I could not wholly approve, and therefore do not imitate. But in general, I see no preaching made very useful for the gathering of souls, where poor sinners are shut out of the discourse. I think one of the closest and most moving addresses to sinners I ever met with, is in Dr. Owen's Exposition of the 130th Psalm (in my edition, from p. 243 to 276). If you get it and examine it, I think you will find it all agreeable to Scripture; and he was a steady, deep-sighted Calvinist. I wish you to study it well, and make it your pattern. He handles the same point likewise in other places, and shows the weakness of the exceptions taken somewhere at large, but I cannot just now find the passage. Many think themselves quite right, because they have not had their thoughts exercised at large, but have confined themselves to one track. There are extremes in every thing. I pray God to show you the golden mean.

I am, etc.

The Rev. Thomas Bowman.

MR. BOWMAN was appointed vicar of Martham, in Norfolk, in November, 1758. As appears from one of his letters to Mr. Newton, it was about the year 1763 that he became savingly acquainted with the truth, and having found the Christ, he at once began to speak to others of him. It was, however, with much diffidence, for there seems to have been a constitutional timidity about him, and so little fluency of speech that he could not utter two or three sentences without hesitation. This led him almost to doubt his call to the ministry. Nevertheless, it was a work he could not give up, and it is manifest that eventually these difficulties were quite overcome. In the meantime it was probably this consciousness of inability in the pulpit which led him to publish a volume of sermons and letters, entitled *The Principles of Christianity as taught in Scripture*, and which passed through four editions. The first must have been published early in the year 1765. Mr. Newton met with it in London, and at the same time received such an account of its author, who, it appears, had read his *Narrative*, as induced him to write to Mr. Bowman. Referring to his work, which was very decided in its evangelical views, Mr. Newton says, in his first letter, "Though we have no acquaintance we are already united in the strictest ties of friendship, partakers of the same hope, servants of the same Lord, and in the same part of his vineyard. I therefore hold all apologies needless. I rejoice in the Lord's goodness to you, I pray for his abundant blessing on your labours, I need an interest in your prayers, I have an affectionate desire to know more concerning you. These are my motives for writing."

In 1768, Mr. Newton went into Norfolk to visit his friend, and writing on that occasion to Mr. Cowper he says, "I see here fresh reason to be thankful for my situation at Olney. Poor Mr. Bowman has as yet few or none to pray for him or strengthen his hands. How glad would he be to be encompassed as I am." The county of Norfolk was at that time in much spiritual darkness, and Mr. Bowman was not a little discouraged by the state of things around him, and the apparent want of success attending his own efforts; but in 1774 he tells Mr. Newton of a great awakening at Martham, and he began to reap the fruits of his many prayers and earnest labours. About the same time, as we read in *The Life and Times of the Countess of Huntingdon*, her ladyship having engaged the Tabernacle at Norwich, it is there recorded that "Mr. Shirley, Mr. Glasscott, and Mr. Bowman were the first clergymen who preached after it came into the possession of the countess," and again, "The labours of Mr. Glasscott and Mr. Bowman were abundantly successful at this time in exciting a spirit of inquiry" (vol. ii. pp. 343, 5).

It may be added that Mr. Bowman published a second work, in 1791, entitled, *Caustonia; or, Twelve Discourses addressed to the Inhabitants of Cawston*. He also communicated several papers to the *Gospel Magazine*. The labours of this good man were brought to a close in the year 1792.

To the REV. T. BOWMAN.

LETTER I.—Divine help in the work of the ministry—Guarding against extremes—Christian prudence.

November 2, 1765.

VERY DEAR SIR,—Your letter of the 4th ult. gave me great pleasure. I thank you for the particular account you have favoured me with. I rejoice with you, sympathize with you, and find my heart opened to correspond with unreserved freedom. May the Lord direct our pens, and help us to help each other. The work you are engaged in is great, and your difficulties many; but faithful is He that hath called you, who also will do it. The weapons which He has now put into your hands are not carnal, but mighty through God to the pulling down of strongholds. Men may fight, but they shall not prevail against us, if we are but enabled to put our cause simply into the Lord's hands, and keep steadily on in the path of duty. He will plead our cause, and fight our battles; He will pardon our mistakes, and teach us to do better. My experience as a minister is but small, having been but about eighteen months in the vineyard; but for about twelve years I have been favoured with an increasing acquaintance among the people of God, of various ranks and denominations, which, together with the painful exercises of my own heart, gave me opportunity of making observations which were of great use to me when I entered upon the work myself; and ever since, I have found the Lord graciously supplying new lights and new strength, as new occurrences arise. So I trust it will be with you. I endeavour to avail myself of the examples, advice, and sentiments of my brethren, yet at the same time to guard against calling any man master. This is the peculiar of Christ. The best are but men; the wisest may be mistaken; and that which may be right in another might be wrong in me, through a difference of circumstances. The Spirit of God distributes variously, both in gifts and dispensations; and I would no more be tied to act strictly by others' rules, than to walk in shoes of the same size. My shoes must to be found among some of that system, which I do not choose to imitate. I dislike those sentiments against which you have borne your testimony in the note at the end of your preface; but having known many precious souls in that party, I have been taught, that the kingdom of God is not in names and sentiments, but in righteousness, faith, love, peace, and joy in the Holy Ghost. I should, however, upon some occasions, oppose those tenets, if they had any prevalence in my neighbourhood: but they have not; and in general, I believe, the surest way to refute or prevent error, is to preach the truth. I am glad to find you are aware of that spirit of enthusiasm which has so often broken loose and blemished hopeful beginnings, and that the foundation you build upon is solid and scriptural: this will, I hope, save you much trouble, and prevent many offences. Let us endeavour to make our people acquainted with the Scripture, and to impress them with a high sense of its authority, excellence, and sufficiency. Satan seldom remarkably imposes on ministers or people, except where the word of God is too little consulted or regarded. Another point in which I aim at a medium is in what is called *prudence*. There is certainly such a thing as Christian prudence, and a remarkable deficiency of it is highly inconvenient. But caution too often degenerates into cowardice; and if the fear of man, under the name of prudence, gets within our guard, like a chilling frost, it nips every thing in the bud. Those who trust the Lord, and act openly with an honest freedom and consistency, I observe He generally bears them out, smoothes their way, and makes their enemies their friends, or at least restrains their rage; while such as halve things, temporize, and aim to please God and man together, meet with double disappointment, and are neither useful nor respected. If we trust to him, He will stand by us; if we regard men, He will leave us to make the best we can of them. . . .

May we, dear Sir, live and feed upon the precious promises, John xiv. 16, 17, 26, and xvi. 13—15. There is no teacher like Jesus, who by his Holy Spirit reveals himself in his word to the understanding and affections of his children. When we thus behold his glory in the gospel-glass, we are changed into the same image. Then our hearts melt, our eyes flow, our stammering tongues are unloosed. That this may be your increasing experience, is the prayer of, dear Sir,

Yours, etc.

To the Rev. T. Bowman.

LETTER II.—Experimental knowledge — Owen, Leighton, Edwards — Spread of the truth.

January 21, 1766.

DEAR SIR,—Your letters give me the sincerest pleasure. Let us believe that we are daily thinking of and praying for each other, and write when opportunity offers without apologies. I praise the Lord that he has led you so soon to a settled judgment in the leading truths of the gospel. . . . It is a mercy likewise, to be enabled to acknowledge what is excellent in the writings or conduct of others, without adopting their singularities, or discarding the whole on account of a few blemishes. We should be glad to receive instruction from all, and avoid being led by the *ipse dixit* of any. *Nullius jurare in verbum,** is a fit motto for those who have one master, even Christ. We may grow wise apace in opinions, by books and men; but vital, experimental

* Freely rendered—To call no man Master.

knowledge can only be received from the Holy Spirit, the great instructor and comforter of his people. And there are two things observable in his teaching: 1. That He honours the means of his own appointment, so that we cannot expect to make any great progress without diligence on our parts. 2. That He does not teach all at once, but by degrees. Experience is his school; and by this I mean the observation and improvement of what passes within us and around us in the course of every day. The word of God affords a history in miniature of the heart of man, the devices of Satan, the state of the world and the method of grace. And the most instructing and affecting commentary on it to an enlightened mind, may be gathered from what we see, feel, and hear, from day to day. . . . We are favoured with many excellent books in our tongue; but I, with you, agree in assigning one of the first places (as a teacher) to Dr. Owen. I have just finished his *Discourse on the Holy Spirit*, which is an epitome, if not the masterpiece of his writings. As to Archbishop Leighton, . . . I set the highest value upon his *Prælectiones Theologiæ*. He has wonderfully united the simplicity of the gospel with all the captivating beauties of style and language. Bishop Burnet says, he was the greatest master of the Latin tongue he ever knew, of which, together with his compass of learning, he has given proof in his lectures; yet in his gayer dress, his eminent humility and spirituality appear to no less advantage than when clad in plain English. I think it may be said to be a diamond set in gold. . . .

"Edwards on Free Will," I have read with pleasure, as a good answer to the proud reasoners in their own way; but a book of that sort cannot be generally read: where the subject matter is unpleasing, and the method of treating it requires more attention than the Athenian spirit of the times would bear, I wonder not if it is uncalled for. . . .

You send us good news indeed, that two more of your brethren are declaring on the gospel side. The Lord confirm and strengthen them, add yet to your numbers, and make you helps and comforts to each other. Surely He is about to spread his work. Happy those whom He honours to be fellow-workers with him. Let us account the disgrace we suffer for his name's sake to be our great honour. Many will be against us; but there are more for us. All the praying souls on earth, all the glorified saints in heaven, all the angels of God, yea, the God of angels himself, are all on our side. Satan may rage, but he is a chained enemy. Men may contradict and fight, but they cannot prevail. Two things we shall especially need, courage and patience, that we neither faint before them, nor upon any provocation act in their spirit. . . .
As the Lord brings you out a people, witnesses for you to the truth of his word, you will find advantage in bringing them often together. The interval from sabbath to sabbath is a good while, and affords time for the world and Satan to creep in. Intermediate meetings for prayer, etc., when properly conducted, are greatly useful. I could wish for larger sheets and longer leisure; but I am constrained to say adieu, in our dear Lord and Saviour.

Yours, etc.

Daniel West, Esq.

THE letters addressed to Mr. West, some of them in their author's happiest vein, show in how much esteem he was held by Mr. Newton, and everything that is recorded of his friend proves how just that estimate was. It is stated of Mr. West, in an obituary notice in the *Evangelical Magazine*, for 1796, that he was, for many years, a happy subject of Divine grace, and a zealous and approved friend of the gospel.

Mr. West was a friend of the Rev. George Whitefield, and that excellent man left him joint trustee, with Mr. Keene, of the Tabernacle, and Tottenham Court Chapel. The subject of our notice is said to have been with his co-trustee, "always regular and exact in the weighty duties devolving upon him. It was ever his study to conciliate the affections of the ministers, to promote the glory of Christ, and the spiritual interests of the congregation."

For the last thirteen years of his life, Mr. West was afflicted with a very painful malady; but he is said never to have deserted his post, or to have uttered a murmuring expression, but to have endured his trial with great patience and fortitude of mind. He was, moreover, an eminent example of Christian humility and thankfulness.

In September, 1796, he was taken very ill at Tottenham Court Chapel-house. He ventured, however, on the following sabbath, to attend at the Tabernacle; but while there, his complaint returned with such severity, that he was too ill to be removed, and after lingering some days, died on the 30th of September. During this time he strikingly exhibited the strength of his trust in God. He looked upon death with the greatest cheerfulness, and thanked God that his work was done. A very interesting account of Mr. West's last hours will be found in the publication referred to above.

To DANIEL WEST, ESQ.

LETTER I.—*How to regard our earthly comforts.*

January 25, 1766.

DEAR SIR,—You (and, consequently, Mrs. West, for you cannot suffer alone,) have lately been in the furnace, and are now brought safely out. I hope you have much to say of the grace, care, and skill of the great Refiner, who watched over you; and that you have lost nothing but dross. Let this experience be treasured up in your hearts for the use of future times. Other trials will come, but you have found the Lord faithful to his promise, and have good encouragement to trust him again. I would take the liberty to address myself particularly to dear Mrs. West, upon a theme my heart is so well acquainted with. You know your weak side; endeavour to set a double guard of prayer there. Our earthly comforts would be doubly sweet, if we could but venture them without anxiety in the Lord's hands. And where can we lodge them so safely? Is not the first gift, the continuance, the blessing, which makes them pleasing, all from him? Was not his design in all this, that we should be happy in them? How then can we fear that He will threaten them, much less take them away, but with a view to our further benefit? Let us suppose the thing we are most afraid of actually to happen. Can it come a moment sooner, or in any other way, than by his appointment? Is He not gracious, and faithful, to support us under the stroke? Is He not rich enough to give us something better than ever He will take away? Is not the light of his countenance better than life and all its most valued enjoyments? Is not this our time of trial; and are we not travelling towards a land of light? Methinks, when we view things in the light of eternity, it is much the same, whether the separating stroke arrives at the end of seven or seventy years; since, come when it will, it must and will be felt; but one draught of the river of pleasure at God's right hand will make us forget our sorrows for ever; or the remembrance, if any, will only serve to heighten our joys. Further, what life did He lead whom we call our Master and our Lord? Was not He a man of sorrows, and acquainted with grief? Has He marked out *one* way to heaven with his painful footsteps, and shall we expect, or even wish, to walk in another? With such considerations as these, we should endeavour to arm our minds, and pray to the Lord to fix a sense of them in our hearts, and to renew it from time to time; that when changes are either feared or felt, we may not be like the people of the world, who have no hope, no refuge, no throne of grace, but may be enabled to glorify our God in the fire, and give proof that his grace is sufficient for us in every state. It is neither comfortable for ourselves, nor honourable to our profession, to start at every shaking leaf. If we are sensible of this, mourn over our infirmities before the Lord, and faithfully strive in prayer against the fear that easily besets us; He can, and He will, strengthen us with strength in our souls, and make us more than conquerors, according to his sure promise.

A proneness to idolatry is our bosom sin: I have smarted for it. I dare not say I am cured; yet I would hope the Lord's wonderful interchange of comforts and chastisements have not been wholly lost upon me, but have been accompanied with some measure of his sanctifying grace. At present, that is, ever since my settlement at Olney, I have been favoured with an interval of ease. I never had so long and general an exemption from sharp trials. When I consider, and feel what I am, I am amazed at his forbearance. Surely, I deserve to be visited with breach upon breach. But his compassions are infinite. Yet, I must not expect to have always fair weather in a changeable world. I would desire neither to presume that my mountain stands strong, nor yet to afflict myself with needless apprehension of what a day may bring forth. Oh! that I could improve the present, and cheerfully commit the future to him who does all things wisely and well, and has promised that all shall work together for good.

I am, dear Sir,
Your very affectionate and obliged servant.

To D. West, Esq.

LETTER II.—What Christ is to his people, and what unprofitable servants they are to him.

April 12, 1771.

MY DEAR SIR,—I often review my late London visit with much satisfaction, rejoicing that I found so many of my dear friends thriving in the good ways of the Lord. Surely, his service is perfect freedom; his ways are ways of pleasantness, and all his paths are peace. He is a sun and a shield, a hiding-place, and a resting-place, to them that fear him. May we still press forward: we have not yet attained. There are larger measures of grace, establishment, and consolation, set forth in the Gospel, than all we have hitherto received. The Lord has set before us an open door which no man can shut; He has given us exceeding great and precious promises; has bid us open our mouths wide, and has said that He will fill them. He would have us ask great things, and when we have enlarged our desires to the utmost, He is still able to do exceeding more than we can ask or think. May we be as wise in our generation as the children of this world. They are not content with a little, or, even with much, so long as there is any probability of getting more. As to myself, I am but a poor man in the trade of grace; I live from hand to mouth, and procure just enough, (as we say,) to keep the wolf from the door. But I must charge it to my unbelief and indolence, which have been so great that it is a mercy I am not a bankrupt. This would have been the case, but that I have a friend, (whom you know,) who has kindly engaged for me. To tell you the plain truth, I have nothing of my own, but trade wholly upon his stock; and yet, (would you think it possible,) though I often confess to him I am an unprofitable and unfaithful steward, yet I have upon many occasions spoken and acted as if I would have people believe, that what He has committed to me was my own property. Ah! Sir, if you had a servant like me, that should affect to show away at your expense, you would hardly bear with him long. You would be ready to say—What is this I hear? Give an account of thy stewardship, for thou may'st be no longer steward. I learn sometimes, from family relations, to form a little judgment of the Lord's patience towards his people. What a family has He to bear with! Those to whom He stands in the relation of a husband, admit idols in their hearts against him; his friends hold a secret correspondence with his enemies; his children repine against him, and quarrel one with another; his servants serve themselves. I do not wonder that those who are not well acquainted with the freedom and security of the gospel covenant, should live in daily fear of being turned out of doors. I am sure I deserve it every day of my life. But He is God, and not man; his ways are not as ours; and as it has pleased him to receive us as children, He has promised that we shall abide in his house for ever. It is our mercy that we have an atonement of infinite value, and an Advocate who is always heard, and who ever liveth to make intercession for us.

I am, dear Sir,

Your much obliged and affectionate servant.

JOHN NEWTON.

To D. West, Esq.

LETTER III.—*Christ the great Physician—Spiritual prosperity at Olney.*

June 2, 1772.

MY DEAR SIR,—It is true: I confess it. I have been very naughty. I ought not to have been so long in answering your last kind letter. Now I hope you have forgiven me. And therefore I at once recover my confidence without troubling you with such excuses as the old man, ever desirous of justifying himself, would suggest. We were glad to hear of your welfare, and of the prosperity with which the Lord favours you at home, and in the two great houses;* which I hope will continue to be like trees planted by the waters of the sanctuary, maintaining the leaves of Gospel doctrine always green and

* Tottenham Court Road Chapel and the Tabernacle in Moorfields.

flourishing, and abounding with a constant succession of blossoms, green and ripe fruit; I mean believers in the states of babes, young men, and fathers in Christ.

> "Awake, O heavenly wind, and come;
> Blow on these gardens of perfume!
> Spirit divine, descend and breathe
> A gracious gale on plants beneath."

And while you are using your best endeavours in watching for the good of these vineyards, may your own flourish. May your soul rejoice in the Lord and in the success of his work, and every ordinance and providence administer unto you an especial blessing!

The illness under which I have laboured longer than the man mentioned in John v. 5, is far from being removed. Yet I am bound to speak well of my Physician: He treats me with great tenderness; assures me that it shall not be to death, but to the glory of God; and bids me in due time expect a perfect cure. I know too much of him (though I know but little) to doubt either his skill or his promise. It is true I suffer sad relapses, and have been more than once brought in appearance to death's door since I have been under his care; but this fault has not been his, but my own. I am a strange refractory patient; have too often neglected his prescriptions, and broken the regimen He appoints me to observe. This perverseness, joined to the exceeding obstinacy of my disorders, would have caused me to be turned out as an incurable long ago, had I been under any hand but his. But, indeed, there is none like him. When I have brought myself low, He has still helped me. Blessed be his name, I am yet alive; yea, I shall ere long be well; but not here. The air which I breathe is unfavourable to my constitution, and nourishes my disease. He knows this, and intends, at a proper season, to remove me into a better climate, where there are no fogs nor damps, where the inhabitants shall no more say, I am sick. He has brought my judgment to acquiesce with his; and sometimes I long to hear him say, Arise and depart. But to tell you the truth, I am much more frequently pleased with the thought of staying a little and a little longer here, though in my present situation I am kept alive merely by dint of medicine; and though his medicines are all salutary, they are not all pleasant. Now and then He gives me a pleasant cordial; but many things which there is a need-be for my taking frequently, are bitter and unpalatable. It is strange that knowing this is, and must be, the case, I am not more desirous of my dismission. I hope, however, one thing that makes me willing to stay is, that I may point him out as a Physician of value to others. We sometimes see in the newspapers acknowledgments of cures received. What sheets and quires of advertisements would be necessary, if all the Lord's people were to publish their cases. . . .

When will you come and see the flock at Olney? By the blessing of the Good Shepherd, we have had a good number of lambs added to the fold of late, who are in a very promising way. You would like to hear their bleatings. The voice of joy and thanksgivings is heard in our tabernacles, saying, The right hand of the Lord is exalted; the right hand of the Lord bringeth mighty things to pass. Pray for us, that these gracious drops may be the forerunners of a plentiful shower. For, notwithstanding what I have said, wickedness still abounds amongst us in the town. And many, having long resisted the convictions of the Word and Spirit, are hardened and bold in sinning to a great degree. So that Olney is like the two baskets of Jeremiah's figs, the good are very good, and the bad are exceedingly bad.

I am, my dear Sir,

Your affectionate and obliged servant,

J. NEWTON.

To D. WEST, ESQ.

LETTER IV.—The life of faith a happy life.

April 20, 1773.

MY DEAR SIR,—It is time to thank you for your kind letter, but I am so much taken up, that I can hardly pay my debts of correspondence in due season. However, I do not love to let yours be long unanswered, because till I have quitted scores, I have but little hopes of hearing from you again.

We were glad to hear that you and Mrs. West were well, and to find by your writing, that the Lord makes your feet like hinds' feet in his good ways, and leads you in the paths of pleasantness and peace. I doubt not but you likewise have your share of trials; but when the love of God is shed abroad in the heart by the Holy Ghost, it sweetens what bitter things the Lord puts into our cup, and enables us to say, None of these things move us. Yea, the life of faith is a happy life, and if attended with conflicts, there is an assurance of victory; if we sometimes get a wound, there is healing balm near at hand; if we seem to fall, we are raised again; and if tribulations abound, consolations shall abound likewise. Is it not happiness to have an infallible Guide, an invincible Guard, an Almighty Friend? to be able to say *of* the

Maker of heaven and earth, He is my Beloved, my Shepherd, my Saviour, and my Husband; and to say *to* him,

> Let waves and thunders mix and roar,
> Be thou my God, I ask no more:
> While thou art Sovereign, I'm secure;
> I shall be rich till thou art poor?

Oh the peace that flows from believing that all events in which we are concerned are under his immediate disposal; that the hairs of our head are all numbered; that He delights in our prosperity; that there is a *need be*, if we are in heaviness, and that all things shall surely work for our good! How happy to have such views of his sovereignty, wisdom, love, and faithfulness, as will enable us to meet every dispensation with submission, and to look through the changes of the present life, to that unchangeable inheritance to which the Lord is leading us, when all evil shall cease, and where joy shall be perfect and eternal. I trust He who loves you strengthens you in this life of faith, and fills you with a peace that passes all understanding.

Perhaps you have heard that I have not been well. My illness was not so great as to confine me from my work, and the Lord was pleased to give me a peaceful frame of mind under his hand, so that I did not suffer much. For about a week I was set to learn the value of hearing by the want of it; for I was so deaf that I could join in no conversation; but now, thanks to the great Physician, my complaints are all removed. . . .

I am your much obliged and affectionate servant,

J. NEWTON.

To D. WEST, ESQ.

LETTER V.—A striking portrait.

August 13, 1773.

MY DEAR SIR,—We are always glad to hear from you, because your paper is perfumed with the name of Jesus. You speak well of him, and you have reason, for he has been a good friend to you. I likewise am enabled to say something of him; and I trust the chief reason why I would wish my life to be prolonged is, that I may employ more of my breath in his praise. But, alas! while I endeavour to persuade others, that He is the chief among ten thousand and altogether lovely, I seem to be but half persuaded of it myself; I feel my heart so cold and unbelieving. But I hope I can say this is not I, but sin that dwelleth in me. Did you ever see my picture? I have it drawn by a masterly hand. And though another person, and one whom I am far from resembling, *sat* for it, it is as like me as one new guinea is like another. The original was drawn at Corinth, and sent to some persons of *distinction* at Rome. Many copies have been taken, and though perhaps it is not to be seen in any of the London print-shops, it has a place in most public and private libraries, and I would hope in most families. I had seen it a great many times before I could discover one of my own features in it; but then my eyes were very bad. What is remarkable, it was drawn long before I was born, but having been favoured with some excellent eye-salve, I quickly knew it to be my own. I am drawn in an attitude which would be strange and singular, if it were not so common with me, looking two different and opposite ways at once, so that you would be puzzled to tell whether my eyes are fixed upon heaven or upon earth: I am aiming at things inconsistent with each other at the same instant, so that I can accomplish neither. According to the different light in which you view the picture, I appear to rejoice and mourn, to choose and refuse, to be a conqueror or a captive. In a word, I am a double person; a riddle. It is no wonder if you know not what to make of me, for I cannot tell what to make of myself. I would and I would not; I do and do not; I can and I cannot. I find the hardest things easy, and the easiest things impossible: but while I am in this perplexity, you will observe in the same piece, a hand stretched forth for my relief, and may see a label proceeding out of my mouth with these words.—"I thank God, through Jesus Christ my Lord." The more I study this picture, the more I discover some new and striking resemblance, which convinces me that the painter knew me better than I knew myself. . . .

I am sincerely yours,

J. NEWTON.

To D. West, Esq.

LETTER VI.—A blessed habitation.

August 29, 1774.

MY DEAR SIR,—I have been often with you in spirit in your new habitation. In my idea of it, it is a grand place; a temple where the Lord is worshipped; a castle guarded by Almighty Power. If I mistake not, it has several privileges beyond most of the houses in your neighbourhood. Does not the sun often shine into it in the night season? Have you not some rooms so far exceeding the gallery of St. Paul's, that if you speak but

in a whisper, your voice is heard beyond the clouds?
Have you not a very fine prospect from it, when the air is
clear? According to my notion of the situation when
you look one way, you have a long vista which would
take one a good number of years to travel over, and a
great number of curious Ebenezers erected (instead of
mile-stones) all along the road. If you look the other
way, there is always a kind of mist, which prevents objects which are near at hand from being clearly seen;
but, what is very extraordinary, I am told you can see
through that mist, to a land that lies a great way off, and
that the more you look the better you can see. If every
house around you had the like advantages, it would certainly be the finest village in the kingdom — a little
heaven upon earth. All houses from the king's to the
labourer's however they differ in other circumstances,
agree in this, that they must have windows whereby
they may receive the light. A palace without a window
would be little better than a dungeon; and a man would
almost think himself buried alive in it. Many splendid
houses are dungeons with respect to spiritual light. A
believer could not bear the thoughts of living in any situation, unless he enjoyed the light of the Sun of Righteousness, and with this any situation is tolerable. You know
the value of this light, and you are favoured with it.
Therefore I doubt not your house is a good one. May
you enjoy it more and more, and now you are withdrawn
from the noise of the town, and (as I suppose) in some
measure from the hurry of business, may your leisure be
sanctified, and a sense of the Lord's presence brighten
every hour of your future life; and may you dwell, as
Jacob lodged for one night at the gate of heaven, till the
appointed moment when the gate shall open and let you

in, to be for ever with the Lord. In the mean time you are happy that the Lord has favoured you with many opportunities and advantages of promoting his glory, and the good of his people, and giving you a heart to improve them.

As to myself, I would tell you how it is with me if I could: at the best, it would be an inconsistent account. . . . I am a sinner, believing in the name of Jesus. I am a silly sheep, but I have a gracious, watchful Shepherd. I am a dull scholar, but I have a Master who can make the dullest learn. He still bears with me, He still employs me, He still enables me, He still owns me. Oh for a coal of heavenly fire to warm my heart, that I might praise him as I ought! As a people, we have much cause of complaint in ourselves, and much cause of thankfulness to him. In the main I hope we are alive, though not as we could wish: our numbers rather increase from year to year, and some flourish. In the ordinances, we are favoured in a measure with his presence. But, oh for a day of his power,—that his work may run broader and deeper, and the fire of grace spread from heart to heart, till the whole town be in a flame! To this I hope you will give a hearty Amen, and often remember us in your prayers.

I am sincerely yours,
JOHN NEWTON.

Captain Scott.

CAPT. SCOTT was a member of an ancient and highly respectable family in Salop. When he was seventeen he obtained a commission as cornet in a regiment of dragoons, and in due course became captain. Though at first he led a dissipated life, he was brought to some serious thoughts by considering the dangers to which, as a soldier, he was exposed; but he was utterly ignorant of the gospel, and vainly thought by acts of self-righteousness to approve himself in the sight of God. His good resolutions were constantly broken, and he was dissatisfied and without rest. When in this state of mind his regiment was quartered at Oathall in Sussex, where Lady Huntingdon had a preaching station. Being out one day on a shooting excursion, Capt. Scott was driven by a storm to seek shelter in the house of a farmer, who was a pious man. He talked with the Captain in a manner that surprised him; and, upon asking him where he had learned those things, the farmer told him that he was in the habit of attending at a neighbouring hall where a famous man, Mr. Romaine, was preaching for Lady Huntingdon; and the good man urged him to go and hear for himself. Capt. Scott accordingly went the next Sunday, and was deeply impressed by the whole service. The truth preached seemed exactly to meet his particular case, and was the means of his conversion to God. With the energy characteristic of him, he at once felt it his duty to use every opportunity of doing good to others. This he did, unmindful of opposition and reproach. Being stationed at Northampton in Aug. 1766, and having heard, we suppose, of Mr. Newton's religious character and efforts, and especially that he was not forgetful to entertain strangers, Capt. Scott, with a brother officer, went to Olney to spend the sabbath. Such was the commencement of a life-long friendship between these good men.

In the following year the religious doings of Capt. Scott awakened the notice and dislike of his commanding officer, and at length perceiving that there was a wish to get rid of him from the army, he sold his commission, and so gave up all hope of promotion in that quarter. At first he had thoughts of entering the church; but feeling he should have less liberty there, he resolved to join the dissenters. When he quitted the army he took up his residence at Wollaston near Wem. Here he lived for several years, full of activity and zeal, introducing the gospel into several places in the neighbourhood and being instrumental in building chapels in many of them. But his labours were not confined to that locality. At Chester, Lancaster, and other places in their vicinity he was alike active and successful. He was at length invited to settle at Lancaster, but this he declined, considering that his work was rather that of an *Evangelist*, and as such he was ordained at the above-mentioned place in 1776. From this time Mr. Scott was in labours more abundant. Three years afterwards he was introduced to Lady Glenorchy, who largely assisted him in the erection of chapels. Dying in 1786 this excellent woman bequeathed to Mr. Scott a chapel and dwelling house at Matlock in Derbyshire. Thither he removed, and, beginning to feel the infirmities of age, he divided his labours between Matlock and Nantwich. At length his eminently useful life was closed, May 28, 1807.

This brief notice supplies abundant evidence of the zeal and devotedness of Mr. Scott, as also of his sincere piety. It is said of him that he possessed much of the spirit of prayer, and that his conversation was peculiarly spiritual and edifying. His pulpit talents were popular, and as a preacher he was greatly blessed of God. He regularly supplied the Tabernacle in Moorfields for upwards of twenty years.

To Captain Scott.

Letter I.—A letter of encouragement in circumstances of trial.

August 8, 1766.

My dear Friend,—I am very willing to meet you with a letter at York, though I have no particular advice to offer. It seems probable, as you say, that your expected interview with the General will afford you some further light into your future path. I am in no pain about the event.* Man is a proud creature, and prone to please himself with the imagination of influence and power; but in reality he has none any further than as it is given him from above. The General, or whoever else are displeased with you, have their commission, and limits assigned them by one whom they little think of; and when they seem to think they can do most, they shall in effect do nothing but as instruments of his will. I trust the Lord will stand by you, put his love into your heart, and suitable words into your mouth, and overrule the minds of them with whom you have to do. And if He has further service for you in that situation, you will find that his hook and bridle will hold them in, so that they shall not be able to hurt you. As you know whom you have believed, and where to apply for strength suited to your day, according to his promise, I am so far from trembling for the event, that I congratulate you on the honourable opportunity that is before you of witnessing a good confession

---

* There is a very interesting letter from Captain Scott to Mr. Newton, which will be found in the life of the latter, p. 160, etc., giving a detail of the Captain's interview with General Howard, the colonel of his regiment, and showing how the Colonel could find nothing against him except concerning the law of his God.

in such a presence, which I trust the Lord will own, and bless you in. Fear them not. Remember Jesus stood before the high priest, Herod, and Pilate, for you. But, how different are the cases! You may perhaps meet with some expressions of dislike, but the laws of the land will protect you from the full effects of their resentment; and even the laws of politeness will in some degree restrain them. You are not going to be buffeted, blinded, and spit upon. Look at your regimentals, and let them remind you of him who wore a scarlet robe for you, not as a mark of honourable service, but as a badge of infamy. You are a soldier: if you were appointed to march against a battery, though it is a service not agreeable to flesh and blood, yet a sense of honour, and what you owe to your king, your country, and yourself, would prompt you to reject any rising thought of fear, that might betray you to act a part unsuitable to your character, with disdain. But, oh, how much stronger and more animating are the motives which should influence us as Christian soldiers! I trust you will fully feel their influence. There is but a veil of flesh and blood between you and that unseen world where Jesus reigns in all his glory. Perhaps you will be attended with such companies of the heavenly host, as made themselves visible to the shepherds. How will they rejoice to see you fervent and faithful in your Master's cause! Nay, Himself will be there; and though you cannot see him, He will be looking upon you, as He did on his servant Stephen. Then think of the day when He, in his turn, will own and confess you before an assembled world. Yea, perhaps upon the spot, He may witness his approbation; and if you can hear him whispering in your heart, "Well done, good and faithful servant," you will little regard what is said against you. As to consequences, leave them in his hand: they shall be all good and glorious to them that fear him. He may suffer a cloud to appear, but He can blow it away in a moment. He may permit this or that course to be stopped up; but He can open twenty in the room of it. He can show you how little dependence there is to be placed on the friendships and favour of men, when once we are enabled to be active and hearty for him; but these failures shall only give occasion of showing you likewise how all-sufficient He is in wisdom, love, and power, to give more and better than creatures can possibly deprive us of. Fear not, be strong, yea I say unto you be strong: the Lord of hosts is with you.

I am yours, etc.

To Captain Scott.

Letter II.—The benefit of religious exercises.

January 4, 1768.

My dear Friend,—My heart is as much with you, I trust, as it would be had you the most canonical appointment, and the most regular sphere of service. And I would as willingly hear you, in your usual places, as if you preached in St. Paul's. But as I have already answered your letter, this, and more that I could offer from it, now I have it before me, may be little more than repetition. . . .

Exercises of mind are common to all who know any thing of themselves, and have some just views of their obligations to redeeming love. But those who preach to others must expect a double portion. We need them in order to keep us humble, upon which, as a means, our success and comfort especially depend. We need them that we may know to speak a word in season to weary souls. Innumerable are the trials, fears, complaints and temptations which the Lord's people are beset with; some in one way, and some in another; the minister must, as it were, have a taste of all, or it might happen a case might come before him to which he had nothing to say. And we need them likewise to bring our hard hearts into a feeling disposition and sympathy with those who suffer: otherwise we should be too busy or too happy to attend unto their moans. Surely much of that hasty and censorious spirit, too often observable in young converts, arises from their having, as yet, a very imperfect acquaintance with the deceitfulness of their own hearts. But, the old weather-beaten Christian, who has learnt by sorrowful experience how weak he is in himself, and what powerful subtle enemies he has to grapple with, acquires a tenderness in dealing with bruises and broken bones, which greatly conduces to his acceptance and usefulness. I desire therefore to be resigned and thankful, and to give myself up to the Lord to lead me in whatever way he sees best; only I am grieved, that it is so much his appointment to keep me thus low, as it is the necessary consequence of my own folly and remissness.

I am yours, etc.

To Captain Scott.

LETTER III.—On his friend leaving the army—Similarity of the experience in believing.

May 20, 1769.

MY DEAR SIR,—I am more sorry than surprised that you are constrained to leave the army. I was apprehensive from the first that sooner or later, this would be the case. However, as I know you have acted with a simple view to the glory of God and the good of souls, I trust He will give you the reward of those that suffer for righteousness' sake. May He now make you a blessing wherever He shall be pleased to fix or send you, and give you many seals to your labours, that you, and all about you, may rejoice in your present situation. And as you are not now under either military or ecclesiastical restraints, I doubt not but you will gladly spend and be spent for his sake. The campaign is short; the victory already secured: we have but a few skirmishes to pass through, and then He, who has promised to make us more than conquerors, will put a crown of eternal life upon our heads. . . .

As to your complaints, I might transcribe them, and send them back in my name. I seem to have all the causes of grief and shame, that are common to others, and not a few, that I am ready to think peculiar to myself. But, through mercy, I can also follow you in what you say of the all-sufficiency of Jesus. His blood, righteousness, intercession and unchangeable love, keep me from giving way to the conclusions which Satan and unbelief would sometimes force upon me. It is He who must do all things for me, by me, and in me. I long to live more above the influence of a legal spirit and an unbelieving heart. But, indeed, I groan being burdened. I have no reason to complain of a want of liberty in public, but I wish I could be more concerned for success, and more affected to see poor sinners hardening under the sound of the gospel. I am afraid that if I am enabled to fill up my hour, and to come off with tolerable acceptance, I am too easily satisfied. Indeed this is a mercy which demands my thankfulness; but the great concern should be, that neither my preaching nor their hearing may be in vain. However, the Lord grant me to be faithful.

I am yours, etc.

Miss Thorpe.

WE have very little to communicate of Miss Thorpe. She is twice referred to in Mr. Newton's *Diary*, once while he was in London previous to his residence at Liverpool, and again in the latter place when he gives thanks to God that one so unworthy as he was made the instrument of good to another.

The letter on the theatre and other places of public amusement may not be without its value in these days of loose religious profession.

To Miss Thorpe.

The theatre.

MY DEAR MADAM,—Let what has been said on the subject of acquaintanceship, etc., suffice. It was well meant on my side, and well taken on yours. You may perhaps see that my hints were not wholly unnecessary, and I ought to be satisfied with your apology, and am so. The circumstances of your being seen at the playhouse has nothing at all mysterious in it; as you say you have not been there these six or seven years, it was neither more nor less than a mistake. I heard you had been there within these two years: I am glad to find I was misinformed. I think there is no harm in your supposing, that of the many thousands who frequent public diversions, some may in other respects be better than yourself; but I hope your humble and charitable construction of their mistake will not lead you to extenuate the evil of those diversions in themselves. For though I am persuaded, that a few, who know better what to do with themselves, are, for want of consideration, drawn in to expose themselves in such places, yet I am well satisfied, that, if there is any practice in this land sinful, attendance on the playhouse is properly and eminently so. The theatres are fountains and means of vice; I had almost said, in the same manner and degree as the ordinances of the gospel are the means of grace; and I can hardly think there is a Christian upon earth who would dare to be seen there, if the nature and effects of the theatre were properly set before him. Dr. Witherspoon of Scotland has written an excellent piece upon the stage, or rather against it, which I wish every person, who makes the least pretence to fear God, had an opportunity of perusing. I cannot judge much more favourably of Ranelagh, Vauxhall, and all the innumerable train of dissipations, by which the god of this world blinds the eyes of multitudes, lest the light of the glorious gospel should shine in upon them. What an awful aspect upon the present times have such texts as Isaiah xxii. 12—14; iii. 12; Amos vi. 3, 6; James iv. 4! I wish you, therefore, not to plead for any of them, but use all your influence to make them shunned as pest-houses, and dangerous nuisances to precious souls; especially if you know any who you hope, in the main, are seriously disposed, who yet venture themselves in those purlieus of Satan, endeavour earnestly and faithfully to undeceive them.

The time is short; eternity at the door: was there no other evil in these vain amusements than the loss of precious time (but alas! their name is legion), we have not leisure in our circumstances to regard them. And, blessed be God, we need them not. The gospel opens a source of purer, sweeter, and more substantial pleasures: we are invited to communion with God: we are called to share in the theme of angels, the songs of heaven; and the wonders of redeeming love are laid open to our view. The Lord himself is waiting to be gracious, waiting with promises and pardons in his hands. Well then may we bid adieu to the perishing pleasures of sin; well may we pity those who can find pleasure in those places and parties where he is shut out; where his name is only mentioned to be profaned; where his commandments are not only broken, but insulted; where sinners proclaim their shame, as in Sodom, and attempt not to hide it; where at best wickedness is wrapt up in a disguise of delicacy, to make it more insinuating; and nothing is offensive that is not grossly and unpolitely indecent.

I sympathize with all your complaints; but if the Lord is pleased to make them subservient to the increase of your sanctification, to wean you more and more from this world, and to draw you nearer to himself, you will one day see cause to be thankful for them, and to number them amongst your choicest mercies. A hundred years hence it will signify little to you whether you were sick or well the day I wrote this letter.

I am, etc.

William Cowper, Esq.

To attempt the slightest sketch of the life of the poet Cowper is needless, and would be quite out of place here. It may suffice to refer to some points of interest in the relation subsisting between Mr. Cowper and Mr. Newton. When Mr. Cowper came to Olney, in the year 1766, it was a source of great pleasure to each party. There was very much that was congenial between them, rendering their intercourse more than usually happy. Referring some time after to this period, at first so joyous and then so sad, Mr. Newton says, "The Lord who had brought us together had so knit our hearts and affections that for nearly twelve years (*i. e.* till Mr. Newton left Olney), we were seldom separated for twelve hours at a time when we were awake and at home. The first six I passed in daily admiring and trying to imitate him; during the second six I walked pensively with him in the valley of the shadow of death." It is abundantly evident from the whole tenor of their correspondence, how strong was the mutual attachment of these friends; and how little there was of the assumption and "direction" attributed to Mr. Newton is manifest enough from the passage quoted above.

After a visit to Olney in 1783, when Mr. Newton found his friend more than usually depressed, Mr. Cowper writes, "You know not what I suffered while you were here, nor is there any reason you should. . . . The friend of my heart, the person with whom I had formerly taken sweet counsel no longer useful to me as a minister, no longer pleasant to me as a Christian, was a spectacle that must necessarily add the bitterness of mortification to the sadness of despair." Again, Mr. Cowper writes, in 1795: "There is no day in which you are excluded from my thoughts." Even when the deepening gloom of his terrible melancholy had to a great extent beclouded and blunted the sensibilities of that tender and loving heart, when the unhappy poet could say more truly than ever,

> But me scarce hoping to attain that rest
> Always from port withheld, always distress'd—
> Me howling blasts drive devious, tempest toss'd,
> Sails ripp'd, seams opening wide and compass lost,

even then the last sad letter, written in 1799, shows the love that evidently lay hid under its seeming coldness. "Adieu, dear sir, whom in those days (just before referred to), I could call dear friend with feelings that justified the appellation."

Few whose sympathies will be in accordance with the contents of this volume are likely to give heed to the mis-apprehensions and mis-statements which have been too frequently expressed as to the intercourse of these friends, and to the absurd charge of harshness and tyranny exercised by Newton over Cowper, yet such statements have unhappily had an influence on some, not otherwise disposed to think unfavourably of Mr. Newton, but who from lack of better information have been unwittingly deceived. If it be so these few remarks may perhaps lead to a more correct view of the case.*

To WILLIAM COWPER, ESQ.

LETTER I.—Encouragement against doubts and fears.

July 30, 1767.

DEAR SIR,—Your letter gave me much pleasure, and increases my desire (if it be the Lord's will), of having you so near us. As I hope it will not be long before I have the pleasure of seeing you, I shall be the less solicitous if my frequent engagements should constrain me to close before my paper is filled. I can only advise you to resist to the utmost every dark and discouraging suggestion. The Lord has done great things for you, and wonderfully appeared in your behalf already. Take encouragement

---

* The whole subject is fully discussed in the *Life of Newton*, by the Rev. J. Bull, pp. 187, etc., 285, and 364.

hence to hope, that he will not forsake the work of his own hands; Judges xiii. 23. There is much weight in the apostle's argument in Rom. v. 10. Surely He who showed us mercy before we asked for it, will not withhold it now He has taught us how to plead for it agreeably to his own will. Though sin has abounded in us, grace has superabounded in him; though our enemies are many, and mighty, Jesus is above them all; though He may hide himself from us at times for a moment, He has given us a warrant to trust in him, even while we walk in darkness, and has promised to return, and gather us with everlasting mercies.

The Christian calling, like many others, is easy and clear in theory, but not without much care and difficulty to be reduced to practice. Things appear quite otherwise, when felt experimentally, to what they do, when only read in a book. Many learn the art of navigation (as it is called), by the fire-side at home; but when they come to sea, with their heads full of rules, and without experience, they find that the art is only to be thoroughly learnt upon the spot. So, to renounce self, to live upon Jesus, to walk with God, to overcome the world, to hope against hope, to trust the Lord when we cannot trace him, and to know that our duty and privilege consist in these things, may be readily acknowledged or quickly learned; but, upon repeated trial, we find that saying and doing are two things. We think at setting out that we sit down and count the cost; but alas! our views are so superficial at first, that we have occasion to correct our estimate daily. For every day shows us some new thing in the heart, or some new turn in the management of the war against us which we were not aware of; and upon these accounts, discouragements may arise so high as to bring us (I speak for myself) to the very point of throwing down our arms, and making either a tame surrender or a shameful flight. Thus it would be with us at last, if the Lord of hosts were not on our side. . . . . But if He is the Captain of our salvation, if his eye is upon us, his arm stretched out around us, and his ear open to our cry, and if He has engaged to teach our hands to war and our fingers to fight, and to cover our heads in the day of battle, then we need not fear, though a host rise up against us; but, lifting up our banner in his name, let us go forth conquering and to conquer; Rom. xvi. 20.

We hope we shall all be better acquainted soon. We please ourselves with agreeable prospects and proposals; but the determination is with the Lord. We may rejoice that it is, He sees all things in their dependences and connexions, which we see not, and therefore he often thwarts our wishes for our good; but if we are not mistaken, if any measure we have in view would, upon the whole, promote our comfort or his glory, He will surely bring it to pass in answer to prayer, how improbable soever it may appear; for He delights in the satisfaction and prosperity of his people, and without a *need-be*, they shall never be in heaviness. Let us strive and pray for a habitual resignation to his will; for He does all things well. It is never ill with us but when our evil hearts doubt or forget this plainest of truths.

I beg an interest in your prayers, and that you will believe me to be,

            Dear Sir, your affectionate servant.

To WILLIAM COWPER, ESQ.

LETTER II.—Engagements in London—Desire to return home—Messages of kindness to his people.

MY VERY DEAR FRIEND,—I *feel* myself already in London. Forced to lie in bed, and straitened for leisure and retirement when up, I steal a few minutes before breakfast to tell you, that as soon as that is finished we go into the City to hear Mr. Brewer, at Pinner's Hall. We are to dine with Mrs. Wilberforce at Mr. West's*, and in the evening I am to speak to the little company there. There I trust we shall meet you, Mr. Foster, and all my dear people, in the spirit.

Pray for me that my heart may be looking to Jesus for peace, wisdom, and strength. Without him all is waste and desert. And every thought in which He has not a place or rule is treason. I trust, yea, I know He will be with you. He will cover your head in the day of battle, and give you many a song of triumph before the great day of decision, when all enemies shall be finally bruised under your feet.

On Tuesday evening I spoke (*vice* Mr. Brewer) to the society at Mr. West's. On Wednesday preached at the Lock; Friday at St. Antholin's. Sunday morning at Blackfriars; afternoon in Bishopsgate Street. In the several public services the Lord was pleased to give me liberty. He can touch the rock and make the waters flow forth. I thank you for yours of the 21st. I pity your conflicts, and I try not to envy your comforts. You are in safe hands. All your combats and all your victories are

---

* See letters to Captain Clunie, p. 61.

already marked out for you. I hope Molly Coles is recovering apace, and that the quarantine between the two houses, will soon be taken off. Please to give my love to her, as likewise to Molly Mole (who I hope will be a very good girl), and to all the Marys, Mollys, Sallys, Sarahs, etc., that come in your way, particularly Sally Johnson and Judith.* I trust we live in the daily remembrance of you and dear Mrs. Unwin, and we doubt not we are the better for your prayers. I think we shall be both glad to see Olney again. Yet, as I am abroad, I hope to make myself tolerably easy till the time comes. Please to give our love to Miss Unwin, Mr. Foster, Mr. Palmer, etc. To Mrs. Unwin and Sir Cowper we join in more than a common salutation. We are bound to you both by the fourfold cord of esteem, friendship, communion, and obligation. Judge then, how warmly and sincerely we can assure you that we are most affectionately yours,

JOHN AND M. NEWTON.

To WILLIAM COWPER, ESQ.

LETTER III.—Franks—An accident—The spring—Hope of his friend's restoration.

CHARLES SQUARE: *April* 29, 1780.

MY DEAR FRIEND,—We seldom send anything to a friend with a more interested and selfish view than a frank, for we expect not only to have it returned, but that what we send empty should be returned full. I hope when the weather will not allow you to be all day in the garden, you are preparing a cargo for my frank—letters, essays, thoughts, bons mots, tales, fables, in a word, miscellanies of

* Mr. Newton's servants.

all kinds, in prose or verse. Whatever bears the signature of your hand, or of your manner, will be welcome; and as long as you find materials, I will endeavour to find franks, and to send you pepper-corns of thanks in return as often as I can.

The recovery of my arm has advanced happily without interruption. I can now put on my great-coat, have almost done with my sling, and hope in a few days more, to be released from the bandages. Blessed be the Lord, my best physician and friend, my present and all-sufficient help. I have seen no reason yet to regret my fall, nor have I been permitted to do it; yet I may consider it as a chastisement, though of a gentle and merciful kind. A sinner need not spend much time in searching out the cause of an affliction; but that the afflictions of such a sinner as I should be so seldom, so moderate, so soon removed, depends upon reasons, which I should never have known but by the word of God. There I am taught to spell his name. "The Lord, the Lord God, long suffering, abundant in mercy, forgiving iniquity, transgression and sin;" and thus I read the reason why I am not consumed.

The spring long retarded, begins to force its way, and to make its appearance in the trees that surround our square. The close behind our garden seems as green as your meadows, and the cows that are feeding in it, have very much the look of country cows. St. Luke's church affords us a sort of substitute for Olney steeple. Islington (by the help of an imagination which loves to concur in putting an agreeable deception upon itself), passes for Emberton; and the New River, if it did not run underground hereabouts, would soon obtain a new name, and be called the Ouse. We take the same liberty with persons as with places, and cannot walk much in the streets without meeting a somebody that recalls somebody else to our minds. But to impose upon ourselves so far as to think any place like Orchard Side, or any persons like Mrs. Unwin or Mr. Cowper, exceeds our present attainment in the art of substitution. In other respects our situation is, upon the whole, so well, that I may apply to either of you

"*Excepto quod non simul esses, cætera lætus.*"*

But, indeed, a removal from two such dear friends is a dislocation, and gives me at times a mental feeling, something analogous to what my body felt when my arm was forced from its socket. I live in hopes that this mental dislocation will one day be happily reduced likewise, and that we shall come together again *as bone to its bone*. The connexion which the Lord himself formed between us, was undoubtedly formed for *eternity;* but I trust we shall have more of the pleasure and comfort of it *in time*, and that I shall yet hear you say, "Come, magnify the Lord with me, and let us exalt his name together; for He hath turned my mourning into joy, and He hath taken off my sackcloth and girded me with gladness."

I am, dearest Sir,

Your most affectionate and obliged.

To WILLIAM COWPER, ESQ.

LETTER IV.—Beating the parish boundaries—Further reference to his friend's state of mind—Request for some sketches.

CHARLES SQUARE: *May* 6, 1780.

MY DEAR SIR,—You will have no reason to apply to me Luke vii. 42. For when you pipe I am ready to

* Sincerely blest, but that I want my friend.—*Francis.*

dance; and when you mourn, a cloud comes over my brow, and a tear stands a-tiptoe in my eye. I observe your letters usually begin and end in the allegro strain, and you put the most serious part in the middle; as this seems the fittest place for it, I will try to imitate you, though it be something, if either my beginning or my close should entitle me to your smile, except you smile at the presumption of your humble imitator, and recollect the fable of the frog, who tried to imitate the ox.

On Thursday I attended, in my robes, the churchwardens and several of the gentlemen of the parish. We had large nosegays in our hands, and, all but myself, favours in their hats, accompanied by a number of little boys smartly dressed, and carrying white wands. Thus marshalled and accoutred, we paraded the streets, and a tall man who has some other name, but is best known to me by that of the organ-blower, pointing successively to the marks, corners, and abutments which distinguished ours from the circumjacent parishes, proclaimed at each, "The boundary of the parish of St. Mary Woolnoth." The chorus, consisting of a number of huzzas, was performed by the youths, who likewise beat the marks and walls with their wands. This ostentatious service draws abundance of eyes; ladies, gentlemen, porters, and carters, all stop and turn and stare. After the procession, and distributing ribbons and cakes to the parishioners, we divided into two parties for dinner. All passed with much decorum and courtesy, and nothing happened that made me sorry I was among them. This little parochial farce is acted annually on Ascension-day. I am afraid my overture is very dull, but if you could suppose it the translation of a fragment dug out of Herculaneum, giving an account of some custom that obtained (*mutatis mutandis**),

---

* Making the necessary changes.

in ancient Rome, then both the ears of your classical attention would doubtless be nailed to the subject.

Do not wonder that I prize your letters. Besides the merit which friendship puts on them, as being yours, you always send me something I should value from a stranger. Some thoughts in your last I shall be the better for, if it be not my own fault. How wonderful is that tincture, the inexpressible something, which gives your sentiments when you speak of yourself so gloomy a cast, while in all other respects it leaves your faculties in full bloom and vigour! How strange that your judgment should be clouded on one point only, and that a point so obvious and strikingly clear to everybody who knows you! How strange that a person who considers the earth, the planets, and the sun itself as mere baubles, compared with the friendship and favour of God their Maker, should think the God who inspired him with such an idea, could ever forsake and cast off the soul which He has taught to love him! How strange is it I say, that you should hold tenaciously both parts of a contradiction! Though your comforts have been so long suspended, I know not that I ever saw you for a single day since your calamity came upon you, in which I could not perceive as clear and satisfactory evidence, that the grace of God was with you, as I could in your brighter and happier times. In the midst of all the little amusements, which you call trifling, and which I would be very thankful you can attend to in your present circumstances, it is as easy to see who has your heart, and which way your desires tend, as to see your shadow when you stand in the sun. . . .

I shall enlarge my commission for filling the franks and parcels which I hope to receive from you. I have a little back parlour which bears the name of my study. It is at present much unfurnished, and I must beg you, therefore, to send me in a few mountains and valleys, woods, streams and ducks to ornament the walls; in return I will join my praises to Mrs. ———'s and your own, which, indeed, considering how destitute I am of taste and vertû, will be but like putting a cipher on the wrong side of a significant figure, which adds a round O to the line, but nothing to the sum.* But let the great boast of their Raphaels and their Titians, it shall suffice for me if I may inscribe on the pieces in my study—W. C. *pinxit*.

My bandage is taken off, and my arm almost *in statu quo*. I wish to be thankful to him who maketh sore and bindeth up, who woundeth and his hands make whole.

Accept our best love, and believe me to be,

Most affectionately yours,

J. N.

---

* Whether Mr. Newton's request was complied with we know not. There is a letter addressed at a somewhat later period to Mrs. King by Mr. Cowper, in which he says, "I even had the hardiness to take in hand the pencil, and studied a whole year the art of drawing. Many figures were the fruit of my labours, which had at least the merit of being unparalleled by any production either of art or nature. But before the year was ended I had occasion to wonder at the progress that may be made in spite of natural deficiency, by dint alone of practice; for I actually produced three landscapes which a lady thought worthy to be framed and glazed. I then judged it high time to exchange this occupation for another, lest by any subsequent productions of inferior merit I should forfeit the honour I had so fortunately acquired."—*Southey's Cowper*, vi. 196. An engraving from one of these drawings, originally presented to Lady Austin and given by her to Mr. J. A. Knight, will be found in the *Gentleman's Magazine* for June, 1804.

To William Cowper, Esq.

Letter V.—Interruptions in his work—Thelyphthora—Present of oysters — Congregation at St. Mary Woolnoth.

My dear Friend, . . . I feel the propriety of your advice to keep on and on with anything I have in hand, because intermissions breed unfitness and disinclination. But I feel likewise the impossibility of complying with it. This day fortnight I began with some eagerness the sermons I mentioned, but have not been able to return to the task but one hour since. And then I was so awkward that what I, with much scratching and puzzling my head, wrote in that hour must be out of the book, for the next time I saw it I was not pleased with it. Sometimes I can drive away *currente calamo*,* without a minute's hesitation from sheet to sheet. Sometimes every line is uphill work, *invitâ Minervâ*.† Oh what toiling and panting and straining when invention and imagination flounder in the mud and cannot get through! Thus I learn that what I have is not my own, and that what I do (if tolerable) is not my doing. At the best I am but like a ship whose rigging is useless, and sails spread to no purpose, unless the wind blow and it is tolerably fair. However, I cannot yet proceed. Next week I am to be at Ramsgate, the following at Reading. A fortnight's absence from home will produce as many necessary engagements when I come back as can be well dispatched

* With a ready pen.
† Minerva (the goddess of wisdom) refusing her aid.

in a month. Some must visit us, others must be visited; letters must be answered; every day forestalled, every hour too short. What can I do? especially as indolence and a sort of dissipation and unsteadiness increase upon one as business increases. I believe I shall make but a poor figure as an author henceforward. Then heaps of folk would persuade me that I can attempt nothing so seasonable, needful, and with equal probability of usefulness, as an answer to *Thelyphthora*.* I am not yet of this mind, and besides that I am not satisfied with the expediency of an answer. Mr. Indolence uses all his influence with me, which is considerable, to keep me quiet; Mr. Prudence cautions me against meddling with one above my match; and Mr. Delicacy says, Surely you would not write against your friend. However, this triumvirate may prevent my writing; notwithstanding all that Prudence and Delicacy urge, and whether they are pleased or not, I must bear my testimony against Thelyphthora to-morrow night *vivâ voce*. I shall not so much mind Indolence, except he should actually follow me into the pulpit, which he seldom does, though I am pestered with him everywhere else. But in the course of sermons I lately began on relative duties I must enter on the relation of husband and wife to-morrow night; and it would be high treason, or at least misprision of treason against the truth, when expressly preaching on the subject of marriage, to leave the dangerous and novel doctrine of the present lawfulness of polygamy unnoticed, because I have a love for the person who presumed to broach it.

A small but (as I am told) a select company, from Pyfleet, will set out to-day by Rogers' waggon for Olney, and I expect they will take up their quarters with Mrs.

* A work by the Rev. Dr. Madan, advocating polygamy.

Unwin. I hope they will not disturb you, for they are as mute as fishes, and though they will be as well at your house as anywhere, you will perceive, as soon as you see them, that they are not in their proper element. So far from being forward, a degree of violence will be necessary to make them open their mouths, at least upon their first coming down. But when properly treated they show themselves to greater advantage than might be expected from the roughness of their appearance. They were all lately resident in my parish.

The two five-toed feathered inhabitants of Olney came safe to us, but had not been long in town before they went to pot. We thank you and Mrs. Unwin for feeding them that have since supplied us with food.

In every nation they that fear God and work righteousness are accepted of him. In the number of my hearers there are some in connection with Mr. Wesley. They come to me as often as they can, and some of them with whom I am acquainted are very excellent people indeed. It is generally allowed that the congregation at St. Mary Woolnoth is remarkably serious, attentive, and respectable. How unlike the gaping, staring, sleepy mortals who made the bulk of our auditory at Olney. Some say there is not such a congregation in London as mine; that it is the flower and picking of all the denominations of professors. However that may be we are through mercy very comfortable together. And such of my own parish as do attend behave apparently as well as the rest. But we are indeed a medley as to names. My turn is peaceable, and the peaceable of all sorts seem disposed to hear me. I had but few materials for a letter, but I have worked them up and made the most of them I could, in hopes of getting towards the bottom of the page. Having succeeded so well in my enterprise as to leave no room for making apologies, I heartily present our joint love to Mrs. Unwin and you, and retire the moment I have assured you that I am your most affectionate Achates,

JOHN NEWTON.

HOXTON: *Sept.* 30, 1780.

To WILLIAM COWPER, ESQ.

LETTER VI.—*Disappointment of authors—The praise or blame of mortals of little account.*

MY DEAR FRIEND,—I have given you more respite than I intended, and think, notwithstanding an agreement not to insist upon form, some apology is almost necessary for the delay. *Truditur dies die.** Something occurs every day which pleads for putting off something else till to-morrow, and so on, till (as Austin in his quaint way expresses it), *Modo et modo non habet modum.*† It is a proof of our depravity that good habits are much more easily lost than acquired, whereas bad habits are acquired with ease but laid aside with difficulty. My propensity to write to you I account a good habit, which I should be very sorry to lose.

I wish you good dispatch and much success with Homer. But the apprehensions I hinted lest you should be so much taken up with your work as to expose you to painful feelings in case of any disappointment, is not abated by that part of your letter where you say, "He knows my frame, and will consider that I am but dust, dust into the bargain that has been so trampled under foot and beaten, that a storm less violent than an unsuccessful issue of such a business would be sufficient to blow me quite away. This

---

* Day presses on the heels of day.—*Francis.*
† Now and now has no now.

acknowledgment rather increases than abates my fear for you. But I hope and pray that the Lord who has supported you under and brought you through many storms, which were violent and terrible indeed, would enable you to consider the failure of a poem (if it should be so, which I hope it will not) as no more than the breath of an infant, compared with the tempests by which I have seen you assaulted.

I am an author likewise, and am soon to launch forth into the public notice a new book.* I can therefore have a fellow-feeling with you. Some approbation I may hope for. A portion of censure and dislike I may likewise expect. Suppose we join in ordering our imagination, to balloon us to Liliput. Surely were we there we should be too *Big*, if not too *Great*, to pay much regard to the judgment of a parcel of little things, not more than five or six inches high, who might presume to give themselves airs about *Us*. Yet I can conceive a possibility that mannikins or womankins of those small dimensions might possess as much wisdom, goodness, and truth as the taller animals who inhabit Great Britain. But were our admirers and censurers as tall as Brobdignags, their applause and their petulance will soon be stifled in the dust. These are in a manner but creatures of a day; and indeed so are we. But we belong to another world. We are going where their praise and their obloquy can do us neither good nor harm. *In eternitatem pingimus.*† Let our ambition be of the noblest kind: let our aim be to please God. If the great Judge shall be pleased to receive us with approbation, we shall be little concerned what the emmets we have left behind may think of us after we are gone. In his favour is life. His smile would amply overbalance the frown

---

* His *Messiah*.   † We paint for eternity.

of the whole creation. Yes, my friend, when the Lord shall break the fetters that have so long entangled your spirit (and of this happy event you have yourself conceived and expressed a hope) you will rejoice, and I shall rejoice with you, whatever reception our books may meet with.

. . . . My dear has been often and much indisposed of late, but is at present better. Sick or well we always feel the same unabated regard for you and for dear Mrs. Unwin. We leave Charles Square as soon as may be after Ladyday, and remove to Coleman Street Buildings. In all places no less than in all seasons I hope to approve myself,

Yours indeed and in truth,

JOHN NEWTON.

March 11, 1786.

The Rev. Joshua Symonds.

MR. SYMONDS was born at Kidderminster, in January, 1739. His father was a medical man, and eminent for his piety, as were others of his ancestors. He was originally designed for agricultural pursuits, but his religious character and talents led some Christian friends to suggest his engaging in the work of the ministry. Consequently, after fitting deliberation, he entered the academy of Dr. Conder at Mile End, near London, at the same time uniting himself to the church of Mr. Brewer, at Stepney. Towards the close of his academical career he was invited to the vacant church at Bedford, where the celebrated John Bunyan once ministered. The result was his settlement there as its pastor. The contiguity of Bedford to Olney, and the fact that Mr. Symonds had become acquainted with Mr. Brewer, were probably the means of his introduction to Mr. Newton, who speaks thus of him in his *Diary*:—" March 12, '66. A visit from Mr. Symonds. He is supplying a vacancy at Bedford. I shall be glad if the Lord sees fit to fix him there. I think him a sensible, spiritual, humble young man, and believe he would make an agreeable and useful neighbour. Heard him preach in the evening from John xii. 21."

Mr. Symonds was a truly good man and devoted to his work. Family cares and severe bodily affliction sometimes cast a gloom over his spirit and led him to take desponding views of himself;* yet for the most part he glorified God in the fire; and though afflictions abounded, grace did much more abound. After being at Bedford some years, Mr. Symonds changed his views on the subject of infant baptism. Hence the references of Mr. Newton in his third letter. He died in November, 1788, at the early age of forty-nine, especially in his last illness glorifying God by patience under extreme suffering, and by his steadfast reliance, notwith-

---

* See Letter II. of this series, and *Life of Newton*, p. 199.

standing many temptations, on the Saviour, who, to use his own words, "filled him with a steady, constant peace, and sometimes with unutterable joy and transport."

To the REV. JOSHUA SYMONDS.

LETTER I.—Degrees of glory—Christians not to be measured by gifts or services.

February 17, 1769.

DEAR SIR,—I cannot agree with your friends, or with Witsius, respecting the degrees of glory. Perhaps we are not capable of stating the question properly in this dark world. I see no force in the argument drawn from 1 Cor. xv. 40, 41; or, rather, that does not appear to me the sense of the passage; or that the apostle had any respect to degrees of glory. The text in Matt. xix. 28, may be compared with Rev. iii. 21. However, admitting such degrees, perhaps they will not be distributed (according to human expectation) to such as have been most employed in active life, Matt. x. 41. As wickedness is rated by the judgment of God, not according to the number of outward acts, but by what the heart would do had opportunity offered, Matt. v. 28; so the Lord will graciously accept the desires of his people, and they shall in no wise lose their reward because his providence has appointed them a narrower sphere.

One man, like Mr. Whitefield, is raised up to preach the gospel with success through a considerable part of the earth. Another is called to the humbler service of sweeping the streets, or cleaning this great minister's shoes. Now, if the latter is thankful and content in his poor station,—if he can look without envy, yea, with much love on the man that is honoured,—if he can rejoice in the good that is done, or pray for the success of those whom the Lord sends,—I see not why he may not be as great a man in the sight of God as he who is followed and admired by thousands.

Upon a supposition of degrees of glory, I should think it probable, the best Christian will have the highest place; and I am inclined to think that if you and I were to travel in search of the best Christian in the land, or were qualified to distinguish who deserved the title, it is more than two to one we should not find the person in a pulpit, or any public office of life. Perhaps some old woman at her wheel, or some bed-rid person, hid from the knowledge of the world, in a mud-walled cottage, would strike our attention more than any of the doctors or reverends with whom we are acquainted. Let us not measure men, much less ourselves, by gifts or services. One grain of grace is worth abundance of gifts. To be self-abased, to be filled with a spirit of love, and peace, and gentleness; to be dead to the world; to have the heart deeply affected with a sense of the glory and grace of Jesus, to have our will bowed to the will of God; these are the great things, more valuable, if compared in the balance of the sanctuary, than to be an instrument of converting a province or a nation. See 1 Cor. xiii. 1–3. In a word, I should think, from Luke vii. 47, that those who love most will be most happy; that those who have most forgiven will love most. And, as in the present life every believer thinks himself a peculiar instance of mercy, and sees his sins in a peculiar light of aggravation, I apprehend it to be so hereafter. The sin of nature is equal in all; and so I think would actual sin be likewise, but for the differences made by the restraining grace and providence of God. He is not, perhaps, in the sight of God, the greatest sinner, who has committed the most notorious acts of sin in the sight of man. We should not judge one wolf to be fiercer than another because he had opportunity of devouring more sheep. Any other wolf would have done the same in the same circumstances. So in sin; so (think I) in grace. The Lord's people, every one of them, would be glad to do him as much service, and to yield him as much honour, as any of the number have attained to. But He divides severally, to one sixty, to one thirty, to one a hundred as he pleases; but they are all accepted in the same righteousness; equally united to Jesus; and, as to the good works on which a supposed difference is afterwards to be founded, I apprehend those that have most will gladly do by them as Paul did by his legal righteousness,—count them loss and dung for the excellency of Jesus Christ, the Lord. Matt. xxv. 37. But it may be said, Is nothing, then, to be expected for so many trials and sufferings, as some ministers are called to for the sake of the gospel? In my judgment, he that does not find a reward in being excited, supported, and enabled by the Holy Spirit of God in the work of the gospel; who does not think that to have multiplied labours owned to the conversion of even a few souls is a great reward; who does not account the ministry of the gospel, with grace to be faithful in the discharge of it, a reward and honour in itself sufficient to overbalance all the difficulties it may expose him to; whoever, I say, does not thus think of the service of Jesus in the gospel, has some reason to question his right to the lowest degree of glory; or, at least, has little right to look for eminence in glory, even though he should preach with as much power and acceptance, and in the midst of as many hardships as St. Paul did.

You will hardly think by my letter that I am straitened for time at present, yet this is indeed the case; but I have dropped into a gossip with you insensibly. I am glad the Lord has visited you and comforted you of late. Think it not strange if such seasons are followed by temptations and darkness. St. Paul was in danger of being exalted above measure; and you know the means the Lord employed to preserve him. You are no better than he, and need not desire to be more graciously dealt with. His grace shall be sufficient for you. As to everything else, submit yourself to him.

I am, yours, etc.

To the REV. JOSHUA SYMONDS.

LETTER II.—On evidences of our spiritual state.

MY DEAR FRIEND,—I might defer answering your last till I see you; yet, because I love you I will write. I apprehend your mind is darkened with temptation; for your views of the gospel, when you preach, are certainly clearer than your letter expresses. You may think you distinguish between evidences and conditions; but the heart is deceitful, and often beguiles our judgment when we are judging concerning ourselves.

You say, " I hope it is my desire to cast myself upon the free promise in Jesus Christ; but this alone does not give assurance of my personal interest in his blood." I ask, Why not? Because you lean to conditions, and do not think yourself good enough. It appears to me, that if I cast myself upon his promise, and if his promise is true, I must undoubtedly be interested in his full redemption; for He has said, " Him that cometh I will in no wise cast out." If you can find a case or circumstance which the words *in no wise* will not include, then you may despond.

It is certainly a delusion to imagine oneself of the number of elect, without scriptural evidence. But have you not that evidence? I think, as the saying is, you cannot see the wood for trees. You tell me what evidences you want, namely, spiritual experiences, inward holiness, earnest endeavours. All this I may allow in a right sense; but in judging on these grounds, it is common and easy in a dark hour to turn the gospel into a covenant of works. But take it your own way. If a fear of being deceived, a mourning under a sense of vileness, a hungering and thirsting after righteousness, a sense of the evil and danger of sin, a persuasion of the preciousness and suitableness of Christ in his offices, etc.; if these are not spiritual experiences, I know not what are. And will you dare deny that God has given you these? As to inward holiness, when we meet, you shall define, if you please, what you mean by it. The holiness of a sinner seems principally to consist in self-abasement, and in admiring views of Jesus as a complete Saviour. These are the main principles whence any gracious fruit is derived. In proportion as we have these, we shall be humble, meek, patient, weaned from the world, and devoted to God. But if you will look for a holiness that shall leave no room for the workings of corruption and temptation, you look for what God has nowhere promised, and for what is utterly inconsistent with our present state. If you say, you must doubtless expect to feel evil in your heart; but that you are discouraged by feeling so much,—I ask, further, if you can find, from the word of God, how much a holy person *may* feel. For my own part, I believe the most holy people feel the most evil. Indeed, when faith is strong and in exercise, sin will not much break out to the observation of others; but it cuts them out work enough within.

Indeed, my friend, you will not be steadily comfortable till you learn to derive your comfort from a simple apprehension of the person, work, and offices of Christ. He is made unto us of God, not only righteousness, but sanctification also. One direct appropriating act of faith in him will strengthen you more than all the earnest endeavours you speak of. Evidences, as you call them, are of use in their place; but the best evidence of faith is the shutting our eyes equally upon our defects and our graces, and looking directly to Jesus as clothed with authority and power to save to the very uttermost. So you preach to others; so you deal with exercised consciences; why not preach so to yourself? Will you point out a ground for their hopes, upon which you are afraid to venture your own? Has He not kept you sound in the faith in wavering times? Does He not preserve you unspotted from the world? Does He not enable and own you in your ministry? Has He not often refreshed you with his consolations? Do you not tell others that the blood of Jesus cleanseth from all sin? Why then do you give way to doubts and fears? I would have you humbled before the Lord for your own unworthiness. In this I wish I was more like you; but rejoice in Christ Jesus, and resist every temptation to doubt your interest in his love, as you would resist a temptation to adultery or murder. Plead the apostle's argument, Rom. viii. 31–39, before the Lord and against Satan; and do not dishonour Christ so as to imagine He will disappoint the desire which no power but his could implant in your heart.

  Yours, in the best bonds, etc.

To the Rev. Joshua Symonds.

LETTER III.—Regret at not speaking to edification.—The Moravians.

June 24, 1774.

MY DEAR FRIEND, ... Though I was very glad to see you and our friends at your house, I was not pleased with myself when there. Particularly, I was sorry I gave way to the discourse about baptism, which, as we all seemed well persuaded in our own minds, was little better than idle talk. When tea was almost over, it occurred to me how easily I might have turned it to a more profitable subject; but then it was too late. Methinks it did not require much study to find out that we were but poorly employed. Perhaps I may be wiser hereafter; but one word draws on another so strangely, that we are liable to be entangled before we are aware, for Mr. Self loves to speak last.

I thought of you yesterday. I hope you had a pleasant visit. I should have been glad to have been with you. I love that house.* There seems to be no leisure in it to talk about persons or opinions. The inquiry there is concerning Jesus; how to love him more, and serve him better; how to derive from him, and render to him. If this is to be a Moravian, I do not wonder they are reproached and scorned. Where the spirit of the gospel is there the cross will be. But as I am acquainted only with two families, I cannot say how it is with the rest; but why should I not hope they are all in the same

* Mr. Foster Barham's.

way? If they have, notwithstanding, some little peculiarities, I apprehend very few of those societies which are ready to censure them, can exceed them in the real fruits of the Spirit.

I am, your sincerely affectionate.

To the REV. JOSHUA SYMONDS.

LETTER IV.—Satan's opportunity—Our ingratitude—The Divine patience.

November 18, 1778.

DEAR SIR,— I have observed that most of the advantages which Satan is recorded to have gained against the Lord's servants, have been after great and signal deliverances and favours; as in the cases of Noah, Lot, David, and Hezekiah. And I have found it so repeatedly in my own experience. How often, if my history were written by an inspired pen, might this proof of the depravity of my heart be inserted: "But John Newton rendered not again according to the benefits received; for his heart was lifted up." May it be far otherwise with you. May you come out of the furnace refined; and may it appear to yourself and all around you that the Lord has done you good by your afflictions. Thus vile are our natures; to be capable of making the Lord such perverse returns as we often do. How should we blush if our earthly friends and benefactors could bring such charges of ingratitude against us, as He justly might! No; they could not bear a thousandth part; the dearest and kindest of them would have been weary of us, and cast us off long ago, had we behaved so to them. We may well say, Who is a God like unto Thee, that pardonest iniquity, and passest by the transgression of the remnant of thine heritage. It seems that the prophet selects the Lord's patience towards his own people, as the most astonishing of all his perfections, and that which eminently distinguishes him from all other beings. And, indeed, the sins of believers are attended with aggravations peculiar to themselves. The inhabitants of Sodom and Gomorrah were great sinners, but they did not sin against light and love and experience. Pharaoh was proud; but he had not been humbled at the foot of the cross. Ahab killed Naboth for his vineyard; but not altogether so basely as David killed Uriah for his wife. I see many profligate sinners around me; but the Lord has not followed them with mercies, instructions, and pardons, as He has followed me. My outward life, through mercy, is not like theirs; but if the secrets of my heart were laid open, they who are favourable to me would not think me much better than the worst of them. Especially at some times and seasons, since I first tasted that He was gracious. And yet He has borne with me, and is pleased to say, He will never leave me nor forsake me.

Well, when we have said all we can of the aboundings of sin in us, grace still more abounds in Jesus. We cannot be so evil as He is good. His power is a good match for our weakness; his riches for our poverty; his mercy for our misery. We are vile in ourselves; but we are complete in him. In ourselves we have cause to be abased; but in him we may rejoice. Blessed be God for Jesus Christ.

I am, sincerely, yours,

To the Rev. Joshua Symonds.

LETTER V.—Happiness of his situation in London—Sympathy with all true Christians, whatever their name.

March 29, 1781.

DEAR SIR,—It is certain I did not wish to leave Olney, and likewise that, if the Lord had left me to choose my situation, London would have been almost the last place I should have chosen. But since it was the Lord's choice for me, I am reconciled and satisfied. He has, in this respect, given me another heart; for, now I am fixed here, I seem to prefer it. My sphere of service is extremely enlarged, and my sphere of usefulness likewise. And not being under any attachment to systems and parties, I am so far suited to my situation. My hearers are made up of all sorts, and my connexions are of all sorts likewise. I mean of those who hold the head. My inclination and turn leads me chiefly to insist on those things in which all who are taught of God agree. And my endeavour is to persuade them to love one another, to bear with one another, to avoid dispute; and if they must strive, to let their strife and emulation be who shall most express the life of the Son of God in their temper and conduct.

I preach my own sentiments plainly but peaceably, and directly oppose no one. Accordingly, Churchmen and Dissenters, Calvinists and Arminians, Moravians and Methodists, now and then I believe Papists and Quakers, sit quietly to hear me. I can readily adopt "No Popery" for my motto; but popery with me has a very extensive sense. I dislike it, whether it be on a throne, as at Rome, or upon a *bench* or at a *board*, as sometimes in London. Whoever wants to confine me to follow his sentiments, whether as to doctrine or order, is so far a papist. Whoever encourages me to read the Scriptures, and to pray for the teaching of the Holy Spirit, and then will let me follow the life the Lord gives me, without being angry with me because I cannot or will not see with his eyes, nor wear his shoes, is a consistent Protestant. The depravity of human nature; the deity of the Saviour; the influences of the Holy Spirit; a separation from the world, and a devotedness to God — these are principles which I deem fundamental; and though I would love and serve all mankind, I can have no religious union or communion with those who deny them. But whether a *surplice* or a *band* be the fittest distinction of a minister, whether he be best ordained by the *laying on* or the *holding up* of hands; whether water-baptism should be administered by a spoonful or tubfull, or in a river, or in Jordan (as Constantine thought), are to me points of no great importance. I will go further. Though a man does not accord with my views of election; yet if he gives me good evidence that *he* is *effectually called of God*, he is my brother. Though he seems afraid of the doctrine of final perseverance; yet if grace enable him to persevere, he is my brother still. If he loves Jesus, I will love him; whatever hard name he may be called by, and whatever incidental mistakes I may think he holds. His differing from me will not always prove him to be wrong, except I am infallible myself.

I praise the Lord for preserving you from harm when you fell. I have had such falls from horses, and received no hurt. When I dislocated my shoulder, I was at my own door and in the greatest apparent safety. But we are only safe, naturally or spiritually, while the Lord holds us up.

I am yours, etc.

The Rev. Matthew Powley.

COMING to Oxford about the year 1760, Mr. Powley was led to attend the ministry of the Rev. Dr. Haweis, then preaching at Magdalen church. He thus became experimentally acquainted with the truths of religion. It becoming known that Mr. Powley entertained Methodistical tenets, he was excluded from the foundation of his college, and threatened with expulsion. Mr. Venn, hearing of this, became interested in his case, and promised to present him to the first vacant chapelry in his church; and, accordingly, three years afterwards, in 1767, he became perpetual curate of Staithwaite, in the parish of Huddersfield. The case also came to the knowledge of Lady Huntingdon, and Mr. Powley supplied her chapel at Bath, in 1768, where his labours were crowned with great success, for he was a man of superior talent and earnest piety. His acquaintance with Mr. Newton was, probably, through Dr. Haweis, though no mention of it appears. At any rate, Mr. Powley's name is found as supplying Mr. Newton's pulpit not long after his coming to Olney, and frequently on subsequent occasions.

In August, 1767, Mr. Powley had left home on account of ill health; and Mr. Newton writes to him in the following terms:—"I read your letter at the Great Room. Our people feel and pray for you, and remember your labours among them with much affection. I thank the Lord, and I thank you as the instrument, that when I came home from Yorkshire, I found them all in peace, and, in general, in a thriving way. You will always be a welcome visitant at Olney, to the people, and particularly to your affectionate friend and brother."

Mr. Powley's visits to Olney, led to an acquaintance with Miss Unwin, to whom he was married in 1774. Three years afterwards, through the interest of Lord Dartmouth, he was presented to the living of Dewsbury, in Yorkshire. The *Christian Observer* says of him,—"For meekness and humbleness of mind, for sincerity and integrity of heart and life; for love to God and the souls of men, and for a faithful and laborious discharge of his professional duties, the subject of this memoir was eminently distinguished." He died in December 1806. Mrs. Powley survived him nearly nine-and-twenty years.

To the REV. MATTHEW POWLEY.

LETTER I.—Baxter—What a Christian ought to be.

January 26, 1775.

DEAR SIR,—I lately read a sermon of Mr. Baxter's (in the fifth volume of the *Morning Exercises*) on Matthew v. 16. My mind is something impressed with the subject, and with his manner of treating it. Some of Mr. Baxter's sentiments in divinity are rather cloudy, and he sometimes upon that account met with but poor quarter from the staunch Calvinists of his day. But by what I have read of him where he is quiet and not ruffled by controversy, he appears to me, notwithstanding some mistakes, to have been one of the greatest men of his age, and perhaps in fervour, spirituality, and success, more than equal, both as a minister and a Christian, to some twenty taken together, of those who affect to undervalue him in this present day. There is a spirit in some passages of his *Saints' Rest*, his *Dying Thoughts*, and other of his practical treatises, compared with which, many modern compositions, though well written and well meant, appear to me to a great disadvantage. But I was speaking of his sermon. He points out the way at which we should aim to let our light shine in the world, for the glory of God, and the conviction and edification of men. I have mentioned where it is to be found, that, if you have the *Morning Exercises,* or they should come in your way, you may look at it. I think you would like it. The perusal suggested to me some instruction and much reproof. Alas! my friend, are we not too often chargeable with a sad shameful selfishness and narrowness of spirit, far, very far different from that activity, enlargement, and generosity of soul, which such a gospel as we have received might be expected to produce? For myself, I must plead guilty. It seems as if my heart was always awake, and keenly sensible to my *own* concernments, while those of my Lord and Master affect me much less forcibly, at least only by intervals. Were a stranger to judge of me by what I sometimes say in the pulpit, he might think that, like the angels, I had but two things in view, to do the will of God and to behold his face. But alas! would he not be almost as much mistaken, as if, seeing Mr. Garrick in the character of a tragedy hero, he should suppose him to be the very person whom he only represents. I hope Satan will never be able to persuade me that I am a *mere hypocrite* and *stage-player;* but sure I am, that there is so much hypocrisy in me, so many littlenesses and self-seekings insinuating into my plan of conduct, that I have humbling cause to account myself unworthy and unprofitable, and to say, Enter not into judgment with thy servant, O Lord. I have some tolerable ideas of what a Christian ought to be, and it is, I hope, what I desire to be. A Christian should be conformable to Christ in his spirit and in his practice; that is, he should be spiritually minded, dead to the world, filled with zeal for the glory of God, the spread of the gospel, and the good of souls. He should be humble, patient, meek, cheerful, thankful under all events and changes. He should account it the business and honour of his life to imitate him who pleased not himself, who went about doing good, and has expressed to us the very feelings of his heart, in that divine aphorism, which surpasses all the fine admired sayings of the philosophers, as much as the sun outshines a candle, " It is more blessed to give than to receive." The whole deportment of a Christian should show that the knowledge of Jesus, which he has received from the gospel, affords him all he could expect from it; a balm for every grief, an amends for every loss, a motive for every duty, a restraint from every evil, a pattern for everything, which he is called to do or suffer, and a principle sufficient to constitute the actions of every day, even in common life, acts of religion. He should (as the children of this world are wise to do in their generation) make every occurrence through which he passes subservient and subordinate to his main design. Gold is the worldly man's god, and his worship and service are uniform and consistent, not by fits and starts, but from morning to night, from the beginning to the end of the year, he is the same man. He will not let slip an opportunity of adding to his pelf to-day, because he may have another to-morrow, but he heartily and eagerly embraces both; and so far as he carries his point, though his perseverance may expose him to the ridicule or reproach of his neighbours, he thinks himself well paid, and says,

*Populus me sibilat; at mihi plaudo
Ipse domi, simul ac nummos contemplor in arca.**

I am, etc.

---

* ———— Let them hiss on, he cries,
 While in my own opinion fully blest
 I count my money, and enjoy my chest.
                        Francis.

To the Rev. Matthew Powley.

LETTER II.—Dependence on God—Personal experience.

January —, 1776.

DEAR SIR,—I may learn (only I am a sad dunce) by small and common incidents, as well as by some more striking and important turns in life, that it is not in man that walketh to direct his steps. It is not for me to say, to-day or to-morrow I will do this or that. I cannot write a letter to a friend without leave or without help, for neither opportunity nor ability are at my own disposal. It is not needful that the Lord should raise a mountain in my way, to stop my purpose; if He only withdraw a certain kind of imperceptible support, which in general I have, and use without duly considering whose it is; then, in a moment, I feel myself unstrung and disabled, like a ship that has lost her masts, and cannot proceed till He is pleased to refit me and renew my strength. My pride and propensity to self-dependence render frequent changes of this kind necessary to me, or I should soon forget what I am, and sacrifice to my own drag. Therefore, upon the whole, I am satisfied, and see it best, that I should be absolutely poor and pennyless in myself, and forced to depend upon the Lord for the smallest things as well as the greatest. And if, by his blessing, my experience should at length tally with my judgment in this point, that without him I can do nothing, then I know I shall find it easy, through him to do all things; for the door of his mercy is always open, and it is but ask and have. But, alas! a secret persuasion (though contrary to repeated convictions) that I have something at home, too often prevents me going to him for it, and then no wonder I am disappointed. The life of faith seems so simple and easy in theory, that I can point it out to others in few words; but in practice it is very difficult, and my advances are so slow, that I hardly dare say I get forward at all. It is a great thing indeed to have the spirit of a little child, so as to be habitually afraid of taking a single step without leading.

I have heard of you more than once since I heard from you, and am glad to know the Lord is still with you: I trust He has not withdrawn wholly from us. We have much cause for thankfulness, and much for humiliation. Some have been removed, some are evidently ripening for glory, and now and then we have a new inquirer. But the progress of wickedness amongst the unconverted here is awful. Convictions repeatedly stifled in many, have issued in a hardness and boldness in sinning, which I believe is seldom found but in those places where the light of the gospel has been long resisted and abused. If my eyes suitably affected my heart, I should weep day and night upon this account; but, alas! I am too indifferent. I feel a woful defect in my zeal for God and compassion for souls; and when Satan and conscience charge me with cowardice, treachery, and stupidity, I know not what to reply. I am generally carried through my public work with some liberty; and because I am not put to shame before the people, I seem content and satisfied. I wish to be more thankful for what the Lord is pleased to do amongst us; but, at the same time, to be more earnest with him for a further out-pouring of his Spirit. Assist me herein with your prayers.

As to my own private experience, the enemy is not suffered to touch the foundation of my faith and hope: thus far I have peace; but my conflicts and exercises with the effects of indwelling sin, are very distressing. I cannot doubt of my state and acceptance; and yet it seems no one can have more cause for doubts and fears than myself, if such doubtings were at all encouraged by the gospel: but I see they are not. I see that what I want and hope for, the Lord promises to do, for his own name's sake, and with a *non obstante** to all my vileness and perverseness; and I cannot question but he has given me (for how else could I have it?) a thirst for that communion with him in love and conformity to his image, of which, as yet, I have experienced but very faint and imperfect beginnings. But if He has begun, I venture upon his word that He will not forsake the work of his own hands.

But I must conclude, and am, etc.

To the Rev. Matthew Powley.

LETTER III.—Christian prudence.

DEAR SIR, . . . To combine zeal with prudence is indeed difficult. There is often too much self in our zeal, and too much of the fear of man in our prudence. However, what we cannot *attain* by any skill or resolution of our own, we may hope in measure to *receive* from him who giveth liberally to those who seek him, and desire to serve him. Prudence is a word much abused; but there is a heavenly wisdom, which the Lord has promised to give to those who humbly wait upon him for it. It does not consist in forming a bundle of rules and maxims, but in a spiritual taste and discernment, derived from an experimental knowledge of the truth, and of the heart of man, as described in the word of God; and its exercises consist

* Notwithstanding—in spite of.

much in a simple dependence upon the Lord, to guide and prompt us in every action. We seldom act wrong, when we truly depend upon him, and can cease from leaning to our own understanding. When the heart is thus in a right tune and frame, and his word dwells richly in us, there is a kind of immediate perception of what is proper for us to do in present circumstances, without much painful inquiry; a light shines before us upon the path of duty; and if He permits us in such a spirit to make some mistakes, He will likewise teach us to profit by them; and our reflections upon what was wrong one day, will make us act more wisely the next. At the best, we must always expect to meet with new proofs of our own weakness and insufficiency; otherwise, how should we be kept humble, or know how to prize the liberty He allows us of coming to the throne of grace for fresh forgiveness and direction every day? But if He enables us to walk before him with a single eye, He will graciously accept our desire of serving him better if we could, and His blessing will make our feeble endeavours in some degree successful, at the same time that we see defects and evils attending our best services, sufficient to make us ashamed of them.

I am, etc.

Miss Delafield.

AFTERWARDS MRS. CARDALE.

WE find in the *Evangelical Magazine* for 1816, an obituary notice of Mr. Cardale, a solicitor in Bedford Row, of whom it is said, that he was an intimate friend of Mr. Cecil, and took an active part in the management of St. John's Chapel. Miss Delafield was married to a Mr. Cardale in 1776; and we believe it was to this gentleman. There is nothing in the following letters which suggest any further information respecting this correspondent of Mr. Newton.

To Miss Delafield.

LETTER I.—Blessing of God's presence—Frames and faith.

May 4, 1773.

. . . . My heart was once like a dungeon, out of the reach of day, and always dark: the Lord, by his grace, has been pleased to make this dungeon a room, by putting windows in it; but I need not tell you, that though windows will transmit the day-light into a room, they cannot supply the want of it. When the day is gone, windows are of little use; when the day returns, the room is enlightened by them again. Thus, unless the Lord shines, I cannot retain to-day the light I had yesterday; and though his presence makes a delightful difference, I have no more to boast of in myself at one time than another; yet when it is dark, I am warranted to expect the return of light again. When He is with me, all goes on pleasantly; when He withdraws, I find I can do nothing without him. I need not wonder that I find it so, for it must be so of course, if I am what I confess myself to be,—a poor, helpless, sinful creature in myself. Nor need I be overmuch discouraged, since the Lord has promised to help those who can do nothing without him, not those who can make a tolerable shift to help themselves. Through mercy He does not so totally withdraw as to leave me without any power or will to cry for his return. I hope He maintains in me at all times a desire of his presence; yet it becomes me to wait for him with patience, and to live upon his faithfulness, when I can feel nothing but evil in myself.

In your letter, after having complained of your inability, you say you converse with many who find it otherwise, who can go whenever they will to the Father of mercies with a child-like confidence, and never return without an answer, an answer of peace. If they only mean that they are favoured with an established faith, and can see that the Lord is always the same, and that their right to the blessings of the covenant is not at all affected by their unworthiness, I wish you and I had more experience of the same privilege. In general, the Lord helps me to aim at it, though I find it sometimes difficult to hold fast my confidence. But if they speak absolutely with respect to their frames, that they not only have something to support them under their changes, but meet with no changes that require such support, I must say it is well that they do not live here; if they did, they would not know how to pity us, and we should not know how to understand them. We have an enemy at Olney that fights against our peace, and I know not one amongst us but often groans under the warfare. I advise you not to be troubled by what you hear of other folks experience, but keep close to the written word, where you will meet with much to encourage you, though you often feel yourself weary and heavy laden. For my own part, I like that path best which is well beaten by the footsteps of the flock, though it is not always pleasant and strewed with flowers. In *our* way we find some hills, from whence we can cheerfully look about us; but we meet with deep valleys likewise, and seldom travel long upon even ground.

I am, etc.

To Miss Delafield.

Letter II.—Christian intercourse—Disadvantages of being from home—The path of duty the right path.

January 10, 1775.

There is hardly anything in which the Lord permits me to meet with more disappointment, than in the advantage I am ready to promise myself from creature converse. When I expect to meet any of my Christian friends, my thoughts usually travel much faster than my body. I anticipate the hour of meeting, and my imagination is warmed with expectation of what I shall say and what I shall hear; and sometimes I have had seasons for which I ought to be more thankful than I am. It is pleasant indeed when the Lord favours us with a happy hour, and is pleased to cause our hearts to burn within us while we are speaking of his goodness. But often it is far otherwise with me: I carry with me a dissipation of spirit, and find that I can neither impart nor receive. Something from within or from without crosses my schemes; and when I retire, I seem to have gained nothing but a fresh conviction, that we can neither help nor be helped, unless the Lord himself is pleased to help us. With his presence in our hearts, we might be comfortable and happy if shut up in one of the cells of Newgate: without it, the most select company, the most desirable opportunities, prove but clouds without water.

I have sometimes thought of asking you, whether you find that difference between being abroad and at home that I do? But I take it for granted that you do not: your connexions and intimacies are, I believe, chiefly with those who are highly favoured of the Lord; and if you can break through, or be upon your guard against the inconveniences which attend frequent changes and much company, you must be very happy in them. But I believe, considering my weakness, the Lord has chosen wisely and well for me, in placing me in a state of retirement, and not putting it in my power, were it ever so much my inclination, to be often abroad. As I stir so seldom, I believe when I do it is not upon the whole to my disadvantage; for I meet with more or less upon which my reflections afterwards may, by his blessing, be useful to me, though at the time my visits most frequently convince me how little wisdom or skill I have in improving time and opportunities. But were I to live in London, I know not what might be the consequence. Indeed, I need not puzzle myself about it, as my call does not lie there; but I pity and pray for those who do live there, and I admire such of them as, in those circumstances which appear so formidable to me, are enabled to walk simply, humbly, and closely with the Lord. They remind me of Daniel, unhurt in the midst of lions, or of the bush which Moses saw, surrounded with flames, yet not consumed, because the Lord was there. Some such I do know, and I hope you are one of the number.

This is certain, that if the light of God's countenance, and communion with him in love, afford the greatest happiness we are capable of, then whatever tends to indispose us for this pursuit, or to draw a vail between him and our souls, must be our great loss. If we walk with him, it must be in the path of duty, which lies plain before us when our eye is single, and we are waiting with attention upon his word, Spirit, and providence. Now, wherever the path of duty leads we are safe: and it often does lead and place us in such circumstances as no other consideration would make us choose. We are not designed to be mere recluses, but have all a part to act in life. Now, if I find myself in the midst of things disagreeable enough in themselves to the spiritual life; yet if, when the question occurs, What dost thou here? my heart can answer, I am here by the will of God, I believe it to be, all things considered, my duty to be here at this time rather than elsewhere. If I say I am tolerably satisfied of this, then I would not burden and grieve myself about what I cannot avoid or alter, but endeavour to take all such things up with cheerfulness, as a part of my daily cross, since I am called, not only to do the will of God, but to suffer it; but if I am doing my own will rather than his, then I have reason to fear lest I should meet with either a snare or a sting at every step. May the Lord Jesus be with you.

I am, etc.

The Rev. William Howell.

MR. HOWELL preached at Knaresborough, in Yorkshire. It appears that the Independent chapel at this place was originally built by Lady Hewley, but that it was afterwards shut up for many years. On the occasion of Mrs. Thornton, the wife of John Thornton, Esq., visiting Harrogate, and finding the chapel at Knaresborough thus circumstanced, she resolved to put it in a state of repair and to secure the services of a stated minister. These efforts resulted in the settlement of Mr. Howell. Through his devoted labours the aspect of things was entirely changed, and spiritual prosperity succeeded the former desolation; and not only in Knaresborough, but in the neighbourhood around.

In the year 1770, it pleased God heavily to afflict this good man, and he sank into a state of great mental depression. It was under these circumstances that the letters in the following pages, were written—see the first letter especially. The health of Mr. Howell was however restored, and he again betook himself with his wonted diligence to the work in which he so greatly delighted.

Deeply interested in the subject of missions to the heathen, which about this time awakened the earnest attention of the Christian church, Mr. Howell made an offer of his services to the London Missionary Society. He was appointed to superintend the mission to the South Seas on the second voyage of the ship "Duff." This was in 1799. The vessel, as is well known, was captured by a French privateer, and the missionaries were carried to Monte Video. This resulted in Mr. Howell's return to England, where he resumed his charge at Knaresborough; and in the providence of God he was enabled to fulfil his duties there till the year 1835.

He was a man of great devotedness and zeal, humble and retiring in his habits; but of a truly catholic spirit, and beloved by good men of all parties. He died at the advanced age of 89.

To the Rev. Wm. Howell.

LETTER I.—Depression arising from affliction—Christ our helper—The imperfection of our services no reason for despair.

DEAR SIR,—You are not wholly a stranger to me, though we are not personally acquainted. My late honoured friend, Mrs. Thornton, informed me of you upon your first settlement at Knaresborough. I had from her frequent accounts, during her life, of your diligence in preaching the gospel, and of the success with which the Lord honoured your labours, which gave me much pleasure.

I have not heard much of you since her removal. I hoped, however, that you were going on comfortably, and with a prospect of growing usefulness. It was, therefore, with real concern that I read your last two letters to Mr. Samuel Thornton, which he put into my hands yesterday, expressing, at the same time, his desire that I should write to you.

If your own apprehensions respecting yourself are justly formed you may possibly not be living, or not able to open or read my letter. But I am willing to hope otherwise, as the mournful strain in which you write is not the usual manner in which the Lord's faithful servants express themselves when drawing very near to the close of life. Should it be his pleasure to call you home by this illness, I trust, before your departure, you will be enabled to bear a comfortable testimony to the power of those truths in your own soul, by which, in the course of your ministry, you have been instrumental to the comfort of others. But with submission to his will I pray that this sickness may not be unto death, but to the glory of God, for the sake both of your people and your children; and, as I have hinted, I take some encouragement to pray thus from the state of your mind when you wrote your last letter. However the event may prove, I trust that you have a good right to say, " Whether I live, I shall live unto the Lord, or whether I die, I shall go to the Lord; so that living or dying, I am the Lord's." The right to say this and the power of saying it are distinct things, and may, upon some occasions, be separated for a season. For from the near and intimate union between body and mind, sickness and pain often darken and obstruct the actings of the soul, and afford the enemy, if he is permitted, some peculiar advantages of assaulting it with temptations. But though he may disturb, he cannot destroy those who have committed themselves to Jesus and devoted themselves to his service.

Is not the case of Joshua the high priest, described by the prophet Zech. iii. 1—5, applicable to you, as it has been to many before you. When he stood before the Lord in his filthy garments Satan was at his right hand to resist him. Joshua had nothing to offer in his own behalf. He could not deny the charge, or pretend that his filthy garments were white and clean. But he had a powerful friend to plead for him, who claimed him as a brand plucked out of the fire, silenced his adversary, and clothed him with a change of raiment.

Thus totally undeserving are we, thus abundantly gracious is the Lord. Do not therefore speak of yourself as without hope, but rather say, " Why art thou cast down, O my soul? Hope thou in God, for I shall yet praise Him!"

Your expression, "O that I had lived more to God and less to myself," is what becomes me also to adopt. Surely when I draw near to the gates of the grave, I shall (if sensible) feel the force of that thought more than I do at present. I am a debtor for innumerable blessings for which I have made no suitable acknowledgment, and for innumerable sins which I have committed. "If thou, Lord, wert strict to mark what is amiss, O Lord, who could stand? I could not answer to one of a thousand." But our comfort lies in the solemn assurance given, " There is forgiveness with thee."   .   .   .   It is true I have sinned. My best service is defective, my all is defiled, my heart is deceitful and desperately wicked, my every power is disordered and depraved, so that my services and duties, my preaching and my prayers are sufficient to ruin me, if the Lord should enter into judgment. But it is true Christ died for sinners, that He is risen, ascended, that He is able and willing and determined to save to the uttermost all that come unto God by him. His precious blood cleanseth from all sin; his grace is sufficient for us, and where He has begun a good work He will carry it on. Upon this gospel ground I desire to stand, and I trust you likewise will find a firm footing, solid rock, a sure foundation; and that when your enemy sees you resolved to take rest and refuge in Jesus Christ crucified, he will be put to shame and flight.   .   .   .   Many causes of humiliation we have. We have been poor, unprofitable servants; but not wholly so, because He has been pleased to work in and by us; and our services are not the ground of our acceptance. We are not under the law but under grace, and are invited and encouraged to look to him alone for our salvation, who so loved us as to obey and suffer for us.

Cheer up, sir, and commit yourself to the Almighty Shepherd and Saviour. He knows your sorrows, your fears, and your feelings. All your enemies are under his control, and cannot distress you a moment longer than He permits them. I shall be glad to hear that though the Lord has chastened you sore He has not given you over to death, but that you are to live and to declare his wonderful works. If He appoint otherwise, you have but done with cares and trials the sooner. You have sown in tears, but the harvest will be unspeakable joy. I wish the knowledge I have received of your illness may be sanctified to quicken me in my work and warfare, that I may abound in the Lord's service while it is day, for the night cometh. Perhaps I may not see you in this world, but I hope to meet you at last, and join with you in the song before the throne, "To him who loved us and washed us from our sins in his own blood." I commend you to his care and keeping.

I remain,
Your affectionate friend and brother,
JOHN NEWTON.

LONDON: *May* 21, 1770.

To the REV. WILLIAM HOWELL.

LETTER II.—Christ saves to the uttermost—Sin of unbelief—True grace.

DEAR SIR,—I am glad to find I was not mistaken in thinking your illness would terminate better than your apprehensions. . . .

I imputed your fears and complaints very much to the weakness of your bodily frame, and the lowness and hurry of your animal spirits. My judgment is confirmed by what you have written to me. I am ready to take it for granted that you did not preach to your people such a scheme of the gospel as you seem to have proposed to yourself during your illness. Did you ever try to persuade them that our Lord Jesus Christ could save little sinners and forgive little sins (if such there be), but that great sinners (like you), and scarlet sins (like yours), were beyond the limits of his power and mercy? Or have you not rather often told them that all manner and degrees of sin are forgiven for the Son of man's sake, and that He will in no wise cast out him that cometh, and that He is able to save to the uttermost? If you preached thus, you said the truth; and if this be the truth, what solid ground of discouragement can you justly draw from any peculiarity in your own case? You were willing to come to him; if, therefore, you had been cast out, it must have been in some wise. If you must have been lost, why were you told, or why did you tell others, that He saves to the uttermost?

Satan seldom transforms himself more in the resemblance of an angel of light than when he would impress us with a counterfeit humility, and persuade us that it would be presumption in such great sinners as we are to believe the promises of God. I apprehend every person who is truly convinced of sin thinks he has reason to deem himself the chief of sinners, because he knows more of the nature, number, and aggravations of the evils of his own heart and life than he can possibly know, or has any just right to suspect of his fellow-sinners. But in what part of the Bible do we find a distinction made between few or many, great or small sins, in the article of forgiveness? Could we suppose a person who had committed but one sin, he would need faith in the blood of the Saviour to cleanse him from that one; for the Scripture tells us of no other name by which the sinner can be saved. And if all the sins committed in Yorkshire, or in London, were chargeable upon a single person, if that person was wrought upon by the Holy Spirit sincerely to seek salvation in God's appointed way, the blood of Jesus Christ is able to cleanse him from them all. This humbling doctrine which appoints one and the same way, and but one way of salvation, for all sorts and sizes of sinners, is very offensive to our natural pride and self-righteousness; but it is a source of consolation and encouragement to all who are acquainted with the plague of their own hearts.

When the brazen serpent was erected in the wilderness, to cure those who must otherwise have died, the benefit was not restrained to those who had been bitten by the fiery serpent but once or a few times. The worst case amongst the people was relieved as soon and as certainly as the very slightest. The remedy was universally proposed to every person. The application was easy; it was only, look and live. But if a man had spent all his time in measuring or counting his wounds, instead of looking to the ordinance of God, he might have died, though the means of life were within his view. The sense of the evil of sin is given to quicken our application to Christ, and not to discourage our approach. The Scripture has concluded all under sin, and as such we are all condemned already. But the Gospel proclaims a free pardon to every one who, with the eye of his mind, looks for life to him who hung upon the cross.

When we burden ourselves with our many sins, we are apt to overlook the very greatest of them—unbelief; for what can be a greater proof of stubbornness and pride than to dare to contradict the express Word of God, to say that He will not pardon, when he declares that He will; to persist in it that He will make differences when He has assured us that He will make none? We read that Noah being warned of God, prepared an ark. The Lord condescended to give very particular directions for building it. When it was finished and the deluge approaching, Noah entered, and the Lord himself shut him in. Now, suppose it possible that history had terminated something in this way, "And it came to pass after these things, that the ark was dashed to pieces upon the mountains of Ararat, and Noah and his family all perished," how would this event have astonished us? What! did the Lord appoint the ark, command Noah to go into it, and shut him carefully in, and Noah perished at last? Did not the Lord mean to save him? or did He not know how to save him? Our doubts and unbelief are founded upon a supposition no less absurd and impossible than that I have mentioned. Did Jesus die for sinners? Did He say to my heart, at a time when I thought not of him, "Seek ye my face, and live?" Did He incline and constrain my heart to answer, "Thy face, Lord, will I seek." And will He, can He disappoint the desires which only He could raise? Did He open the door of his mercy and invite me to draw near, only to shut it against me when I came? Impossible. Neither you nor I, who are evil, could treat a beggar so. If we were not disposed to relieve him, we should not take pains to persuade him that we would. Yet this is the horrid charge which unbelief would fix upon the God of mercy and truth. If He had been pleased to kill us, He would not have shown us such things as these—

> Would He have given me eyes to see
> My danger and my remedy,
> Reveal his name, and bid me pray,
> Had He resolved to say me, Nay?

It seems you have found out, though you have not only preached the gospel to a flourishing poor people, but loved them and delighted in them, that you never possessed grace. It is, indeed possible to preach the gospel without grace, but not to love and delight in those who receive it.

I mean not to persuade you into a good opinion of yourself, but if what you relate of your own feelings and desires in the latter part of your letter, be not descriptive of grace, I am at a loss to know what the word grace means. I do hope and believe that your late afflictions have been sanctified to you, and that you will be brought out of the furnace refined like gold. The simplicity of our dependence upon God, and of our intention to promote his glory is always capable of increase; for everything here is in a state of imperfection. But the Lord does not despise the day of small things, nor should we. The kingdom of heaven is like a grain of mustard seed—like the dawn of day. The beginnings are small, but the latter end shall greatly increase. The seed is grace, or the tree which springs from it would not be gracious. Yea the desire of grace is actual grace; for sin is our natural element, and nature can no more desire grace than a fish could long live upon the dry land. During the eleven years you have preached with acceptance and usefulness, and maintained a conversation becoming the gospel, you have either supported and preserved yourself, or the Lord has been with you. If all this has been done without grace, you have something to boast of. If the Lord has done it, He should have the praise. This, likewise, is a species of false humility, when we are tempted to deny or to depreciate what the Lord has already done for us, because it is not that which He has taught us to desire. But though there is a great difference between the earnest and the full sum, yet an earnest from him who cannot change is a strong security for the whole.

But why should I write as if the objections you stated against your peace were properly your own, when I am aware they were partly owing to the weakness of your nerves, and partly to the power of temptation which indeed (unless the Lord signally interposes) are seldom quite separate. Be thankful for the past and the present. Trials no less than comforts are the tokens of his love. All is regulated by infinite wisdom. You will find cause to praise him even for the severe.

I shall be glad to hear from you and occasionally to write to you; but I cannot promise to be always so speedy and punctual. May the Lord bless you with increase of strength both in body and mind, and make you a blessing to many.

I am, your affectionate friend and brother,
JOHN NEWTON.

To the REV. WILLIAM HOWELL.

LETTER III.—The only true satisfaction in religion—Humility learned by suffering—Hutchinsonianism.

DEAR SIR, . . . How little do the thoughtless and the gay know of that intercourse which passes between believers and the invisible world! The conflicts which they are exposed to with the powers of darkness, and the consolations by which their wounds are healed and their strength renewed, are equally treated as enthusiastic. If they had one hour's experience of either, how greatly would they prize the gospel, which alone can support us in the day of trouble, or even enable us to find satisfaction in a state of prosperity! For, until we are reconciled to God by the blood of Jesus, everything to which we look for satisfaction will surely disappoint us. God formed us originally for himself, and has therefore given the human mind such a vastness of desire, such a thirst for happiness as He alone can answer; and therefore, till we seek our rest in him, in vain we seek it elsewhere. Neither the hurries of business, nor the allurements of pleasure, nor the accomplishment of our wishes, can fill up the mighty void that is felt within. Oh that they were wise, that they understood this! I hope and believe that He who brought you out of your troubles will enable you to profit by them and that your profiting will be visible to others. But I am not surprised that you do not think better of yourself than before. The highest attainment we can reach in this life is a broken and a contrite spirit arising from a deep conviction how very disproportionate our best returns are to our obligations, and how far our obedience and holiness fall short of the standard, the revealed law and will of God. Job was commended by the Lord himself before his great trials came upon him, and in a calm moment he expressed a persuasion that when he was fully tried he should come forth as gold. But when he was at last brought forth, he did not say, "Behold I am perfect," but, "Behold I am vile." And the great lesson he learnt by his sufferings and his deliverance was, to abhor himself and to repent in dust and ashes. I apprehend they are the most favoured and most eminent Christians who come the nearest to the spirit with which he spoke these words.

. . . . The New Testament is a plain book designed for plain people. The gospel is to be preached to the poor and simple who are as capable of receiving it as the wise, and in some sense more so. I therefore lay little stress upon any sentiments that lie out of the common road, that depend upon a knowledge of languages and criticism, or require a degree of capacity and genius to be understood.

In this view I judge of Mr. Hutchinson's writings, I mean on theological subjects. I think their tendency is rather to amuse the understanding than to warm the heart.

Mr. Romaine is much of a Hutchinsonian; but when he preaches in that strain I do not think his sermons so edifying as those which he delivers in the more usual and popular way. The whole of religion may be summed up in the love of God in Christ, and of man for God's sake. This was aimed at, and in a measure obtained, before Mr. Hutchinson was born, and is still, by many who have no knowledge of him or his writings.* As a minister, I endeavour to avoid all nostrums, singularities, and new discoveries. I wish to advance nothing which I cannot maintain upon the authority of the Bible in our mother tongue, which I deem sufficient to make us and our hearers wise unto salvation; though I have heard Mr. Romaine in his zeal for Hutchinsonianism unguardedly style it, "a vile translation." . . .

That the Lord may be the light of your eye, the strength of your arm, and the joy of your heart, and may give an increasing blessing to your ministry is the sincere prayer of

Dear Sir,

Your affectionate brother and friend,

JOHN NEWTON.

LONDON: *October* 18.
6, *Coleman Street Buildings.*

---

* Hutchinsonianism is so called from John Hutchinson, a learned layman, who, about 1724, published a work entitled, *Moses' Principia.* He regarded the Hebrew Scriptures as comprising a complete system of physical science as well as of theological truth, and so he endeavoured to controvert the Newtonian system as at variance with the philosophy there taught. He maintained that the Hebrew language contains in its etymological construction and radical terms the most important hidden truths; that it is the only language capable of adequately expressing the essence of Jehovah; and that the Scriptures of the Old Testament are to be interpreted in a typical sense, according to the radical import of the Hebrew expressions.

This new system of philology and philosophy was advocated with a great deal of learning and ingenuity, and was adopted to a greater or less extent by some few scholars and men of true piety; but Hutchinsonianism belongs to those systems which have almost passed away before more rigid principles of philosophy and Scripture interpretation.

The Rev. John Ryland, Jun.

AFTERWARDS DR. RYLAND.

THE following letters, with some others in *Cardiphonia*, are addressed to the son of the Rev. John Ryland, Baptist minister at Northampton, a man who combined with some eccentricities very extraordinary powers of mind and great piety. For the father, Mr. Newton in his *Diary* frequently expresses his great admiration, for the son he had a very loving regard. The correspondence commenced when Mr. Ryland was only nineteen, while Mr. Newton was more than twice that age, yet was there the most thorough sympathy between them. The letters which are omitted, are of less general interest, yet show how entirely Mr. Ryland gave his confidence to Mr. Newton, and how thoroughly that confidence was appreciated.

The subject of our notice was born at Warwick where his father was then settled. He was a remarkably precocious child. It is said of him, that he read a chapter in the Hebrew Bible to the celebrated Hervey before he was five years old. What is of more importance, he was early converted to God, and eventually became co-pastor with his father at Northampton. In 1773 he removed to Bristol undertaking the joint offices of President of the Baptist Theological Institution, and the pastorate of the church at Broadmead.

In the funeral sermon preached by the Rev. Robert Hall on occasion of the death of Dr. Ryland in 1825, he is spoken of as a man remarkably endowed with the distinguishing graces of the Christian character, of a religion eminently fruitful in all good works, and of a spirit of devotion which was the very element of his being. "Where," says Mr. Hall, addressing his sorrowing flock, "where will you look for another whose life is a luminous commentary on his doctrine, and who can invite you to no heights of piety but what you are conscious he himself has attained?"

To the Rev. John Ryland, Jun.

Letter I.—The church safe in the keeping of Christ—Falls of professors.

July 31, 1773.

Dear Sir,—I received your sorrowful epistle yesterday, and in order to encourage you to write, I answer it to-day.

The ship was safe when Christ was in her, though He was *really* asleep. At present I can tell you good news, though you know it: He is wide awake, and his eyes are in every place. You and I, if we could be pounded together, might perhaps make two tolerable ones. You are too anxious, and I am too easy in some respects. Indeed I cannot be too easy, when I have a right thought that all is safe in his hands; but if your anxiety makes you pray, and my composure makes me careless, you have certainly the best of it. However, the ark is fixed upon an immoveable foundation; and if we think we see it totter, it is owing to a swimming in our heads. Seriously, the times look dark and stormy, and call for much circumspection and prayer; but let us not forget that we have an infallible Pilot, and that the power, and wisdom, and honour of God, are embarked with us.

At Venice they have a fine vessel, called the *Bucentaur*, in which, on a certain day of the year, the Doge and nobles embark, and go a little way to sea, to repeat the foolish ceremony of marriage between the Republic and the Adriatic (in consequence of some lying, antiquated Pope's bull, by which the banns of matrimony between Venice and the Gulf were published in the dark ages), when, they say, a gold ring is very gravely thrown overboard. Upon this occasion, I have been told, when the honour and government of Venice are shipped on board the *Bucentaur*, the pilot is obliged by his office to take an oath that he will bring the vessel safely back again, *in defiance of wind and weather.* Vain mortals! If this be true, what an instance of God's long-suffering is it, that they have never yet sunk as lead in the mighty waters! But my story will probably remind you, that Jesus has actually entered into such an engagement in behalf of his church. And well He may, for both wind and weather are at his command; and He can turn the storm into a calm in a moment. We may therefore safely and confidently leave the government upon his shoulders. Duty is our part, the care is his. . . .

The miscarriages of professors are grievous; yet such things must be; how else could the Scriptures be fulfilled? But there is one who is able to keep *us* from falling. Some who have distressed us, perhaps never were truly changed: how then could they stand? We see only the outside. Others who are sincere are permitted to fall for our instruction, that we may not be high-minded, but fear. However, he that walketh humbly walketh surely.

Believe me, etc.

To the Rev. John Ryland, Jun.

Letter II.—A sight of the heavenly King.

May 28, 1775.

Dear Sir, . . . You must not expect a long letter this morning; we are just going to court in hopes of seeing the King, for He has promised to meet us. We can say He is mindful of his promise; and yet it is not strange, that though we are all in the same place, and the King in the midst of us, it is but here and there one (even of those who love him) can see him at once. However, in our turns we are all favoured with a glimpse of him, and have had cause to say, How great is his goodness! How great is his beauty! We have the advantage of the Queen of Sheba, a more glorious object to behold, and not so far to go for the sight of it. If a transient glance exceeds all that the world can afford for a long continuance, what must it be to dwell with him! If a day in his courts be better than a thousand, what will eternity be in his presence! I hope the more you see, the more you love; the more you drink, the more you thirst; the more you do for him, the more you are ashamed you can do so little; and that the nearer you approach to your journey's end, the more your pace is quickened. Surely, the power of spiritual attraction should increase as the distance lessens. Oh that heavenly loadstone! may it so draw us, that we may not creep, but run. In common travelling, the strongest become weary if the journey be very long; but in the spiritual journey, we are encouraged with a hope of going on from strength to strength. *Instaurabit iter vires*,* as Johnson expresses it. No road but the road to heaven can thus communicate refreshment to those who walk in it, and make them more fresh and lively when they are just finishing their course than when they first set out.

I am, etc.

To the Rev. John Ryland, Jun.

Letter III.—Following Christ—The soul a besieged city.

April 18, 1776.

Dear Sir,—Are you sick, or lame of your right hand, or are you busy in preparing a folio for the press, that I hear nothing from you? You see by the excuses I would

* The way will renew our strength.

contrive I am not willing to suppose you have forgotten me, but that your silence is rather owing to a *cannot* than a *will not*.

I hope your soul prospers. I do not ask you, if you are always filled with sensible comfort; but do you find your spirit more bowed down to the feet and will of Jesus, so as to be willing to serve him, for the *sake* of serving him, and to follow him, as we say, through thick and thin; to be willing to be anything or nothing, so that He may be glorified? I could give you plenty of good advice upon this head; but I am ashamed to do it, because I so poorly follow it myself. I want to live with him by the day, to do all for him, to receive all from him, to possess all in him, to leave all to him, to make him my hiding-place and my resting-place. I want to deliver up that rebel self to him in chains; but the rogue, like Proteus, puts on so many forms, that he slips through my fingers: but I think I know what I would do if I could fairly catch him.

My soul is like a besieged city: a legion of enemies without the gates, and a nest of restless traitors within, that hold a correspondence with them without; so that I am deceived and counteracted continually. It is a mercy that I have not been surprised and overwhelmed long ago: without help from on high, it would soon be over with me. How often have I been forced to cry out, O God! the heathen are got into thine inheritance: thy holy temple have they defiled, and defaced all thy work. Indeed it is a miracle that I still hold out. I trust, however, I shall be supported to the end, and that my Lord will at length raise the siege, and cause me to shout deliverance and victory.

Pray for me, that my walls may be strengthened, and wounds healed. We are all pretty well as to the outward man, and join in love to all friends.

Joseph Foster Barham, Esq.

BETWEEN this gentleman, who resided at Bedford, and Mr. Newton, a very close intimacy subsisted. Mr. Newton formed his acquaintance in the year 1773. He speaks of his first interview with the family as exceedingly pleasant, and some time afterwards, having made a longer stay at Mr. Barham's house, he writes in his *Diary*, "Such a happy family perhaps I never saw, where the peace and love of God seem to dwell in every heart. I spoke every morning after breakfast and attended the chapel (Moravian) every evening." So in a letter to his friend Mr. Bull, when there was a probability that the latter might leave the neighbourhood, Mr. Newton says, "I certainly should miss you, for excepting a friend, twelve miles off (referring to Mr. Barham), I have no person in these parts with whom my heart so thoroughly unites in spirituals, though there are many I love."

The family of the Fosters was descended from an ancient and distinguished house in Northumberland. John Foster held a military command in the expedition to Jamaica under Penn and Venables in 1655. He received a grant of extensive estates in the parish of St. Elizabeth, in that island, the greater part of which are still in the possession of the family. The subject of this notice was the great grandson of John. He was born in the year 1729, and subsequently assumed the name of Barham. At an early period he united himself to the Moravian church, and several of his relatives followed his example.

Mr. Barham was held in much esteem by the church of the United Brethren. He had the extension of the Redeemer's kingdom much at heart, and was liberal in the support of every institution for the welfare of mankind.

The last two letters in this series are addressed to Miss Mary Barham, the youngest daughter of Mr. Barham.

To J. Foster Barham, Esq.

LETTER I.—How trials are to be estimated.

October 15, 1774.

MY DEAREST SIR,—I think the greatness of trials is to be estimated, rather by the impressions they make upon our spirits, than by their outward appearance. The smallest will be too heavy for us if we are left to grapple with it in our own strength, or rather weakness; and if the Lord is pleased to put forth his power in us, He can make the heaviest light. A lively impression of his love, or of his sufferings for us or of the glories within the vail, accompanied with a due sense of the misery from which we are redeemed; these thoughts will enable us to be not only submissive, but even joyful, in tribulations. When faith is in exercise, though the flesh will have its feelings, the spirit will triumph over them. But it is needful we should know that we have no sufficiency in ourselves, and in order to know it we must feel it; and therefore the Lord sometimes withdraws his sensible influence, and then the buzzing of a fly will be an overmatch for our patience: at other times He will show us what He can do in us and for us; then we can adopt the apostle's words, and say, I can do or suffer all things through Christ strengthening me. He has said, My grace is sufficient for thee. It is observable, that the children of God seldom disappoint our expectations under great trials; if they show a wrongness of spirit, it is usually in such little incidents that we are ready to wonder at them. For which, two reasons may be principally assigned. When great trials are in view, we run simply and immediately to our all-sufficient Friend, feel our dependence, and cry in good earnest for help: but if the occasion seems small, we are too apt secretly to lean to our own wisdom and strength, as if in such slight matters we could make shift without him. Therefore in these we often fail. Again, the Lord deals with us as we sometimes see mothers with their children. When a child begins to walk he is often very self-important; he thinks he needs no help, and can hardly bear to be supported by the finger of another. Now, in such a case, if there is no danger or harm from a fall, as if he is on a plain carpet, the mother will let him alone to try how he *can* walk. He is pleased at first, but presently down he comes; and a few experiments of this kind convince him he is not so strong and able as he thought, and make him willing to be led. But was he upon the brink of a river or a precipice, from whence a fall might be fatal, the tender mother would not trust him to himself, no not for a moment. I have not room to make the application, nor is it needful. It requires the same grace to bear with a right spirit a cross word as a cross injury; or the breaking of a china plate, as the death of an only son.

I am, etc.

To J. Foster Barham, Esq.

LETTER II.—The lessons of Christian experience.

November 23, 1771.

MY DEAR SIR,—I hope to be informed in due time, that the Lord has given you full health and cure. He has preserved me hitherto from the hands of surgeons; but I feel as if my flesh would prove, as you say, a very coward, were it needful to submit to a painful operation. Yet I observe, when such operations are necessary, if people are satisfied of a surgeon's skill and prudence, they will not only yield to be cut at his pleasure, without pretending to direct him where, or how long he shall make the incision, but will thank and pay him for putting them in pain, because they believe it for their advantage. I wish I could be more like them in my concerns. My body, as I said, is, through mercy, free from considerable ailments, but I have a soul that requires surgeon's work continually. . . .

I thank you for your letter; I never receive one from you without pleasure, and I believe seldom without profit, at least for the time. I believe with you, that there is much of the proper and designed efficacy of the gospel mystery which I have not yet experienced. And I suppose they who are advanced far beyond me in the divine light, judge the same of their utmost present attainments. Yet I have no idea of any *permanent* state in this life that shall make my experience cease to be a state of warfare and humiliation. At my first setting out, indeed, I thought to be better, and to feel myself better from year to year; I expected by degrees to attain every thing which I *then* comprised *in my idea* of a saint. I thought my grain of grace, by much diligence and careful improvement, would, in time, amount to a pound, that pound in a further space of time to a talent, and then I hoped to increase from one talent to many; so that, supposing the Lord should spare me a competent number of years, I pleased myself with the thought of dying rich. But, alas! these my golden expectations have been like South Sea dreams; I have lived hitherto a poor sinner, and I believe I shall die one. Have I then gained nothing by waiting upon the Lord? Yes, I have gained that, which I once would rather have been without, such accumulated proofs of the deceitfulness and desperate wickedness of my heart, as I hope, by the

Lord's blessing, has in some measure taught me to know what I mean when I say, Behold I am vile. And in connexion with this, I have gained such experience of the wisdom, power, and compassion of my Redeemer, the need, the worth of his blood, righteousness, attention, and intercession, the glory that He displays in pardoning iniquity and sin, and passing by the transgression of the remnant of his heritage, that my soul cannot but cry out, Who is a God like unto thee? Thus, if I have any meaner thoughts of myself, Ezek. xvi. 63, and any higher thoughts of him than I had twenty years ago, I have reason to be thankful; every grain of this experience is worth mountains of gold. And if, by his mercy, I shall yet sink more in my own esteem, and He will be pleased to rise still more glorious to my eyes, and more precious to my heart. I expect it will be much in the same way. I was ashamed when I began to seek him; I am more ashamed now; and I expect to be most of all ashamed when he shall appear to destroy my last enemy. But, oh! I may rejoice in him, to think that He will not be ashamed of me.

I am, etc.

To J. Foster Barham, Esq.

Letter III.—Self-complaints.

May 19, 1775.

My dear Sir,—I hope you will find the Lord present at all times, and in all places. When it is so, we are at home everywhere; when it is otherwise, *home* is a prison, and *abroad* a wilderness. I know what I ought to desire, and what I do desire. I point him out to others as the All-in-all; I esteem him as such in my own judgment; but, alas! my experience abounds with complaints. He is my sun; but clouds, and sometimes walls, intercept him from my view. He is my strength; yet I am prone to lean upon reeds. He is my friend; but on my part there is such coldness and ingratitude, as no other friend could bear. But still He is gracious, and shames me with his repeated multiplied goodness. Oh for a warmer heart, a more simple dependence, a more active zeal, a more sensible deliverance from the effects of this body of sin and death! He helps me in my endeavours to keep the vineyards of others! but, alas! my own does not seem to flourish as some do around me. However, though I cannot say I labour more abundantly than they all, I have reason to say with thankfulness, By the grace of God I am what I am. My poor story would soon be much worse, did not He support, restrain, and watch over me every minute. Let me intreat your praises and prayers on the behalf of me and mine; and may the Lord bless you and yours with an increase in every good.

I am, etc.

To J. Foster Barham, Esq.

LETTER IV.—Divine sovereignty in the sufferings of believers—Christian friendship.

September 2, 1776.

My dear Sir,—The young woman I spoke of is still living, and not much weaker than when I left her. The Lord was pleased to relieve her on Tuesday evening, and she was comfortable the remainder of the week. But yesterday her conflicts returned, and she was in great distress. The enemy, who always fights against the peace of the Lord's children, finds great advantage against them when their spirits are weakened and worn down by long illness, and is often permitted to assault them. The reasons are hidden from us, but they are doubtless worthy of his wisdom and love, and they terminate in victory, to the praise of his glorious grace, which is more signally manifested by his leading them safely through fire and water than if their path was always smooth. He is sovereign in his dispensations, and appoints some of his people to trials and exercises, to which others, perhaps, are strangers all their days. Believers are soldiers: all soldiers, by their profession, are engaged to fight if called upon; but who shall be called to sustain the hottest service, and be most frequently exposed upon the field of battle, depends upon the will of the general or king. Some of our soldiers are now upon hard service in America, while others are stationed round the palace, see the king's face daily, and have no dangers or hardships to encounter. These, however, are as liable to a call as the others; but, if not called upon, they may enjoy with thankfulness the more easy post assigned them. Thus, the Captain of our salvation allots to his soldiers such stations as he thinks proper. He has a right to employ whom He will, and where He will. Some are comparatively at ease; they are not exposed to the fiercest onsets, but live near his presence; others are, to appearance, pressed above measure, beyond strength, so that they despair even of life; yet they are supported, and in the end made more than conquerors through him who hath loved them. Long observation convinces me, that the temptations which some endure are not chastisements brought upon them by unfaithfulness, or for any thing remarkably wrong in their spirit or walk: I often rather consider that, in *his* warfare, as in worldly wars, the post of danger and difficulty is the post of honour, and as such, assigned to those whom He has favoured with a peculiar measure of his grace. . . . . Possibly some suffer for the instruction of the rest, that we may learn to be more thankful to him for the peace we enjoy, and to be more humbly dependent upon him for the continuance of it. The Lord's way is in the deep, and his path in the great waters, untraceable by our feeble reasonings; but faith brings in a good report. We need not doubt but He does all things well, and in due time we shall see it. In the mean while He checks our vain inquiries, and calls upon us to be still, and know that He is God.

I brought home with me a thankful sense of the kindness and friendship I am favoured with from you and all yours. I account this connexion one of the great comforts of my life; and I hope it has been, and will be, not only pleasant but profitable to me. Though I am but an unapt scholar, I hope I am not unwilling to learn; and the Lord, in his merciful providence, appoints me many teachers. There is little praise due to us, if we either communicate or receive benefit in our intercourse with our fellow-disciples. In both we are but instruments under the influence of a higher hand. Were Christians to meet together without their Lord, they would either trifle or quarrel their time away. But as He has said, "Where two or three are met, there am I in the midst of them," we may well be glad of opportunities of coming together. And though, for my own part, I am so poor an improver of such seasons, that the recollection of them, when past, is generally accompanied with shame and regret, yet He is gracious and merciful, and seldom leaves me to complain that they were wholly in vain.

I am, etc.

To Miss Mary Barham.

Letter I.—On Christ carrying on his work in the hearts of his people.

November 11, 1775.

My dear Miss Mary,—Our late visit to Bedford was very pleasant to myself: if any thing that passed was of service to you, we know to whom the thanks are due; for we can neither communicate nor receive anything but so far as He is pleased to enable us. One reason why He often disappoints us is, that we may learn to depend on him alone. We are prone, as you observe, to rest too much upon sensible comforts, yet they are very desirable; only, as to the measure and seasons, it is well to be submissive to his will, to be thankful for them when we have them, and humbly waiting for them when we have them not. They are not, however, the proper ground of our hope; a good hope springs from such a sense of our wants, and such a persuasion of his power and grace, as engages the heart to venture, upon the warrant of his promises, to trust in him for salvation. In a sense, we are often hindering him by our impatience and unbelief; but strictly speaking, when He really begins the good work, and gives us a desire which will be satisfied with nothing short of himself, *He will not be hindered from carrying it on;* for He has said, I will work, and none shall let it. Ah! had it depended upon myself, upon my wisdom or faithfulness, I should have hindered him to purpose, and ruined myself long ago. How often have I grieved and resisted his Spirit! But hereby I have learned more of his patience and tenderness than I could otherwise have known. He knows our frame, and what effect our evil nature, fomented by the artifices of Satan, will have: He sees us from first to last. A thousand evils arise in our hearts, a thousand wrongnesses in our conduct, which, as they do arise, are new to ourselves, and perhaps at some times we were ready to think we were incapable of such things; but none of them are new to him to whom past, present, and future are the same. The foresight of them did not prevent his calling us by his grace. Though He knew we were vile, and should prove ungrateful and unfaithful, yet He would be found of us; He would knock at the door of our hearts, and gain himself an entrance. Nor shall they prevent his accomplishing his gracious purpose. It is our part to be abased before him, and quietly to hope and wait for his salvation in the use of his appointed means. The power, success, and blessing, are wholly from himself. To make us more sensible of this, He often withdraws from our perceptions: and as, in the absence of the sun, the wild beasts of the forest roam abroad; so, when Jesus hides himself, we presently perceive what is in our hearts, and what a poor shift we can make without him; when He returns, his light chases the evils away, and we are well again. However, they are not dead when most controlled by his presence.

It is your great and singular mercy, my dear miss, that He has taught you to seek him so early in life. You are entered in the way of salvation, but you must not expect all at once. The work of grace is compared to the corn, and to a building; the growth of the one, and the carrying forward of the other, are gradual. In a building, for instance, if it be large there is much to be done in preparing and laying the foundation, before the walls appear above ground; much is doing within, when the work does not seem perhaps to advance without; and when it is considerably forward, yet being encumbered with scaffolds and rubbish, a by-stander sees it at a great disadvantage, and can form but an imperfect judgment of it. But all this while the architect himself, even from the laying of the first stone, conceives of it according to the plan and design he has formed; he prepares and adjusts the materials, disposing each in its proper time and place, and views it in idea as already finished. In due season it is completed, but not in a day. The top-stone is fixed, and then the scaffolds and rubbish being removed, it appears to others as he intended it should be. Men indeed often plan what, for want of skill or ability, or from unforeseen disappointments, they are unable to execute. But nothing can disappoint the heavenly Builder; nor will He ever be reproached with forsaking the work of his own hands, or beginning that which He could not or would not accomplish. Phil. i. 6. Let us therefore be thankful for beginnings, and patiently wait the event. His enemies strive to retard the work, as they did when the Jews, by his order, set about rebuilding the temple. Yet it was finished in defiance of them all.

Believe me to be, etc.

To Miss M. Barham.

Letter II.—Christian growth gradual—Special manifestations.

September 3, 1776.

My dear Miss Mary, . . . The Lord is leading you in the good old way, in which you may perceive the footsteps of his flock who have gone before you. They had in their day the same difficulties, fears, and complaints as we have, and through mercy we partake of the same consolation which supported and refreshed them; and the promises which they trusted and found faithful, are equally sure to us. It is still true, that they who believe shall never be confounded. If left to ourselves, we should have built upon sand; but He has provided and revealed a sure foundation, removed our natural prejudices against it; and now, though rains and floods and storms assault our building, it cannot fall, for it is founded upon a rock. The suspicions and fears which arise in an awakened mind, proceed, in a good measure, from remaining unbelief, but not wholly so; for there is a jealousy and diffidence of ourselves, a wariness, owing to a sense of the deceitfulness of our hearts, which is a grace and a gift of the Lord. Some people who have much zeal, but are destitute of this jealous fear, may be compared to a ship that spreads a great deal of sail, but is not properly ballasted, and is therefore in danger of being overset whenever a storm comes. A sincere person has many reasons for distrusting his own judgment; is sensible of the vast importance of the case, and afraid of too hastily concluding in his own favour, and therefore not easily satisfied. However, this fear, though useful, especially to young beginners, is not comfortable; and they who simply wait upon Jesus are gradually freed from it, in proportion as their knowledge of him, and their experience of his goodness increases. He has a time for settling and establishing them in himself, and his time is best. We are hasty, and would be satisfied at once, but his word is, Tarry thou the Lord's leisure. The work of grace is not like Jonah's gourd, which sprang up and flourished in a night, and as quickly withered, but rather like the oak, which, from a little acorn and a tender plant, advances with an almost imperceptible growth from year to year, till it becomes a broad, spreading, and deep-rooted tree, and then it stands for ages. The Christian oak shall grow and flourish for ever. When I see any soon after they appear to be awakened, making a speedy profession of great joy before they have a due acquaintance with their own hearts, I am in pain for them. I am not sorry to hear them afterwards complain that their joys are gone, and they are almost at their wits' end; for without some such check, to make them feel their weakness and dependence, I seldom find them turn out well: either their fervour insensibly abates, till they become quite cold and sink into the world again (of which I have seen many instances), or, if they do not give up all, their walk is uneven, and their spirit has not that savour of brokenness and true humility which is the chief ornament of our holy profession. If they do not feel the plague of their hearts at first, they find it out afterwards, and too often manifest it to others. Therefore, though I know the Spirit of the Lord is free, and will not be confined to our rules, and there may be excepted cases; yet, in general, I believe the old proverb, "Soft and fair goes far," will hold good in Christian experience. Let us be thankful for the beginnings of grace, and wait upon our Saviour patiently for the increase. And as we have chosen him for our physician, let us commit ourselves to his management, and not prescribe to him what He shall prescribe for us. He knows us, and He loves us better than we do ourselves, and will do all things well.

You say, "It never came with power and life to my soul, that he died for me." If you mean, you never had any extraordinary sudden manifestation, something like a vision or a voice from heaven, confirming it to you, I can say the same. But I know he died for sinners; I know I am a sinner: I know He invites them that are ready to perish;

I am such a one; I know, upon his own invitation, I have committed myself to him; and I know by the effects, that He has been with me hitherto, otherwise I should have been an apostate long ago: and therefore I know that He died for me; for had He been pleased to kill me (as He justly might have done), He would not have shown me such things as these.

I know that I am a child, because He teaches me to say, Abba, Father. I know that I am *his*, because He has enabled me to choose him for *mine*. For such a choice and desire could never have taken place in my heart, if He had not placed it there himself. By nature I was too blind to know him, too proud to trust him, too obstinate to serve him, too base-minded to love him. The enmity I was filled with against his government, righteousness, and grace, was too strong to be subdued by any power but his own. The love I bear him is but a faint and feeble spark, but it is an emanation from himself: He kindled it, and He keeps it alive; and because it is his work, I trust many waters shall not quench it.

I have only room to assure you that I am, etc.

Mrs. Talbot.

MRS. TALBOT was the wife of the Rev. W. Talbot, vicar of St. Giles', Reading. In the midst of his devoted labours and in the prime of life this good man was suddenly cut off by a contagious fever caught in the discharge of his ministerial duties. Under date March 11, 1774, Mr. Newton says in his *Diary*. "This evening received an account of the death of my friend Mr. Talbot, who might justly be numbered amongst the first worthies. Considering his character, abilities, and situation, the church of God could hardly have sustained a heavier loss in the removal of one minister."

The first of the following letters is addressed to Mrs. Talbot on this sad occasion. Mrs. Talbot had been a most efficient fellow-helper of her husband in all his efforts to do good, and when, after his death, the living of St. Giles' was given to the Hon. W. B. Cadogan, whose views at that time were quite opposed to those of Mr. Talbot, it was to her a source of the greatest grief. We shall see in the notice of Mr. Cadogan, which appears in a future page, to what an extent Mrs. Talbot was instrumental in his conversion.

Mrs. Talbot is spoken of as a Christian of more than common excellence. She was highly accomplished, possessed of a very sweet disposition, and though of feeble health, evidently endowed with great energy and decision of character. Her acts of benevolence were manifold, and in every way she illustrated the spirit of Christianity. She died as she had lived, full of peace and joy, in 1785, having survived her husband eleven years.

To Mrs. Talbot.

LETTER I.—Consolation in affliction.

March 12, 1774.

MY DEAR MADAM,—My heart is full, yet I must restrain it. Many thoughts which crowd on my mind, and would have vent were I writing to another person, would to you be unseasonable. I write not to remind you of what you have lost, but of what you have which you cannot lose. May the Lord put a word in my heart that may be acceptable; and may his good Spirit accompany the perusal, and enable you to say with the apostle, that as sufferings abound, consolations also abound by Jesus Christ. Indeed I can sympathize with you. I remember too the delicacy of your frame, and the tenderness of your natural spirits; so that were you not interested in the exceeding great and precious promises of the gospel, I should be ready to fear you must sink under your trial. But I have some faint conceptions of the all-sufficiency and faithfulness of the Lord, and may address you in the king's words to Daniel, "Thy God whom thou servest continually, He will deliver thee." Motives for resignation to his will abound in his word; but it is an additional and crowning mercy, that He has promised to apply and enforce them in time of need. He has said, "My grace shall be sufficient for thee; and as thy day is, so shall thy strength be." This I trust you have already experienced. The Lord is so rich and so good, that He can by a glance of thought compensate his children for whatever his wisdom sees fit to deprive them of. If He gives them a lively sense of what He has delivered them from, and prepared for them, or of what He himself submitted to endure for their sakes, they find at once light springing up out of darkness, hard things becoming easy, and bitter sweet. I remember to have read of a good man in the last century (probably you may have met with the story), who, when his beloved and only son lay ill, was for some time greatly anxious about the event. One morning he stayed longer than usual in his closet; while he was there his son died. When he came out, his family were afraid to tell him, but, like David, he perceived it by their looks; and when upon inquiry they said it was so, he received the news with a composure that surprised them. But he soon explained the reason, by telling them, that for such discoveries of the Lord's goodness as he had been favoured with that morning, he could be content to lose a son every day. Yes, madam, though every stream must fail, the fountain is still full and still flowing. All the comfort you ever received in your dear friend was from the Lord, who is abundantly able to comfort you still; and he is gone but a little before you. May your faith anticipate the joyful and glorious meeting you will shortly have in a better world. Then your worship and converse together will be to unspeakable advantage, without imperfection, interruption, abatement, or end. Then all tears shall be wiped away, and every cloud removed; and then you will see, that all your concernments here below (the late afflicting dispensation not excepted), were appointed and adjusted by infinite wisdom and infinite love.

The Lord, who knows our frame, does not expect or require that we should aim at a stoical indifference under his visitations. He allows that afflictions are at present not joyous, but grievous; yea, He was pleased when upon earth to weep with his mourning friends when Lazarus died. But he has graciously provided for the prevention of that anguish and bitterness of sorrow, which is, upon such occasions, the portion of such as live without God in the world; and has engaged that all shall work together for good, and yield the peaceable fruits of righteousness. May He bless you with a sweet serenity of spirit, and a cheerful hope of the glory that shall shortly be revealed.

I intimated that I would not trouble you with my own sense and share of this loss. If you remember the great kindness I always received from Mr. Talbot and yourself, as often as opportunity afforded, and if you will believe me possessed of any sensibility or gratitude, you will conclude that my concern is not small. I feel likewise for the public. Will it be a consolation to you, madam, to know that you do not mourn alone? A character so exemplary as a friend, a counsellor, a Christian, and a minister, will be long and deeply regretted; and many will join with me in praying, that you, who are most nearly interested, may be signally supported, and feel the propriety of Mrs. Rowe's acknowledgment,

> Thou dost but take the dying lamp away,
> To bless me with thine own unclouded day.

We join in most affectionate respects and condolence. May the Lord bless you and keep you, lift up the light of his countenance upon you, and give you peace.

I am, etc.

To Mrs. Talbot.

LETTER II.—On a true estimate of ourselves—Communion of saints.

October 24, 1775.

MY DEAR MADAM,—The manner in which you mention *Omicron's Letters*,* I hope, will rather humble me than puff me up. Your favourable acceptance of them, if alone, might have the latter effect; but alas! I feel myself so very defective in those things, the importance of which I endeavoured to point out to others, that I almost appear to myself to be one of those who say, but do not. I find it much easier to speak to the hearts of others than to my own. Yet I have cause beyond many to bless God, that He has given me some idea of what a Christian ought to be, and I hope a real desire of being one myself; but verily I have obtained but a very little way. A friend hinted to me, that the character I have given of C., or Grace in the full ear, must be from my own experience, or I could not have written it. To myself, however, it appears otherwise; but I am well convinced, that the state of C. is attainable, and more to be desired than mountains of gold and silver. But I find you complain likewise; though it appears to me, and I believe to all who know you, that the Lord has been peculiarly gracious to you, in giving you much of the spirit in which He delights, and by which his name and the power of his gospel are glorified. It seems, therefore, that we are not competent judges either of ourselves or of others. I take it for granted, that they are the most excellent Christians

---

* These letters, originally communicated to the *Gospel Magazine*, were afterwards collected and published by Mr. Newton in the year 1764.

who are most abased in their own eyes; but lest you should think upon this ground that I am something because I can say so many humiliating things of myself, I must prevent your overrating me, by assuring you, that my confessions rather express what I know I ought to think of myself, than what I actually do. Naturalists suppose, that if the matter of which the earth is formed were condensed as much as it is capable of, it would occupy but a very small space; in proof of which they observe, that a cubical pane of glass, which appears smooth and impervious to us, must be exceedingly porous in itself; since in every assignable point it receives and transmits the rays of light; and yet gold, which is the most solid substance we are acquainted with, is but about eight times heavier than glass which is made up (if I may say so) of nothing but pores. In like manner, I conceive, that inherent grace, when it is dilated, and appears to the greatest advantage in a sinner, would be found to be very small and inconsiderable, if it was condensed, and absolutely separated from every mixture. The highest attainments in this life are very inconsiderable, compared with what should properly result from our relation and obligations to a God of infinite holiness. The nearer we approach to him, the more we are sensible of this. While we only hear of God as it were by the ear, we seem to be something; but when, as in the case of Job, He discovers himself more sensibly to us, Job's language becomes ours, and the height of our attainment is, to abhor ourselves in dust and ashes.

I hope I do not write too late to meet you at Bath. I pray that your health may be benefited by the waters, and your soul comforted by the Lord's blessing upon the ordinances, and the converse of his children. If any of the friends you expected to see are still there, to whom we are known, and my name should be mentioned, I beg you to say, we desire to be respectfully remembered to them. Had I wings, I would fly to Bath while you are there. As it is, I endeavour to be with you in spirit. There certainly is a real though secret, a sweet though mysterious, communion of saints by virtue of their common union with Jesus. Feeding upon the same bread, drinking of the same fountain, waiting at the same mercy-seat, and aiming at the same ends, they have fellowship one with another though at a distance. Who can tell how often the Holy Spirit, who is equally present with them all, touches the hearts of two or more of his children at the same instant, so as to excite a sympathy of pleasure, prayer, or praise on each other's account? It revives me sometimes in a dull and dark hour to reflect, that the Lord has in mercy given me a place in the hearts of many of his people; and perhaps some of them may be speaking to him on my behalf, when I have hardly power to utter a word for myself. For kind services of this sort I persuade myself I am often indebted to you. Oh that I were enabled more fervently to repay you in the same way! I can say that I attempt it: I love and honour you greatly, and your concernments are often upon my mind.

We spent most of a week with Mr. Barham since we returned from London, and he has been once here. We have reason to be very thankful for his connexion; I find but few like-minded with him, and his family is filled with the grace and peace of the gospel. I never visit them, but I meet with something to humble, quicken, and edify me. Oh! what will heaven be, where there shall be all who love the Lord Jesus, and they only; where all imperfection, and whatever now abates or interrupts their joy in the Lord and in each other, shall cease for ever? There at least I hope to meet you, and spend an eternity with you, in admiring the riches and glory of redeeming love.

We join in a tender of the most affectionate respects.

I am, etc.

To MRS. TALBOT.

LETTER III.—Our imperfect state here not a ground of distrust—Holiness of sinners and angels—Views of death.

October 28, 1777.

MY DEAR MADAM, ... Your command limits my attention, at present, to a part of your letter, and points me out a subject. Yet, at the same time, you lay me under a difficulty. I would not willingly offend you, and I hope the Lord has taught me not to aim at saying handsome things. I deal not in compliments, and religious compliments are the most unseemly of any. But why might I not express my sense of the grace of God manifested in you as well as in another? I believe our hearts are all alike destitute of every good, and prone to every evil. Like money from the same mint, they bear the same impression of total depravity; but grace makes a difference, and grace deserves the praise. Perhaps it ought not greatly to displease you, that others do, and must, and will think better of you than you do of yourself. If I do, how can I help it, when I form my judgment entirely from what you say and write? I cannot consent that you should seriously appoint me to examine and judge of your state. I thought you knew, beyond the shadow of a doubt, what your views and desires are; yea, you express them in your letter, in full agreement with what the Scripture declares of the principles, desires, and feelings of a Christian. It is true that you feel contrary principles, that you are conscious of defects and defilements; but it is equally true that you could not be right if you did not feel these things. To be conscious of them, and humbled for them, is one of the surest marks of grace; and to be more deeply sensible of them than formerly, is the best evidence of growth in grace. But when the enemy would tempt us to doubt and distrust, because we are not perfect, then he fights, not only against our peace, but against the honour and faithfulness of our dear Lord. Our righteousness is in him, and our hope depends, not upon the exercise of grace in us, but upon the fulness of grace and love in him, and upon his obedience unto death.

There is, my dear Madam, a difference between the holiness of a sinner and that of an angel. The angels have never sinned, nor have they tasted of redeeming love; they have no inward conflicts, no law of sin warring in their members; their obedience is perfect; their happiness is complete. Yet if I be found among redeemed sinners, I need not wish to be an angel. Perhaps God is not less glorified by your obedience, and, not to shock you, I will add, by mine, than by Gabriel's. It is a mighty manifestation of his grace indeed, when it can live, and act, and conquer, in such hearts as ours; when, in defiance of an evil nature and an evil world, and all the force and subtilty of Satan, a weak worm is still upheld, and enabled not only to climb, but to thresh the mountains; when a small spark is preserved through storms and floods. In these circumstances, the work of grace is to be estimated, not merely from its imperfect appearance, but from the difficulties it has to struggle with and overcome; and therefore our holiness does not consist in great attainments, but in spiritual desires, in hungerings, thirstings, and mournings; in humiliation of heart, poverty of spirit, submission, meekness; in cordial admiring thoughts of Jesus, and dependence on him alone for all we want. Indeed these may be said to be great attainments; but they who have most of them are most sensible that they, in and of themselves, are nothing, have nothing, can do nothing, and see daily cause for abhorring themselves, and repenting in dust and ashes.

Our view of death will not always be alike, but in proportion to the degree in which the Holy Spirit is pleased to communicate his sensible influence. We may anticipate the moment of dissolution with pleasure and desire in the morning, and be ready to shrink from the thought of it before night. But though our frames and perceptions vary, the report of faith concerning it is the same. The Lord usually reserves dying strength for a dying hour. When Israel was to pass Jordan, the ark was in the river; and though the rear of the host could not see it, yet as they successively came forward and approached the banks, they all beheld the ark, and all went safely over. As you are not weary of living, if it be the Lord's pleasure, so I hope, for the sake of your friends and the people whom you love, He will spare you amongst us a little longer; but when the time shall arrive which He has appointed for your dismission, I make no doubt but He will overpower all your fears, silence all your enemies, and give you a comfortable, triumphant entrance into his kingdom. You have nothing to fear from death; for Jesus, by dying, has disarmed it of its sting, has perfumed the grave, and opened the gates of glory for his believing people. Satan, so far as he is permitted, will assault our peace, but he is a vanquished enemy: our Lord holds him in a chain, and sets him bounds which he cannot pass. He provides for us likewise the whole armour of God, and has promised to cover our heads himself in the day of battle, to bring us honourably through every skirmish, and to make us more than conquerors at last. If you think my short unexpected interview with Mr. Cadogan may justify my wishing he should know that I respect his character, love his person, and rejoice in what the Lord has done and is doing for him and by him, I beg you to tell him so; but I leave it entirely to you.

We join in most affectionate respects.

I am, etc.

Mrs. Place.

S Mr. Newton became known in the religious world his acquaintance was sought by many Christians like-minded with himself, and by many inquirers after the way of salvation. In his *Diary* there is constant reference not only to letters received from various quarters, but to visitors who were invited or introduced to the vicarage at Olney. Amongst these latter was the lady to whom the following letters are addressed. Towards the close of the year 1773, Mr. Newton writes in his *Diary*, "Accompanied Mrs. Place to Bedford. She stayed much longer than she intended, but I hope the event has been happy. She goes from us not only much better in her health and spirits, but enlightened with views of the gospel which she had not before. I trust the Lord's hand was evident in her coming to Olney, as it was by a remarkable concurrence of providences. The visit has likewise been blessed to her maid."

To Mrs. Place.

LETTER I.—*Prayer in perilous times—The changes and disappointments of the present state contrasted with the glories of the future.*

August, 1775.

MY DEAR MADAM, . . . I hope the good people at Bristol, and everywhere else, are praying for our sinful, distracted land, in this dark day. The Lord is angry, the sword is drawn, and I am afraid nothing but the spirit of wrestling prayer can prevail for the returning it into the scabbard. Could things have proceeded to these extremities, except the Lord had withdrawn his salutary blessing from both sides? It is a time of prayer. We see the beginning of trouble, but who can foresee the possible consequences? The fire is kindled, but how far it may spread, those who are above may perhaps know better than we. I meddle not with the disputes of party, nor concern myself with any political maxims, but such as are laid down in Scripture. There I read, that righteousness exalteth a nation, and that sin is the reproach, and if persisted in, the ruin of any people. Some people are startled at the enormous sum of our national debt: they who understand spiritual arithmetic, may be well startled if they sit down and compute the debt of national sin. *Imprimis,* Infidelity: *item,* Contempt of the gospel: *item,* The profligacy of manners: *item,* Perjury: *item,* The cry of blood, the blood of thousands, perhaps millions from the East Indies. It would take sheets, yea quires, to draw out the particulars under each of these heads, and then much would remain untold. What can we answer, when the Lord saith, "Shall not I visit for these things? Shall not my soul be avenged on such a nation as this?" Since we received the news of the first hostilities in America, we have had an additional prayer-meeting. Could I hear that professors in general, instead of wasting their breath in censuring men and measures, were plying the throne of grace, I should still hope for a respite. . . .

The time when Mr. and Mrs. Cunningham* remove to Scotland drawing near, Mrs. Newton is gone to spend a week or two with them, and take her leave. She feels something at parting with a sister who is indeed a valuable person; and from children they have always lived in the most tender intimacy and uninterrupted friendship. But all beneath the moon (like the moon itself) is subject to incessant change. Alterations and separations are graciously appointed of the Lord, to remind us that this is not

* Mrs. Newton's sister.

our rest, and to prepare our thoughts for that approaching change which shall fix us for ever in an unchangeable state. Oh, madam! what shall we poor worms render to him who has brought life and immortality to light by the gospel, taken away the sting of death, revealed a glorious prospect beyond the grave, and given us eyes to see it? Now the reflection that we must ere long take a final farewell of what is most capable of pleasing us upon earth is not only tolerable, but pleasant. For we know we cannot fully possess our best friend, our chief treasure, till we have done with all below; nay, we cannot till then properly see each other. We are cased up in vehicles of clay, and converse together as if we were in different coaches, with the blinds close drawn round. We see the carriage, and the voice tells us that we have a friend within; but we shall know each other better, when death shall open the coach-doors, and hand out the company successively, and lead them into the glorious apartments which the Lord has appointed to be the common residence of them that love him. What an assembly will there be! What a constellation of glory, when each individual shall shine like the sun in the kingdom of their Father! No sins, sorrows, temptations; no veils, clouds, or prejudices, shall interrupt us then. All names of idle distinction (the fruits of present remaining darkness, the channels of bigotry, and the stumbling-block of the world) will be at an end.

The description you give of your present residence pleases me much, and chiefly because it describes and manifests to me something still more interesting, I mean the peaceable situation of your mind. Had He placed you in an Eden some months ago, it would hardly have awakened your descriptive talent. But He whom the winds and seas obey, has calmed your mind, and I trust will go on to fill you with all joy and peace in believing. It is no great matter where we are, provided we see that the Lord has placed us there, and that He is with us.

I am, etc.

To Mrs. Place.

Letter II.—Danger of London professors—What Jesus is to his people.

1776.

So, my dear madam, I hope we have found you out, and that this letter will reach you in good time to welcome you in our names to London. We are ready to take it for granted, that you will now most certainly make us a visit. Do come as soon, and stay as long, as you possibly can. Methinks you will be glad to get out of the smell and noise as soon as possible. If we did not go to London now and then, we should perhaps forget how people live there. Especially I pity professors; they are exposed to as many dangers as people who live in mines; chilling damps, scorching blasts, epidemical disorders, owing to the impure air. Such are the winds of false doctrines, the explosions of controversy, the blights of worldly conversation, the contagion of evil custom. In short, a person had need have a good constitution of grace, and likewise to be well supplied with antidotes, to preserve a tolerable share of spiritual health in such a situation.

And now, how shall I fill up the rest of the paper? It is a shame for a Christian and a minister to say he has no subject at hand, when the inexhaustible theme of redeeming love is ever pressing upon our attention. I will tell you then, though you know it, that the Lord reigns. He who once bore our sins, and carried our sorrows, is seated upon a throne of glory, and exercises all power in heaven and on earth. Thrones, principalities, and powers, bow before him. Every event in the kingdoms of providence and of grace is under his rule. His providence pervades and manages the whole, and is as minutely attentive to every part, as if there were only that single object in his view. From the tallest archangel to the meanest ant or fly, all depend on him for their being, their preservation, and their powers. He directs the sparrows where to build their nests, and to find their food. He overrules the rise and fall of nations, and bends, with an invincible energy and unerring wisdom, all events; so that, while many intend nothing less, in the issue, their designs all concur and coincide in the accomplishment of his holy will. He restrains with a mighty hand the still more formidable efforts of the powers of darkness; and Satan, with all his hosts, cannot exert their malice a hair's breadth beyond the limits of his permission. This is He who is the head and husband of his believing people. How happy are they whom it is his good pleasure to bless! How safe are they whom He has engaged to protect! How honoured and privileged are they to whom He is pleased to manifest himself, and whom He enables and warrants to claim him as their friend and their portion! Having redeemed them by his own blood, He sets a high value upon them; He esteems them his treasure, his jewels, and keeps them as the pupil of his eye. They shall not want; they need not fear; his eye is upon them in every situation, his ear is open to their prayers, and his everlasting arms are under them for their sure support. On earth He guides their steps, controls their enemies, and directs all his dispensations for their good; while, in heaven, He is pleading their cause, preparing them a place, and communicating down to them reviving foretastes of the glory that shall be shortly revealed. Oh how is this mystery hidden from an unbelieving world! Who can believe it, till it is made known by experience, what an intercouse is maintained in this land of shadows between the Lord of glory and sinful worms? How should we praise him that He has visited us! for we were once blind to his beauty, and insensible to his love, and should have remained so to the last, had He not prevented us with his goodness, and been found of us when we sought him not.

. . . We live as upon a field of battle; many are hourly suffering and falling around us; and I can give no reason why we are preserved, but that He is God, and not man. What a mercy that we are only truly known to him who is alone able to bear us.

May the Lord bless you and yours: may He comfort you, guide you, and guard you. Come quickly to

Yours, etc.

The Rev. Thomas Scott.

THE story of Mr. Newton's *early* intercourse with this excellent man is not without much interest as we gather it from Mr. Scott's narrative (*The Force of Truth*) and Mr. Newton's notes in his *Diary*. The following letters, five in number, selected from the eight in *Cardiphonia*, are very long, and show Mr. Newton's anxiety to be useful to this newly-formed acquaintance. They have been abbreviated, where it was possible, we hope without injury to their character and connection.

"At a visitation in May, 1775," says Mr. Scott, "I exchanged a few words with Mr. Newton on a controversial subject, in the room among the clergy, which I believe drew many eyes upon us. At that time he prudently declined the discourse, but a day or two after he sent me a short note with a little book for my perusal. This was the very thing I wanted, and I gladly embraced the opportunity which seemed now to offer. Professing friendship and a desire to know the truth, I wrote him a long letter, really wishing to provoke a discussion of our religious differences." He then goes on to say, that he thought highly of Mr. Newton's character and conduct, but looked on his religious sentiments as rank fanaticism.

Continuing his statement, Mr. Scott tells us, that Mr. Newton returned a friendly answer, in which he carefully avoided those things he knew would offend me. He stated that he believed me to be under the teaching of the Spirit, that he was in no way inclined to dictate to me, but leaving me to the guidance of the Lord, should be glad, as occasion offered, to bear testimony to the truths of the gospel, and to communicate his sentiments to me on any subjects with all the confidence of friendship. So the correspondence began. From June to December of the year 1775, Mr. Newton wrote to Mr. Scott the letters referred to above, and we find the following notes in the *Diary* relating to them.

Of Mr. Scott's first letter, Mr. Newton says, "Received an unexpected letter from Mr. Scott, my brother curate near me; very long and frank. It seemed dictated by a spirit in search of the truth." Again, "Much of my leisure has been employed in writing to Mr. Scott. Hitherto I gain but little ground. It is Thy prerogative, O Lord, to enlighten and awaken the heart. In dependence upon Thy blessing I persevere." This was in November. December 11th Mr. Newton speaks of another long letter, which he says will "probably close our correspondence, unless the Lord is pleased to work on his heart by what I have already sent, or by some other means."

Speaking of this correspondence Mr. Scott says, "I used every effort to draw Mr. Newton into controversy, disputed almost every thing he advanced, and was much nettled at many things he asserted. A great part of his letters, and some of the books he sent me, were read with much indifference and contempt. His declining controversy I regarded as an acknowledgment of weakness, and when I could not obtain my end, at my instance, the correspondence was dropped." Thus the correspondence and the acquaintance, too, were for a time broken off. "I did not care," says Mr. Scott, "for his company. I did not mean to make any use of him as an instructor, and I was unwilling the world should think us in any way connected. But under discouraging circumstances I had occasion to call on him,* and his discourse so comforted and edified me, that my heart, being by his means relieved from its burden, became susceptible of affection for him. From that time I was inwardly pleased to have him for my friend, though not as now rejoiced to *call* him so. I had, however, even at that time, no thoughts of learning doctrinal truth from him, and was ashamed to be detected in his company."

And now to resume Mr. Newton's notes. September 2, 1777, he speaks of a visit from Mr. Scott, and thanks God that he gets forward in the knowledge of the truth. Again, on the 15th, referring to the darkness of his former view, he says, "he seems now enlightened and established in the most important parts of the gospel." And once

---

* Probably in April, 1777.

more, December 10: "Breakfasted yesterday with Mr. Scott. The Lord has answered my desires and exceeded my expectations in him. How gradually yet how clearly has he been taught the truth of the gospel. . . . What an honour and a mercy should I esteem it to be any way instrumental in this good work! All praise be to God."

In the beginning of the next year (1778) we find Mr. Scott frequently at Mr. Newton's week-day services, both at the church and the Great House. On Mr. Scott preaching for him on one of these occasions, Mr. Newton writes: "My heart rejoiced and wondered. O my Lord, what a teacher art Thou! How soon clearly and solidly is he established in the knowledge and experience of Thy gospel, who but lately was a disputer against every point! I praise Thee for him. Often in my faint manner have I prayed to see some of my neighbours of the clergy awakened. Thou hast answered prayer. Oh, may it please Thee to add to their number."

The next passage has reference to *The Force of Truth*, and was written December, 1778: "Heard him read a narrative of his conversion, which he has drawn up for publication. It is striking and judicious, and will, I hope, by the Divine blessing, be very useful. I think I can see that he has got before me already. Lord, if I have been useful to him, do Thou, I beseech Thee, make him now useful to me." The last extract we will quote is dated January 1, 1779: "Last night heard my friend Scott preach at Weston from 1 Tim. iv. 8. Surely when Thou wilt work, none can let it. What liberty, power, and judgment in so young a preacher! May Thy comforts fill his heart, and Thy blessing crown his labours."

It is not our business to add to this already lengthened notice any account of Mr. Scott's after labours. By them he has acquired a name and a place in the esteem of all Christian denominations, while his *Magnum opus*, his commentary on the Scriptures, will ever be prized for its sound judgment and thoroughly evangelical views, notwithstanding the many more critical and learned expositions since given to the public.

To the Rev. Thomas Scott.

Letter I.—Athanasian Creed—Subscription—Religious knowledge gradual.

June 23, 1775.

Dear Sir,—I have met with interruptions till now, or you would have heard from me sooner. My thoughts have run much upon the subject of your last, because I perceive it has a near connexion with your peace. Your integrity greatly pleases me; far be it from me to shake the *principle* of your conduct. Yet, in the application, I think there is a possibility of carrying your exceptions too far.

From the account you give me of your sentiments, I cannot but wonder you find it so difficult to accede to the Athanasian Creed, when it seems to me you believe and avow what that creed chiefly sets forth. *The doctrine of the Trinity,* some explication of the terms being subjoined, is the Catholic faith, without the belief of which a man cannot be saved. This damnatory clause seems to me proved by Mark xvi. 16. "He that believeth shall be saved," etc. The object of faith must be *truth.* The doctrine of the deity of Christ and of the Holy Spirit in union with the Father, so that they are not three Gods, but one God, is not merely a proposition expressed in words, to which our assent is required, but is absolutely necessary to be known; since without it no one truth respecting salvation can be rightly understood, no one promise duly believed, no one duty spiritually performed. I take it for granted, that this doctrine must appear irrational and absurd in the eye of reason, if by reason we mean the reason of man in his fallen state, before it is corrected and enlightened by a heavenly Teacher. No man can say Jesus is Lord, but by the Holy Ghost. I believe with you, that a man may be saved who never heard of the creed, who never read any book but the New Testament, or perhaps a single Evangelist; but he must be taught of God the things that accompany salvation, or I do not think he can be saved. *The mercies of God in Christ* will not save any (as I apprehend), but according to the method revealed in his word, that is, those who are truly partakers of faith and holiness. For as the religion of the New Testament ascribes all power to God, and considers all goodness in us as the effect of his communication, we being by nature destitute of spiritual life or light; so those whom God himself is pleased to teach, will infallibly attain the knowledge of all that they are concerned to know. This teaching you are waiting for, and it shall be given you; yea, the Lord I trust, has begun to teach you already; but if you consider yourself as a learner, and that it is possible, under the Spirit's increasing illumination, you may hereafter adopt some things which at present you cannot approve, I should think it too early as yet to prescribe to yourself rules and determinations for the government of your future life. Should the will of God appoint you a new path for service, He may, sooner than you are aware, quiet your mind, and enable you to subscribe with as full a persuasion of mind as you now object to subscription. If it depended upon me, I could be content that the creed should rest at the bottom of the sea, rather than embarrass a single person of *your* disposition. Nor am I a warm stickler for subscription in itself: but something of this kind seems necessary, upon the supposition of an establishment.

When I think of an enclosure, some hedge, wall, bank, ditch, etc. is of course included in my idea; for who can conceive of an enclosure without a boundary? So, in a national church, there must be, I apprehend, something marked out, the approbation or refusal of which will determine who do or do not belong to it. And for this purpose articles of some kind seem not improper. You think it would be better to have these articles in scriptural expressions. But if it be lawful to endeavour to exclude from our pulpits men who hold sentiments the most repugnant to the truth, I wish you to consider, whether this can be in any measure secured by articles in which the Scripture doctrines are not explained and stated, as well as expressed. This proposal is strenuously pleaded for by many in our day, upon views very different from yours. The Socinians, for instance, would readily subscribe a Scriptural declaration of the high priesthood, atonement, and intercession of Christ, while they are allowed to put their own sense upon the terms; though the sense they maintain be utterly inconsistent with what those who are enlightened by the Holy Spirit learn from the same expressions.

I acknowledge, indeed, that the end is not answered by the present method; since there are too many like the person you mention, who would easily subscribe 900 articles rather than balk his preferment; yet the profligacy of some seems to be no just reason why the church, why any church, should not be at liberty to define the terms upon which they will accept members or teachers, or why conscientious persons should object to these terms (if they think them agreeable to the truth), merely because they are not expressed in the precise words of Scripture. If allowance may be made for human infirmity in the *Liturgy*, I see not why the *Articles* may not be entitled to the same privilege. For it seems requisite that we should be as well satisfied with the expressions we use with our lips, in frequent solemn prayer to God, as in what we subscribe with our hands. I am persuaded that the leaders of the Association at the Feathers Tavern,* some of them at least, though they begin with the affair of subscription, would not (if they might have their wish) stop there, but would go on with their projected reform, till they had overturned the Liturgy also, or at least weeded from it every expression that bears testimony to the deity of the Saviour, and the efficacious influence of the Holy Spirit. I bless God that you are far otherwise minded.

I hope, however, though you should not think yourself at liberty to repeat your subscription, the Lord will make you comfortable and useful in your present rank as a curate. Preferment is not necessary, either to our peace or usefulness. We may live and die contentedly, without the honours and emoluments which aspiring men thirst after, if He be pleased to honour us with a dispensation to preach *his* gospel, and to crown our endeavours with a blessing. He that winneth souls is wise; wise in the choice of the highest end he can propose to himself in this life; wise in the improvement of the only means by which this desirable end can be attained. . . .

It is the strain of evident sincerity which runs through your letters, that gives me a pleasing confidence the Lord is with you. A disinterested desire of knowing the truth, with a willingness to follow it through all disadvantages, is a preparation of the heart which only God can give.

---

* In the year 1771 an Association was formed by some of the clergy of the Establishment to obtain from Parliament relief in the matter of subscription. It was proposed to substitute a declaration of assent to the sufficiency of the Scriptures instead of subscription to the Thirty-nine Articles and the Book of Common Prayer. From the place of meeting it was called the "Feathers' Tavern Association."

He has directed you to the right method, searching the Scripture, with prayer. Go on, and may his blessing attend you. . . . It will rejoice my soul to be any way assistant to you; but I am afraid I should not afford you much either profit or satisfaction, by entering upon a dry defence of creeds and articles.

The truths of Scripture are not like mathematical theorems, which present exactly the same ideas to every person who understands the terms. The word of God is compared to a mirror, 2 Cor. iii. 18; but it is a mirror in which the longer we look the more we see: the view will be still growing upon us; and still we shall see but in part while on this side eternity. When our Lord pronounced Peter blessed, declaring he had learnt that which flesh and blood could not have taught him, yet Peter was at that time much in the dark. The sufferings and death of Jesus, though the only and necessary means of his salvation, were an offence to him; but he lived to glory in what he once could not bear to hear of. Peter had received grace to love the Lord Jesus, to follow him, to venture all, and to forsake all for him: these first good dispositions were of God, and they led to further advances. So it is still. . . . People may, by industry and natural abilities, make themselves masters of the external evidences of Christianity, and have much to say for and against different schemes and systems of sentiments; but all this while the heart remains untouched. True religion is not a science of the head, so much as an inward and heart-felt perception, which casts down imaginations, and every $ὕψωμα$* that exalteth itself in the mind, and brings every thought into a sweet and willing subjection to Christ by *faith*. Here the learned have no real advantage above

* High thing.—2 Cor. x. v.

the ignorant; both see when the eyes of the understanding are enlightened; till then both are equally blind. And the first lesson in the school of Christ is to become a little child, sitting simply at his feet, that we may be made wise unto salvation.

. . . I set a great value upon your offer of friendship, which I trust will not be interrupted on either side, by the freedom with which we mutually express our difference of sentiments when we are constrained to differ. You please me with entrusting me with the first rough draught of your thoughts; and you may easily perceive, by my manner of writing, that I place equal confidence in your candour. I shall be glad to exchange letters as often as it suits us, without constraint, ceremony, or apology; and may He who is always present with our hearts make our correspondence useful. I pray God to be your sun and shield, your light and strength, to guide you with his eye, to comfort you with his gracious presence in your own soul, and to make you a happy instrument of comforting many.

I am, etc.

To the REV. THOMAS SCOTT.

LETTER II.—Sincere inquirers after truth—The Trinity—The way of salvation not a matter of doubt.

July 14, 1775.

MY DEAR FRIEND,—I gladly adopt your address, and can assure you that the interchange of every letter unites my heart more closely to you. I am glad to find that your views of articles and creeds are not likely to hinder you from going forward in your present situation; and if without contracting your usefulness, they only prove a bar to your preferment, I am sure it will be no grief of mind to you at the hour of death, or the day of judgment, that you were enabled to follow the dictates of conscience in opposition to all the pleas of custom or interest. Since, therefore, I have no desire of shaking your resolves, may we not drop this subject entirely? For, indeed, I act but an awkward part in it, being by no means myself an admirer of articles and creeds, or disposed to be a warm advocate for church power. The propriety of our national establishment, or of any other, is what I have not much to do with; I found it as it is, nor have I influence to alter it were I willing. The question in which I was concerned was simply, Whether I, *rebus sic stantibus*,* could submit to it, so as conscientiously to take a designation to the ministry under it? I thought I could; I accordingly did, and I am thankful that I never have seen cause to repent it.

You seem gently to charge me with a want of candour in what I observed or apprehended concerning the gentlemen of the Feathers Tavern. . . .

I am far from thinking the Socinians all hypocrites, but I think they are all in a most dangerous error; nor do their principles exhibit to my view a whit more of the genuine fruits of Christianity than deism itself. You say, "If they be sincere, and fail not for want of diligence in searching, I cannot help thinking that God will not condemn them for an inevitable defect in their understandings." Indeed, my friend, I have such a low opinion of man in his depraved state, that I believe no one has real sincerity in religious matters till God bestows it; and when He makes a person sincere in his desires after truth, He will assuredly guide him to the possession of it in due time, as our Lord speaks, John vi. 44, 45. To suppose that any persons can sincerely seek the way of salvation, and yet miss it through an inevitable defect of their understandings, would contradict the plain promises of the gospel, such as Matt. vii. 7, 8, John vii. 16, 17; but to suppose that nothing is necessary to be known, which some persons who profess sincerity cannot receive, would be in effect to make the Scripture a nose of wax, and open a wide door for scepticism. I am not a judge of the heart; but I may be sure, that whoever makes the foundation-stone a rock of offence, cannot be sincere in his inquiries. He may study the Scripture accurately, but he brings his own preconceived sentiments with him, and instead of submitting them to the touchstone of truth, he makes them a rule by which he interprets. That they who lean to their own understandings should stumble and miscarry, I cannot wonder; for the same God who has promised to fill the hungry with good things, has threatened to send the rich empty away. So Matt. xi. 25. It is not through defect of understanding, but a want of simplicity and humility, that so many stumble like the blind at noon-day, and can see nothing of those great truths which are written in the gospel as with a sun-beam.

You wish me to explain myself concerning the doctrine of the Trinity. I will try; yet I know I cannot, any further than as He who taught me shall be pleased to bear witness in your heart to what I say. My first principle in religion is what the Scripture teaches me of the utter depravity of human nature, in connexion with the spirituality and sanction of the law of God. I believe we are by nature sinners, by practice universally transgressors; that we are dead in trespasses and sins; and that the bent of our natural spirit is enmity against the holiness, government, and grace of God. Upon this ground, I see, I feel, and acknowledge the necessity of such a salvation as the gospel proposes, which at the same time that it precludes boasting, and stains the pride of all human glory, affords encouragement to those who may be thought, or who may think themselves, the weakest or the vilest of mankind. I believe, that whatever notions a person may take up from education or system, no one ever did, or ever will, feel himself and own himself to be such a lost, miserable, hateful sinner, unless he be powerfully and supernaturally convinced by the Spirit of God. There is, when God pleases, a certain light thrown into the soul, which differs not merely in degree, but in kind, *toto genere*, from anything that can be effected or produced by moral suasion or argument. But (to take in another of your queries), the Holy Spirit teaches or reveals no new truths, either of doctrine or precept, but only enables us to understand what is already revealed in the Scripture. Here a change takes place, the person that was spiritually blind begins to see. The sinner's character, as described in the word of God, he finds to be a description of himself; that he is afar off, a stranger, a rebel; that he has hitherto lived in vain. Now he begins to see the necessity of an atonement, an advocate, a shepherd, a comforter; he can no more trust to his own wisdom, strength and goodness; but, accounting all his former gain but loss, for the excellency of the knowledge of Christ, he renounces every other refuge, and ventures his all upon the person, work, and promise of the Redeemer. In this way, I say, he will find the doctrine of the Trinity not only a proposition, but a principle; that is, from his own wants and situation he will have an abiding conviction, that the Son and Holy Spirit are God, and must be possessed of the attributes and powers of deity, to support the offices the Scriptures assign them, and to deserve the confidence and worship the Scriptures require to be placed in them, and paid to them. Without this awakened state of mind, a divine, reputed orthodox, will blunder wretchedly even in defending his own opinions. I have seen laboured defences of the Trinity, which have given me not much more satisfaction than I should probably receive from a dissertation upon the rainbow composed by a man blind from his birth. In effect, the knowledge of God cannot be attained by studious discussion on our parts; it must be by a revelation on his part, Matt. xi. 27, and ch. xvi. 17; a revelation not objectively of new truth, but subjectively of new light in us. Then he that runs may read. Perhaps you may not quite understand my meaning, or not accede to my sentiment at present; I have little doubt, however, but the time is coming when you will. I believe the Lord God has given *you* that sincerity which he never disappoints.

Far be it from me to arrogate infallibility to myself, or to any writer or preacher; yet, blessed be God, I am not left to float up and down the uncertain tide of opinion, in those points wherein the peace of my soul is nearly concerned. I know, yea I infallibly know whom I have believed. I am under no more doubt about the way of salvation than of the way to London. I cannot be deceived, because the word of God cannot deceive me. It is impossible, however, for me to give you or any other person full satisfaction concerning my evidence, because it is of an experimental nature. Rev. ii. 17. In general, it arises from the views I have received of the power, compassion, and grace of Jesus, and a consciousness that I, from a conviction of my sin and misery, have fled to him for refuge, entrusted and devoted myself and my all to him. Since my mind has been enlightened, everything within me, and everything around me, confirms and explains to me what I read in Scripture; and though I have reason enough to distrust my own judgment every hour, yet I have no reason to question the great essentials, which the Lord himself hath taught me. . . .

Sincerely and affectionately yours.

To the Rev. Thomas Scott.

LETTER III.—The new birth—Its fruits—The gospel designed for man as a sinner—Human depravity—Error respecting the apostle Paul.

August 11, 1775.

MY DEAR FRIEND, ... Your objections neither displease nor weary me. While truth is the object of your inquiry, the more freedom you use with me the better. Nor do they surprise me; for I have formerly made the like objections myself. I have stood upon your ground, and I continue to hope you will one day stand upon mine. As I have told you more than once, I do not mean to dictate to you, or to wish you to receive anything upon my *ipse dixit*; but, in the simplicity of friendship, I will give you my thoughts from time to time upon the points you propose, and leave the event to the divine blessing.

I am glad you do not account the Socinians master builders. However they esteem themselves so, and are so esteemed, not only by a few, (as you think,) but by many. I fear Socinianism spreads rapidly amongst us, and bids fair to be the prevailing scheme in this land, especially with those who profess to be the thinking part. The term *Arminian*, as at present applied, is very indiscriminate, and takes in a great variety of persons and sentiments, amongst whom, I believe there are many who hold the fundamental truths of the gospel, and live a life of faith in the Son of God. I am far from supposing that God will guide every *sincere* person exactly to adopt *all* my sentiments. But there are *some* sentiments which I believe essential to the very state and character of a true Christian. And these make him a Christian, not merely by being his acknowledged sentiments, but by a certain peculiar manner in which he possesses them. There is a certain important change takes place in the heart, by the operation of the Spirit of God, before the soundest and most orthodox sentiments can have their proper influence upon us. . . . It is sometimes called a new birth, sometimes a new creature or new creation, sometimes the causing light to shine out of darkness, sometimes the opening the eyes of the blind, sometimes the raising the dead to life. Till a person has experienced this change, he will be at a loss to form a right conception of it; but it means not being proselyted to an opinion, but receiving a principle of divine life and light in the soul. And till this is received, the things of God, the truths of the gospel, cannot be rightly discerned or understood, by the utmost powers of fallen man, who with all his wisdom, reason and talents, is still but what the apostle calls the natural man, till the power of God visits his heart. 1 Cor. ii. 14. This work is sometimes wrought suddenly, as in the case of Lydia, Acts xvi. 14, at other times very gradually. A person who before was a stranger even to the form of godliness, or at best content with a mere form, finds new thoughts arising in his mind, feels some concern about his sins, some desire to please God, some suspicions that all is not right. He examines his views of religion, hopes the best of them, and yet cannot rest satisfied in them. To-day, perhaps, he thinks himself fixed; to-morrow he will be all uncertainty. He inquires of others, weighs, measures, considers, meets with sentiments which he had not attended to, thinks them plausible, but is presently shocked with objections, or supposed consequences, which he finds himself unable to remove. As he goes on in his inquiry, his difficulties increase. New doubts arise in his mind; even the Scriptures perplex him, and appear to assert contrary things. He would sound the depths of truth by the plummet of his reason; but he finds his line is too short. Yet even now the man is under a guidance which will at length lead him right. The importance of the subject takes up his thoughts, and takes off the relish he once had for the things of the world. He reads, he prays, he strives, he resolves; sometimes inward embarrassments and outward temptations bring him to his wits' end. He almost wishes to stand where he is, and inquire no more. But he cannot stop. At length he begins to *feel* the inward depravity which he had before owned as an opinion: a sense of sin and guilt cut him out new work. Here reasoning will stand him in no stead. This is a painful change of mind; but it prepares the way for a blessing. It silences some objections better than a thousand arguments, it cuts the comb of his own wisdom and attainments, it makes him weary of working for life, and teaches him, in God's due time, the meaning of that text, "To him that worketh not, but believeth on him that justifieth the ungodly, his faith is counted for righteousness." Then he learns, that scriptural faith is a very different thing from a *rational assent* to the gospel; that it is the immediate gift of God, Ephes. ii. 8; the operation of God, Col. ii. 12; that Christ is not only the object, but the author and finisher of faith, Heb. xii. 2; and that faith is not so properly a part of that obedience we *owe to God*, as an inestimable benefit we *receive from him*, for Christ's sake, Phil. i. 29; which is the medium of our justification, Rom. v. 1; and the principle by which we are united to Christ, (as the branch to the vine,) John xvii. 21. I am well aware of the pains taken to put a different sense upon these and other seemingly mysterious passages of Scripture; but thus far we speak that which we know, and testify that which we have seen. I have described a path in which I have known many led, and in which I have walked myself.

The gospel, my dear sir, is a salvation appointed for those who are ready to perish, and is not designed to put them in a way to save themselves by their own works. It speaks to us as condemned already, and calls upon us to believe in a crucified Saviour, that we may receive redemption through his blood, even the forgiveness of our sins. And the Spirit of God, by the gospel, first convinces us of unbelief, sin, and misery; and then by revealing the things of Jesus to our minds, enables us, as helpless sinners, to come to Christ, to receive him, to behold him, or in other words, to believe in him; and expect pardon, life, and grace from him; renouncing every hope and aim in which we once rested, "and accounting all things loss and dung for the excellency of the knowledge of Christ." John vi. 35; Isaiah xlv. 22, with John vi. 40; Col. ii. 6. . . .

Though we have not exactly the same view of human depravity, yet as we both agree to take our measure of it from the word of God, I trust we shall not always differ about it. Adam was created in the image of God, in righteousness and true holiness. Ephes. iv. 24. This moral image, I believe, was totally lost by sin. In that sense, he died the day, the moment he ate the forbidden fruit. God was no longer his joy and delight; he was averse from the thoughts of his presence, and would (if possible) have hid himself from him. His natural powers, though doubtless impaired, were not destroyed. Man by nature is still capable of great things. His understanding, reason, memory, imagination, etc., sufficiently proclaim that the hand that made him is divine. He is, as Milton says of Beelzebub, majestic though in ruins. He can reason, invent, and by application attain a considerable knowledge in natural things. The exertions of human genius, as specified in the characters of some philosophers, poets, orators, etc., are wonderful. But man cannot know, love, trust, or serve his Maker, unless he be renewed in the spirit of his mind. God has preserved in him likewise some feelings of benevolence, pity; some sense of natural justice and truth, etc., without which there could be no society; but these, I apprehend, are little more than instincts, by which the world is kept in some small degree of order; but, being under the direction of pride and self, do not deserve the name of virtue and goodness; because the exercise of them does not spring from a principle of love to God, nor is directed to his glory, nor regulated by the rule of his word, till a principle of grace is superadded. You think, I will not say, "that God, judicially, in punishment of one man's sin, added these corruptions to all his posterity." Let us suppose, that the punishment annexed to eating the forbidden fruit had been the loss of Adam's rational powers, and that he should be degraded to the state and capacity of a brute. In this condition, had he begotten children after the fall in his own likeness, his nature being previously changed, they must have been of course brutes like himself; for he could not convey to them those original powers which he had lost. Will this illustrate my meaning? Sin did not deprive him of rationality, but of spirituality. His nature became earthly, sensual, yea devilish; and this fallen nature, this carnal mind, which is enmity against God, which is not subject to this law, neither indeed can be, Rom. viii. 7, we universally derive from him. Look upon children; they presently show themselves averse from good, but exceedingly propense to evil. This they can learn even without a master; but ten thousand instructors and instructions cannot instil good into them, so as to teach them to love their Creator, unless a divine power co-operates. Just as it is with the earth, which produces weeds spontaneously; but if you only see a cabbage or an apple-tree, you are sure it was planted or sown there, and did not spring from the soil. I know many hard questions may be started upon this subject; but the Lord in due time will clear his own cause, and vindicate his own ways. I leave all difficulties with him. It is sufficient for me that Scripture asserts, and experience proves, that it is thus in fact. Rom. iii. 9—21; Job xiv. 4. Thus we have not only forfeited our happiness by transgression, but are by our depravity incapable of it, and have no more desire or taste for such a state as the Scripture describes heaven to be, than a man born deaf can have for a concert of music. And therefore our Lord declares, that except a man be born again he not only shall not, but cannot see the kingdom of God. Hence a twofold necessity of a Saviour—his blood for the pardon of our sins; his life, spirit, and grace to quicken our souls, and form us anew for himself, that we may feel his love, and show forth his praise.

St. Paul, before his conversion, was not sincere, in the sense I hope you to be: he thought himself in the right, without doubt, as many have done when they killed God's servants. John xvi. 2. He was blindly and obstinately zealous: I think he did not enter into the merits of the cause, or inquire into facts with that attention which sincerity would have put him upon. You think that his sincerity and zeal were the very things that made him a chosen instrument; he himself speaks of them as the very things that made him peculiarly unworthy of that honour, 1 Cor. xv. 9: and he tells us, that he was set forth as a pattern of the Lord's long-suffering and mercy, that the very chief of sinners might be encouraged, 1 Tim. i. 15, 16. Had he been sincerely desirous to know whether Jesus was the Messiah, there was enough in his character, doctrines, miracles, and the prophecies concerning him, to have cleared up the point; but he took it for granted he was right in his opinion, and hurried blindly on, and was (as he said himself) exceedingly mad against them. Such a kind of sincerity is common enough. People believe themselves right, and therefore treat others with scorn or rage; appeal to the Scriptures, but first lay down their own pre-conceived sentiments for truths, and then examine what Scriptures they can find to countenance them. Surely a person's thinking himself right, will not give a sanction to all that he does under that persuasion.

Ignorance and obstinacy are in themselves sinful, and no plea of sincerity will exempt from the danger of being under their influence. Isaiah xxvii. 11; Luke vi. 39. It appears to me, that though you will not follow any man implicitly, you are desirous of discovering your mistakes, supposing you are mistaken in any point of importance. You read and examine the word of God, not to find arms wherewith to defend your sentiments at all events, but to know whether they are defensible or not. You pray for God's light and teaching, and in this search you are willing to risk what men are commonly much afraid of hazarding, character, interest, preferment, favour, etc. A sincerity of this kind I too seldom meet with; when I do, I account it a token for good, and am ready to say, "No man can do this, except God be with him." However, sincerity is not conversion; but I believe it is always a forerunner of it.

. . . .

I am, etc.

To the REV. THOMAS SCOTT.

LETTER IV.—Predestination—Divine sovereignty—Man made willing by the power of God.

November 17, 1775.

MY DEAR FRIEND, . . . My present part is but *actum agere*, to repeat what I have elsewhere expressed, only with some variety and enlargement. You yourself well state the situation of our debate, when you say, "*Nor in truth do you offer any arguments to convince me, nor does it seem very consistent on your grounds so to do.* And if this important change is to be brought about by the intervention of some extraordinary impulse of the Holy Spirit, and cannot be brought about without it, I do not see any thing further that I have to do, than to keep my mind as much unbiassed as I can, and to wait and pray for it." I think my letter from London was to the purport of these your own words, though you seemed dissatisfied with it.

. . . However, to take some notice of your queries as they offer themselves:

The first which occurs is complicated. The substance I think is, whether such belief and aims as you possess, will stand you in no stead unless you likewise believe grace irresistible, predestination absolute, faith in supernatural impulses, etc.? You may have observed, I have several times waved speaking about predestination or election, not that I am ashamed of the doctrine; because if it be indeed absurd, shocking, and unjust, the blame will not deservedly fall upon me, for I did not invent it, but upon the Scriptures, where I am sure it is laid down in as plain terms, as that God created the heavens and the earth. I own I cannot but wonder, that persons professing any reverence for the Bible should so openly and strongly declare their abhorrence of what the Bible so expressly teaches; namely, that there is a discrimination of persons by the grace and good pleasure of God, where by nature there is no difference; and that all things respecting the salvation of these persons is infallibly secured by a divine predestination.

I do not offer this as a rational doctrine, (though it be highly so to me,) but it is scriptural, or else the Scripture is a mere nose of wax, and without a determinate meaning. What ingenuity is needful to interpret many passages in a sense more favourable to our natural prejudice against God's sovereignty! Matt. xi. 25, 26, and xiii. 10—17; Mark xiii. 20—22; John xvii. *passim*; John x. 26; Rom. viii. 28—30, and ix. 13—24, and xi. 7; Eph. i. 4, 5; 1 Pet. i. 2. Were I fond of disputing, as I am not, I think I could put a close reasoner hard to it, to maintain the truth of Scripture prophecies, or the belief of a particular providence, unless he would admit a divine predestination of causes and events as the ground of his arguments. However, as I said, I have chosen to waive the point; because, however true and necessary in itself, the knowledge and comprehension of it is not necessary to the being a true Christian, though I can hardly conceive he can be an established consistent believer without it. . . .

Your two sheets may lead me to write as many quires, if I do not check myself. I now come to the two queries you propose, the solution of which you think will clearly mark the difference of our sentiments. The substance of them is, 1st, Whether I think any sinner ever perished in his sins (to whom the gospel has been preached) because God refused to supply him with such a proportion of his assistance as was absolutely necessary to his believing and repenting, or without his having previously rejected the incitements of his Holy Spirit? A full answer to this would require a sheet. But briefly, I believe, that all mankind being corrupt and guilty before God, He might, without impeachment to his justice, have left them all to perish, as we are assured He did the fallen angels. But He has pleased to show mercy, and mercy must be free. If the sinner has any claim to it, so far it is justice, not mercy. He who is to be our judge assures us, that *few* find the gate that leadeth to life, while many throng the road to destruction. Your question seems to imply, that you think God either did make salvation equally *open to all*, or that it would have been more becoming his goodness to have done so.

But He is the potter, we are the clay; his ways and thoughts are above ours, as the heavens are higher than the earth. The Judge of all the earth *will* do right. He has appointed a day, when He will manifest, to the conviction of *all*, that *He has done right*. Till then, I hold it best to take things upon his word, and not too harshly determine what it becomes Jehovah to do. Instead of saying what *I* think, let it suffice to remind you of what St. Paul thought. Rom. ix. 15—21. But further, I say, that unless mercy were afforded to those who are saved, in a way peculiar to themselves, and what is not afforded to those who perish, I believe no one soul could be saved. For I believe fallen man, universally considered as such, is as incapable of doing the least thing towards his salvation, till prevented by the grace of God, (as our Article speaks,) as a dead body is of restoring itself to life. Whatever difference takes place between men in this respect is *of grace*, that is of God, undeserved. Yea, his first approaches to our hearts are undesired too; for, till He seeks us, we cannot, we will not seek him. Psalm cx. 3. It is in the day of his power, and not before, his people are made willing. But I believe where the gospel is preached, they who do perish, do wilfully resist the light, and choose and cleave to darkness, and stifle the convictions which the truths of God, *when his true gospel is indeed preached*, will, in one degree or other, force upon their minds. The cares of this world, the deceitfulness of riches, the love of other things, the violence of sinful appetites, their prejudices, pride, and self-righteousness, either prevent the reception, or choke the growth of the good seed: thus their own sin and obstinacy is the proper cause of their destruction; they *will* not come to Christ that they may have life. At the same time, it is true that they cannot, unless they are supernaturally drawn of God. John v. 40; vi. 44. They will not, and they cannot come. Both are equally true, and they are consistent. For a man's *cannot* is not a natural but a moral inability: not an impossibility in the nature of things, as it is for me to walk upon the water, or to fly in the air; but such an inability, as, instead of extenuating, does exceedingly enhance and aggravate his guilt. He is so blinded by Satan, so alienated from God by nature and wicked works, so given up to sin, so averse from that way of salvation, which is contrary to his pride and natural wisdom, that he will not embrace it or seek after it; and therefore he cannot, till the grace of God powerfully enlightens his mind, and overcomes his obstacles.—But this brings me to your second query.

II. Do I think that God, in the ordinary course of his providence, grants this assistance in an irresistible manner, or effects faith and conversion without the sinner's own hearty consent and concurrence? I rather chose to term grace *invincible* than *irresistible*. For it is too often resisted even by those who believe; but, because it is invincible, it triumphs over all resistance when He is pleased to bestow it. For the rest, I believe no sinner is converted without his own hearty will and concurrence. But he is not willing till he is made so. Why does he at all refuse? Because he is insensible of his state; because he knows not the evil of sin, the strictness of the law, the majesty of God whom he has offended, nor the total apostasy of his heart; because he is blind to eternity, and ignorant of the excellency of Christ; because he is comparatively whole, and sees not his need of this great Physician; because he relies upon his own wisdom, power, and supposed righteousness. Now in this state of things, when God comes with a purpose of mercy, he begins by convincing the person of sin, judgment, and righteousness, causes him to feel and know that he is a lost, condemned, helpless creature, and then discovers to him the necessity, sufficiency, and willingness of Christ to save them that are ready to perish, without money or price, without doings or deservings.— Then he sees faith to be very different from a rational assent, finds that nothing but the power of God can produce a well-grounded hope in the heart of a convinced sinner; therefore looks to Jesus, who is the author and finisher of faith, to enable him to believe. For this he waits on what we call the means of grace; he prays, he reads the word, he thirsts for God, as the hart pants for the water brooks; and, though perhaps for a while he is distressed with many doubts and fears, he is encouraged to wait on, because Jesus has said, "Him that cometh unto me, I will in no wise cast out." The obstinacy of the will remains while the understanding is dark, and ceases when that is enlightened. Suppose a man walking in the dark, where there are pits and precipices of which he is not aware: *You* are sensible of his danger, and call after him; but he thinks he knows better than you, refuses your advice, and is perhaps angry with you for your importunity. He sees no danger, therefore will not be persuaded there is any; but if you go with a light, get before him, and show him plainly, that if he takes another step he falls beyond the power of recovery, then he will stop of his own accord, blame himself for not minding you before, and be ready to comply with your further directions. In either case man's will acts with equal freedom; the difference of his conduct arises from conviction. Something like this is the case of our spiritual concerns. Sinners are called and warned by the word; but they are wise in their own eyes, and take but little notice till the Lord gives them light, which He is not bound to give to *any*, and therefore cannot be bound to give to *all*. They who have it have reason to be thankful, and subscribe to the apostle's words, "By grace are ye saved, through faith; and that not of yourselves, it is the gift of God."

I have not yet half done with the first sheet; shall consider the rest at leisure, but send this as a specimen of my willingness to clear my sentiments to you as far as I can. Unless it should please God to make what I offer satisfactory, I well know beforehand what objections and answers will occur to you; for these points have been often debated; and, after a course of twenty-seven years, in which religion has been the chief object of my thoughts and inquiries, I am not entirely a stranger to what can be offered on either side. What I write, I write simply and in love; beseeching him, who alone can set a seal to his own truth, to guide you and bless you. This letter has been more than a week in hand: I have been called from it I suppose ten times, frequently in the middle of a period or a line. My leisure, which before was small, is now reduced almost to a nothing. But I am desirous to keep up my correspondence with you, because I feel an affectionate interest in you, and because it pleased God to put it into your heart to apply to me. You cannot think how your first letter struck me: it was so unexpected, and seemed so improbable that you should open your mind to me. I immediately conceived a hope that it would prove for good. Nor am I yet discouraged.

When you have leisure and inclination, write; I shall be always glad to hear from you, and I will proceed in answering what I have already by me, as fast as I can. But I have many letters now waiting for answers, which must be attended to.

I recommend you to the blessing and care of the Great Shepherd; and remain,

Your sincere friend and servant.

To the REV. THOMAS SCOTT.

LETTER V.—Reason and Scripture—Faith and works—God not the Author of sin—Fruits of faith.

December 8, 1775.

MY DEAR FRIEND,—Are you willing I should still call you so, or are you quite weary of me? Your silence makes me suspect the latter. However, it is my part to fulfil my promise, and then leave the event to God. As I have but an imperfect remembrance of what I have already written, I may be liable to some repetitions. I cannot stay to comment upon every line in your letter, but I proceed to notice such passages as seem most to affect the subject in debate. When you speak of the Scripture's maintaining one consistent sense, which, if the word of God, it certainly must do, you say you read and understand it in this one consistent sense; nay, you cannot remember the time when you did not. It is otherwise with me, and with multitudes; we remember when it was a sealed book, and we are sure it would have been so still, had not the Holy Spirit opened our understandings. But when you add, "Though I pretend not to understand the whole, yet what I do understand appears perfectly consistent," I know not how far this exception may extend, for perhaps, the reason why you allow you do not understand some parts, is because you cannot make them consistent with the sense you put upon other parts. You quote my words, "That when we are conscious of our depravity, reasoning stands us in no stead." Undoubtedly, reason always will stand rational creatures in some stead; but my meaning is, that when we are deeply convinced of sin, all our former reasonings upon the ways of God, while we made *our* conceptions the standard by which we judge what is befitting him to do, as if He were altogether such a one as ourselves, all those cobweb reasonings are swept away, and we submit to his αυτος εφη* without *reasoning*, though not without *reason*. For we have the strongest reason imaginable to acknowledge ourselves vile and lost, without righteousness and strength, when we actually feel ourselves to be so.

You speak of the gospel terms of justification. This term is *faith*. Mark xvi. 16; Acts xiii. 39. The gospel propounds, admits no other term. But this *faith*, as I endeavoured to show in my former letter, is very different from rational assent. You speak likewise of the law of

* He himself hath said.

faith; by which, if you mean what some call the remedial law, which we are to obey as well as we can, and that such obedience, together with our faith, will entitle us to acceptance with God, I am persuaded the Scripture speaks of no such thing. Grace and works of any kind, in the point of acceptance with God, are mentioned by the apostles, not only as opposites or contraries, but as absolutely contradictory to each other, like fire and water, light and darkness; so that the affirmation of one is the denial of the other. Rom. iv. 5, and xi. 6. God justifies freely, justifies the ungodly, and him that worketh not. Though justifying faith be indeed an active principle, it worketh by *love*, yet not for acceptance. Those whom the apostle exhorts "to work out their own salvation with *fear* and *trembling*," he considers as justified already; for he considers them as believers, in whom he supposed God had already begun a good work; and if so, was confident He would accomplish it. Phil. i. 6. To them, the consideration, that God (who dwells in the hearts of believers) wrought in them to will and to do, was a powerful motive and encouragement to them to work, that is, to give all diligence in his appointed means, as a right sense of the sin that dwelleth in us, and the snares and temptations around us, will teach us still to work with fear and trembling. . . .

When you desire me to reconcile God's being the author of sin with his justice, you show that you misunderstand the whole strain of my sentiments: for I am persuaded you would not misrepresent them. It is easy to charge harsh consequences, which I neither allow, nor, indeed, do they follow from my sentiments. God cannot be the author of sin in that sense you would fix upon me; but is it possible that, upon your plan, you find no difficulty in what the Scripture teaches us upon this subject? I conceive that those who were concerned in the death of Christ were very great sinners; and that, in nailing him to the cross, they committed atrocious wickedness. Yet, if the apostle may be believed, 'all this was according to the determinate counsel and foreknowledge of God, Acts ii. 23: and they did no more than what his hand and purpose had determined should be done, chap. iv. 28. And you will observe, that this wicked act (wicked with respect to the perpetrators) was not only permitted, but fore-ordained in the strongest and most absolute sense of the word: the glory of God and the salvation of men depended upon its being done, and just in that manner, and with all those circumstances which actually took place; and yet Judas and the rest acted freely, and their wickedness was properly their own. Now, my friend, the arguments which satisfy you, that the Scripture does not represent God as the author of this sin, in this appointment will plead for me at the same time; and when you think you easily overcome me by asking, "Can God be the author of sin?" your imputation falls as directly upon the word of God himself. God is no more the author of sin than the sun is the cause of ice; but it is in the nature of water to congeal into ice when the sun's influence is suspended to a certain degree. So there is sin enough in the hearts of men to make the earth the very image of hell, and to prove that men are no better than incarnate devils, were He to suspend his influence and restraint. Sometimes, and in some instances, He is pleased to suspend it considerably; and so far as He does, human nature quickly appears in its true colours. Objections of this kind have been repeated and refuted before either you or I were born; and the apostle evidently supposes they would be urged against his doctrine, when he obviates the question, Why doth he yet find fault? who hath resisted his will? To which he gives no other answer than by referring it to God's sovereignty, and the power which a potter has over the clay. . . .

You ask If man can do nothing without an extraordinary impulse from on high, is he to sit still and careless? By no means. I am far from saying man can do nothing, though I believe he cannot open his own eyes, or give himself faith. I wish every man to abstain carefully from sinful company, and sinful actions, to read the Bible, to pray to God for his heavenly teaching. And if he persevere thus in seeking, the promise is sure, that he shall not seek in vain. But I would not have him mistake the means for the end; think himself good because he is preserved from gross vices and follies, or trust to his religious course of duties for acceptance, nor be satisfied till Christ be revealed in him, formed within him, and dwell in his heart by faith. . . . True faith, my dear Sir, unites the soul to Christ, and thereby gives access to God, and fills it with a peace passing understanding, a hope, a joy unspeakable and full of glory; teaches us that we are weak in ourselves, but enables us to be strong in the Lord, and in the power of his might. To those who thus believe, Christ is precious, their beloved; they hear and know his voice; the very sound of his name gladdens their hearts, and *He manifests himself to them as He does not to the world.* Thus the Scriptures speak, thus the first Christians experienced; and this is precisely the language which, in our days, is despised as enthusiasm and folly. For it is now as it was then, though *these things* are *revealed* to *babes*, and they are as sure of them as that they see the noon-day sun, they are hidden from the wise and prudent, till the Lord makes them willing to renounce their own wisdom, and to become fools, that they may be truly wise. 1 Cor. i. 18, 19; iii. 8; viii. 2. . . .

Still I find I have not done: you ask my exposition of the parables of the talents and pounds; but at present I can write no more. I have only just time to tell you, that when I begged your acceptance of *Omicron*, nothing was further from my expectation than a correspondence with you. The frank and kind manner in which you wrote presently won upon my heart. In the course of our letters upon Subscription, I observed an integrity and disinterestedness in you which endeared you to me still more. Since that our debates have taken a much more interesting turn; I have considered it as a call, and an opportunity put in my hand, by the especial providence of him who ruleth over all. I have embraced the occasion to lay before you simply, and rather in a way of testimony than argumentation, what (in the main) I am sure is truth. I have done enough to discharge my conscience, but shall never think I do enough to answer the affection I bear you. . . .

I pray that the good Spirit of God may guide you into all truths. He only is the effectual teacher. I still retain a cheerful hope that some things you cannot at present receive, will hereafter be the joy and comfort of your heart; but I know it cannot be till the Lord's own time. . . .

I am still in a manner lost amidst more engagements than I have time to comply with; but I feel and know that

    I am, dear Sir,

      Your affectionate friend and servant.

Mrs. Thornton.

MRS. THORNTON was the wife of the well-known John Thornton, that most benevolent and useful man to whom Mr. Newton was so deeply indebted, and of whom the poet Cowper has so justly written in memoriam—

> "Thou had'st an industry in doing good,
> Keen as the peasant's toiling for his food."

Mrs. Thornton was to a great extent imbued with her husband's spirit. We have already spoken, in the account of Mr. Howell, of the restoration of the chapel at Knaresborough, and of the introduction of a minister there, through her means. And this was not a singular instance of such efforts. Hull was the birthplace of Mrs. Thornton, and here and elsewhere she was known for her benevolence, while the poor generally were the objects of her kind and thoughtful care. These good works were the fruits of a true piety. Mrs. Thornton was a woman of a devout spirit, a diligent student of the Scriptures, and much given to the important duty of self-examination. We have an illustration of her conviction of the importance of such exercises in an allusion in one of Mr. Newton's letters (the third in *Cardiphonia*) to a work containing sacramental meditations which Mrs. Thornton had written: it does not appear that it was ever published. Another very observable trait in Mrs. Thornton's character was her great regard for the ministry of the word. It was a common observation with her, that she never heard a sermon from which she could not derive some benefit. Mrs. Thornton died some years before her excellent husband, whose decease took place at Bath, Nov. 1790.

To Mrs. Thornton.

LETTER I.—On maintaining a right spirit toward those who differ from us—Fault of some evangelical preachers—Divinity of Christ.

November, 1775.

MY DEAR MADAM,—Too much of that impatience which you speak of, towards those who differ from us in some religious sentiments, is observable on all sides. I do not consider it as the fault of a few individuals, or of this or that party, so much as the effect of that inherent imperfection which is common to our whole race. Anger and scorn are equally unbecoming in those who profess to be followers of the meek and lowly Jesus, and who acknowledge themselves to be both sinful and fallible; but too often something of this leaven will be found cleaving to the best characters, and mixed with honest endeavours to serve the best cause. But thus it was from the beginning; and we have reason to confess that we are no better than the apostles were, who, though they meant well, manifested once and again a wrong spirit in their zeal. Luke ix. 54. Observation and experience contribute, by the grace of God, gradually to soften and sweeten our spirits; but then there will always be ground for mutual forbearance and mutual forgiveness on this head. However, so far as I may judge of myself, I think this hastiness is not my most easily besetting sin. I am not indeed an advocate for that indifference and lukewarmness to the truths of God, which seem to constitute the candour many plead for in the present day. But while I desire to hold fast the sound doctrines of the gospel towards the persons of my fellow-creatures, I wish to exercise all moderation and benevolence: Protestants or Papists, Socinians or Deists, Jews,

Samaritans, or Mohammedans, all are my neighbours, they have all a claim upon me for the common offices of humanity. As to religion, they cannot all be right; nor may I compliment them by allowing that the differences between us are but trivial, when I believe and know they are important; but I am not to expect them to see with my eyes. I am deeply convinced of the truth of John Baptist's aphorism, John iii. 27, "A man can receive nothing except it be given him from heaven." I well know, that the little measure of knowledge I have obtained in the things of God has not been owing to my own wisdom and docility, but to his goodness. Nor did I get it all at once: He has been pleased to exercise much patience and long-suffering towards me, for about twenty-seven years past, since He first gave me a desire of learning from himself. He has graciously accommodated himself to my weakness, borne with my mistakes, and helped me through innumerable prejudices, which, but for his mercy, would have been insuperable hinderances: I have therefore no right to be angry, impatient, or censorious, especially as I have still much to learn, and am so poorly influenced by what I seem to know. I am weary of controversies and disputes, and desire to choose for myself, and to point out to others Mary's part, to sit at Jesus's feet, and to hear his words. And, blessed be his name, so far as I have learned from him, I am favoured with a comfortable certainty. I know whom I have believed, and am no longer tossed about by the various winds and tides of opinions, by which I see many are dashed one against the other. But I cannot, I must not, I dare not contend; only, as a witness for God, I am ready to bear my simple testimony to what I have known of his truth whenever I am properly called to it.

I agree with you, that some accounted evangelical teachers have too much confined themselves to a few leading and favourite topics. I think this a fault; and believe, when it is constantly so, the auditories are deprived of much edification and pleasure, which they might receive from a more judicious and comprehensive plan. The whole Scripture, as it consists of histories, prophecies, doctrines, precepts, promises, exhortations, admonitions, encouragements, and reproofs, is the proper subject of the gospel ministry; and every part should in its place and course be attended to; yet so that, in every compartment we exhibit, Jesus should be the capital figure, in whom the prophecies are fulfilled, the promises established: to whom, in a way of type and emblem, the most important parts of Scripture history have an express reference; and from whom alone we can receive that life, strength, and encouragement, which are necessary to make obedience either pleasing or practicable. And where there is *true spiritual faith* in the heart, and in exercise, I believe a person will not so much need a detail of what he is to practise, as to be often greatly at a loss without it. Our Saviour's commandments are plain and clear in themselves; and that love which springs from faith is the best casuist and commentator to apply and enforce them. . . .

There may perhaps be an improper manner of chiming upon the name of Jesus, and I am not for vindicating any impropriety; yet could I feel what I ought to mean when I pronounce that name, I should not fear mentioning it too often. I am afraid of no excess in thinking highly of it, because I read it is the will of God, that all men should honour the Son as they honour the Father. Laboured explications of the Trinity I always avoid. I am afraid of darkening counsel by words without knowledge. Scripture, and even reason, assures me there is but one God, whose name *alone* is Jehovah. Scripture likewise assures me, that Christ is God, that Jesus is Jehovah. I cannot say that reason assents with equal readiness to this proposition as to the former. But admitting what the Scripture teaches concerning the evil of sin, the depravity of human nature, the method of salvation, and the offices of the Saviour; admitting that God has purposed to glorify, not his mercy only, but his justice, in the work of redemption; that the blood shed upon the cross, is a proper, adequate satisfaction for sin; and that the Redeemer is at present the Shepherd of those who believe in him, and will hereafter be the Judge of the world; that, in order to give the effectual help which we need, it is necessary that He be always *intimately with those* who depend upon him, in every age, in every place; must know the thoughts and intents of every heart; must have his eye always upon them, his ear always open to them; his arm ever stretched out for their relief; that they can receive nothing but what He bestows, can do nothing but as He enables them, nor stand a moment but as He upholds them; admitting these and the like promises, with which the word of God abounds, reason must allow, whatever difficulties may attend the thought, that only He who is God over all, blessed for ever, is able or worthy to execute this complicated plan, every part of which requires the exertion of infinite wisdom and almighty power; nor am I able to form any clear, satisfactory, comfortable thoughts of God, suited to awaken my love or engage my trust, but as He has been pleased to reveal himself in the person of Jesus Christ. I believe, with the apostle, that God was once manifested in the flesh upon earth; and that He is now manifested in the flesh in heaven; and that the worship, not only of redeemed sinners, but of the holy angels, is addressed to the Lamb that was slain, and who, in that nature in which He suffered, now exercises universal dominion, and has the government of heaven, earth, and hell upon his shoulders. This truth is the foundation upon which my hope is built, the fountain whence I derive all my strength and consolation, and my only encouragement for venturing to the throne of grace, for grace to help in time of need. . .

I am, etc.

To Mrs. Thornton.

LETTER II.—Sympathy of Jesus.

November 29, 1776.

MY DEAR MADAM, . . . Though I feel grief, I trust the Lord has mercifully preserved me from impatience and murmuring, and that in the midst of all the pleadings of flesh and blood, there is a something within me that aims to say without reserve or exception, "Not my will, but thine be done."

It is a comfortable consideration, that He with whom we have to do, our great High Priest, who once put away our sins by the sacrifice of himself, and now for ever appears in the presence of God for us, is not only possessed of sovereign authority and infinite power, but wears our very nature, and feels and exercises in the highest degree those tendernesses and commiserations, which I conceive are essential to humanity in its perfect state. The whole history of his wonderful life is full of inimitable instances of this kind. His bowels were moved before his arm was exerted; He condescended to mingle tears with mourners, and wept over distresses which He intended to relieve. He is still the same in his exalted state; compassions dwell within his heart. In a way inconceivable to us, but consistent with his supreme dignity and perfection of happiness and glory, He still feels for his people. When Saul persecuted the members upon earth, the head complained from heaven; and sooner shall the most tender mother sit insensible and inattentive to the cries and wants of her infant, than the Lord Jesus be an unconcerned spectator of his suffering children. No, with the eye, and the ear, and the heart of a friend, He attends to their sorrows; He counts their sighs, puts their tears in his bottle; and when our spirits are overwhelmed within us, He knows our path, and adjusts the time, the measure of our trials, and every thing that is necessary for our present support and seasonable deliverance, with the same unerring wisdom and accuracy as He weighed the mountains in scales, and hills in a balance, and meted out the heavens with a span. Still more, besides his benevolent, He has an experimental sympathy. He knows our sorrows, not merely as He knows all things, but as one who has been in our situation, and who, though without sin himself, endured, when upon earth, inexpressibly more for us than He will ever lay upon us. He has sanctified poverty, pain, disgrace, temptation, and death, by passing through these states; and in whatever states his people are, they may by faith have fellowship with him in their sufferings, and He will, by sympathy and love, have fellowship and interest with them in theirs. What, then, shall we fear, or of what shall we complain? when all our concerns are written upon his heart, and their management, to the very hairs of our head, are under his care and providence; when He pities us more than we can do ourselves, and has engaged his almighty power to sustain and relieve us. However, as He is tender, He is wise also; He loves us, but especially with regard to our best interests. If there were not something in our hearts and our situation that required discipline and medicine, He so delights in our prosperity, that we should never be in heaviness. The innumerable comforts and mercies with which He enriches even those we call our darker days, are sufficient proofs that He does not willingly grieve us; but when He sees a need-be for chastisement, He will not withold it because He loves us; on the contrary, that is the very reason why He afflicts. He will put his silver into the fire, to purify it; but He sits by the furnace as a refiner, to direct the process, and to secure the end He has in view, that we may neither suffer too much, nor suffer in vain.

I am, etc.

To Mrs. Thornton.

LETTER III.—How to bear affliction.

August, 1778.

MY DEAR MADAM,—Your obliging favour of the 22nd from Bath, which I received last night, demands an immediate acknowledgment. Many things which would have offered by way of answer, must for the present be postponed; for the same post brought us information which turns my thoughts to *one* subject. What shall I say? Topics of consolation are at hand in abundance; they are familiar to your mind; and was I to fill the sheet with them, I could suggest nothing but what you already know. Then are they consolatory indeed, when the Lord himself is pleased to apply them to the heart. This He has promised, and therefore we are encouraged to expect it. This is my prayer for you: I sincerely sympathize with you: I cannot comfort you; but He can; and I trust He will.

How impertinent would it be to advise you to forget or suspend the feelings which such a stroke must excite! who can help feeling? nor is sensibility in itself sinful. Christian resignation is very different from that stoical stubbornness, which is most easily practised by those unamiable characters whose regards centre wholly in self: nor could we in a proper manner exercise submission to the will of God under our trials, if we did not feel them. He who knows our frame is pleased to allow, that afflictions for the present are not joyous, but grievous. But to them that fear him He is near at hand to support their spirits, to moderate their grief, and in the issue to sanctify it; so that they shall come out of the furnace refined, more humble, and more spiritual. There is, however, a part assigned us; we are to pray for the help in need; and we are not wilfully to give way to the impression of overwhelming sorrow. We are to endeavour to turn our thoughts to such considerations as are suited to alleviate it; our deserts as sinners, the many mercies we are still indulged with, the still greater afflictions which many of our fellow-creatures endure, and, above all, the sufferings of Jesus, that man of sorrows, who made himself intimately acquainted with grief for our sakes.

When the will of the Lord is manifested to us by the event, we are to look to him for grace and strength, and be still to know that He is God, that He has a right to dispose of us and ours as He pleases, and that in the exercise of this right He is most certainly good and wise. We often complain of losses; but the expression is rather improper. Strictly speaking, we can lose nothing, because we have no real property in any thing. Our earthly comforts are lent us; and when recalled, we ought to return and resign them with thankfulness to him who has let them remain so long in our hands. But, as I said above, I do not mean to enlarge in this strain: I hope the Lord, the only Comforter, will bring such thoughts with warmth and efficacy upon your mind. Your wound, while fresh, is painful; but faith, prayer, and time, will, I trust, gradually render it tolerable. There is something fascinating in grief; painful as it is, we are prone to indulge it, and to brood over the thoughts and circumstances which are suited (like fuel to fire) to heighten and prolong it. When the Lord afflicts, it is his design that we should grieve; but in this as in all other things, there is a certain moderation which becomes a Christian, and which only grace can teach; and grace teaches us, not by books or by hearsay, but by experimental lessons: all beyond this should be avoided and guarded against as sinful and hurtful. Grief, when indulged and excessive, preys upon the spirits, injures health, indisposes us for duty, and causes us to shed tears which deserve more tears. This is a weeping world. Sin has filled it with thorns and briars, with crosses and calamities. It is a great hospital, resounding with groans in every quarter. It is as a field of battle, where many are falling around us continually: and it is more wonderful that we escape so well, than that we are sometimes wounded. We *must* have some share; it is the unavoidable lot of our nature and state; it is likewise needful in point of discipline. The Lord will certainly chasten those whom He loves, though others may seem to pass for a time with impunity. That is a sweet, instructive, and important passage, Heb. xii. 5, 11. It is so plain, that it needs no comment; so full, that a comment would but weaken it. May the Lord inscribe it upon your heart, my dear Madam, and upon mine.

I am, etc.

Mrs. Gardiner.

It appears from the letter addressed to Mrs. Gardiner that she was the subject of much affliction. Whether or not this was the means of weaning her from the gay world to which she was once attached we are unable to say. In a letter to Mr. Coffin, Mr. Newton says of her, "She is one of the most excellent women I know, but her spirit is much broken by trial and sickness, and therefore her better judgment is sometimes clouded by temptations and unbeliefs. And in another letter to Mrs. Dawson he says more particularly, "My friend Mrs. Gardiner has been confined to her drawing-room and chamber for these five years. For so long a time she has not been able to set a foot down a single stair, nor does she ever expect it. Yet I think a more lively, cheerful, exemplary Christian than she, is scarcely to be found in London. And since it is the will of God to confine her, she seems to have no more desire to go out of the door than out of the chamber window." This letter was written 1788. Mrs. Gardiner died in 1795.

To Mrs. Gardiner.

LETTER I.—Deprivation of ordinances—Simplicity of Gospel truth—Doubts and fears.

June 20, 1776.

MADAM,—It would be both unkind and ungrateful in me, to avail myself of any plea of business, for delaying the acknowledgment I owe you for your acceptable favour.

. . . .

A sure effect of the grace of God is a desire and longing for gospel ordinances; and when they are afforded, they cannot be neglected without loss. But the Lord sees many souls who are dear to him, and whom He is training up in a growing meetness for his kingdom, who are by his providence so situated, that it is not in their power to attend upon gospel preaching; and perhaps they have seldom either Christian minister or Christian friend to assist or comfort them. Such a situation is a state of trial; but Jesus is all-sufficient, and He is always near. They cannot be debarred from his word of grace, which is everywhere at hand, nor from his throne of grace; for they who feel their need of him, and whose hearts are drawn towards him, are always at the foot of it. Every room in the house, yea, every spot they stand on, fields, lanes, and hedge-rows, all is holy ground to them; for the Lord is there. The chief difference between us, and the disciples when our Saviour was upon earth, is in this: They then walked by sight, and we are called to walk by faith. They could see him with their bodily eyes, we cannot; but He said before He left them, "It is expedient for you that I go away." How could this be, unless that spiritual communion which He promised to maintain with his people after his ascension, were preferable to that intercourse He allowed them whilst he was visibly with them? But we are sure it is preferable, and they who had tried both were well satisfied He had made good his promise; so that though they had known him after the flesh, they were content not to know him so any more. Yes, madam, though we cannot see him, He sees us, He is nearer to us than we are to ourselves. In a natural state, we have very dark, and indeed dishonourable thoughts of God; we conceive of him as at a distance. But when the heart is awakened, we begin to make Jacob's reflection, "Surely the Lord is in this place, and I knew it not." And when we receive faith, we begin to know that this ever-present God is in Christ; that the government of heaven and earth, the dispensations of the kingdom of nature, providence, and grace, are in the hands of Jesus; that it is He with whom we have to do, who once suffered agony and death for our redemption, and whose compassion and tenderness are the same; now he reigns over all blessed for ever, as when he conversed amongst men in the days of his humiliation. Thus God is made known to us by the gospel, in the endearing views of a Saviour, a Shepherd, a Husband, a Friend; and a way of access is opened for us through the vail, that is, the human nature of our Redeemer, to enter, with humble confidence, into the holiest of all, and to repose all our cares and concerns upon the strength of that everlasting arm which upholds heaven and earth, and upon that infinite love which submitted to the shame, pain, and death of the cross, to redeem sinners from wrath and misery.

Though there is a height, a breadth, a length, and a depth, in this mystery of redeeming love, exceeding the comprehension of all finite minds; yet the great and leading principles which are necessary for the support and comfort of our souls, may be summed up in a very few words. Such a summary we are favoured with in Titus ii. 11—14, where the whole of salvation, all that is needful to be known, experienced, practised, and hoped for, is comprised within the compass of four verses. If many books, much study, and great discernment were necessary in order to be happy, what must the poor and simple do? Yet for them especially is the gospel designed; and few but such as these attain the knowledge and comfort of it. The Bible is a sealed book till the heart be awakened, and then he that runs may read. The propositions are few; I am a sinner, therefore I need a Saviour, one who is able and willing to save to the uttermost; such a one is Jesus; He is all that I want, wisdom, righteousness, sanctification, and redemption. But will He receive me? Can I answer a previous question? Am I willing to receive him? If so, and if his word may be taken, if He meant what He said, and promised no more than He can perform, I may be sure of a welcome; He knew long before, the doubts, fears, and suspicions, which would arise in my mind when I should come to know what I am, what I have done, and what I have deserved; and therefore He declared, before He left the earth, "Him that cometh to me I will in no wise cast out." I have no money or price in my hand, no worthiness to recommend me; and I need none, for He saveth freely for his own name's sake. I have only to be thankful for what He has already shown me, and to wait upon him for more. It is my part to commit myself to him as the physician of sin-sick souls, not to prescribe to him how He shall treat me. To begin, carry on, and perfect the cure, is his part.

The doubts and fears you speak of, are, in a greater or less degree, the common experience of all the Lord's people, at least for a time; whilst any unbelief remains in the heart, and Satan is permitted to tempt, we shall feel these things. In themselves they are groundless and evil; yet the Lord permits and overrules them for good. They tend to make us know more of the plague of our own hearts, and feel more sensibly the need of a Saviour, and make his rest (when we attain it) doubly sweet and sure. And they likewise qualify us for pitying and comforting others. Fear not: only believe, wait, and pray. Expect not all at once. A Christian is not of hasty growth, like a mushroom, but rather like the oak, the progress of which is hardly perceptible, but in time becomes a great deep-rooted tree. If my writings have been useful to you, may the Lord have the praise. To administer any comfort to his children is the greatest honour and pleasure I can receive in this life. I cannot promise to be a very punctual correspondent, having many engagements; but I hope to do all in my power to show myself, madam,

Yours, etc.

To Mrs. Gardiner.

LETTER II.—Satan's assaults, and how to meet them.

August 20, 1776.

MADAM, . . . Your exercises have been by no means singular, though they may appear so to yourself, because, in your retired situation, you have not (as you observe) had much opportunity of knowing the experience of other Christians; nor has the guilt with which your mind has been so greatly burdened been properly your own. It was a temptation forced upon you by the enemy, and he shall answer for it. Undoubtedly it is a mournful proof of the depravity of our nature, that there is that within us which renders us so easily susceptive of his suggestions; a proof of our extreme weakness, that after the clearest and most satisfying evidences of the truth, we are not able to hold fast our confidence, if the Lord permits Satan to sift and shake us. But I can assure you these changes are not uncommon. I have known persons, who, after walking with God comfortably in the main for forty years, have been at their wits' end from such assaults as you mention, and been brought to doubt, not only of the reality of their own hopes, but of the very ground and foundation upon which their hopes were built. Had you remained, as it seems you once were, attached to the vanities of a gay and dissipated life, or could you have been content with a form of godliness, destitute of the power, it is probable you would have remained a stranger to these troubles. Satan would have employed his arts in a different and less perceptible way, to have soothed you into a false peace, and prevented any thought or suspicion of danger from arising in your mind. But when he could no longer detain you in his bondage, or seduce you back again into the world, then of course he would change his method, and declare open war against you. A specimen of his power and malice you have experienced; and the Lord whom you loved, because He first loved you, permitted it, not to gratify Satan, but for your benefit, to humble and prove you, to show you what is in your heart, and to do you good in the issue. These things, for the present, are not joyous, but grievous; yet in the end they yield the peaceable fruits of righteousness. In the mean time his eye is upon you; He has appointed bounds both to the degree and the duration of the trial; and He does and will afford you such supports, that you shall not be tried beyond what you are enabled to bear. I doubt not but your conflicts and sorrows will in due time terminate in praise and victory, and be sanctified to your fuller establishment in the truth. . . .

Take courage, madam; resist the devil and he will flee from you. If he were to tempt you to any thing criminal, you would start at the thought, and renounce it with abhorrence. Do the same when he tempts you to question the Lord's compassion and goodness. But there he imposes upon us with a show of humility, and persuades us that we do well to oppose our unworthiness as sufficient exception to the many express promises of the word. It is said, the blood of Jesus cleanseth from all sin; that all manner of sin shall be forgiven for his sake; that whoever cometh He will in no wise cast out; and that He is able to save to the uttermost. Believe his word, and Satan shall be found a liar. . . .

Though our sins have been deep dyed like scarlet, and crimson, enormous as mountains, and countless as the sands, the sum total is but *sin has abounded:* but where sin hath abounded, grace has much more abounded. After all, I know the Lord keeps the key of comfort in his own hands, yet He has commanded us to attempt comforting one another. I should rejoice to be his instrument of administering comfort to you. I shall hope to hear from you soon; and that you will then be able to inform me He has restored to you the joys of his salvation. But if not yet, wait for him, and you shall not wait in vain.

I am, etc.

The Rev. William Rose.

MR. NEWTON speaks of Mr. Rose as a most remarkable instance of the distinguishing grace of God. While a student at Oxford he came under the influence of religious truth, but through what instrumentality does not appear. His acquaintance with Mr. Newton led to his introduction to the family of Mr. Barham, to whose eldest daughter he was married in 1777. "I doubt not," says his friend, "that your union with Miss Barham will be a mutual blessing, and on your part heightened by being connected with such a family."

Mr. Rose became rector of Beckenham, Kent, and vicar of Codrington. He died in the year 1829.

To the Rev. William Rose.

LETTER I.—On being kept by the power of God.

April 15, 1776.

MY DEAR SIR, . . . I often rejoice on your behalf. Your call out of the world was a singular comfortable instance of the power of grace. And when I consider the difficulties and snares of your situation, and that you have been kept in the middle path, preserved from undue compliances on the one hand, and unnecessary singularities on the other, I cannot doubt but the Lord has hitherto helped and guided you. Indeed you have need of his guidance. At your years, and with your expectations in life, your health firm, and your natural spirits lively, you are exposed to many snares: yet if the Lord keeps you sensible of your danger, and dependent upon him, you will walk safely. Your security, success, and comfort, depend upon him; and in the way of means, chiefly upon your being preserved in an humble sense of your own weakness. It is written, "Fear not, I am with thee." It is written again, "Blessed is the man who feareth always." There is a perfect harmony in those seemingly different texts. May the wisdom that cometh from above teach you and me to keep them both united in our view. If the Lord be with us, we have no cause of fear. His eye is upon us, his arm over us, his ear open to our prayer; his grace sufficient, his promise unchangeable. Under his protection, though the path of duty should lie through fire and water, we may cheerfully and confidently pursue it. On the other hand, our hearts are so deceitful, fallible, and frail; our spiritual enemies so subtle, watchful, and powerful; and they derive so many advantages from the occasions of every day, in which we are unavoidably and unexpectedly concerned; there is so much combustible within, and so many temptations arising from without, capable of setting all in a flame, that we cannot be too jealous of ourselves and our circumstances. The Duke of Devonshire's motto (if I mistake not) well suits the Christian, *Cavendo tutus.** When we can say, in the Psalmist's spirit, *Hold thou me up*, we may warrantably draw this conclusion, *and I shall be safe;* but the moment we lean to our own understanding, we are in imminent danger of falling. The enemy who wars against our souls is a consummate master in his way, fertile in stratagems, and equally skilful in carrying on his assaults by sap or by storm. He studies us, if I may so say, all round, to discover our weak sides, and he is a very Proteus for changing his appearances, and can appear as a sly serpent, a roaring lion, or an angel of life, as best suits his purpose. It is a

---

* Safe by caution.

great mercy to be in some measure acquainted with his devices, and aware of them. They who wait humbly upon the Lord, and consult carefully at his word and throne of grace, are made wiser than their enemy, and enabled to escape and withstand his wiles. I know you will not expect me to apologize for putting you in mind of these things, though you know them. I have a double warrant; the love I bear you, and the Lord's command. Heb. iii. 13. Use the like freedom with me, I need it, and hope to be thankful for it, and accept it as one of the best proofs of friendship.

The Lord bless and keep you. Pray for us, and believe me to be sincerely yours.

To the Rev. William Rose.

Letter II.—Congratulation—Danger of prosperity—World at its best state vanity.

December 21, 1776.

My dear Friend,—Your letter brought me tidings of joy, and then furnished me with materials for a bonfire upon the occasion. It was an act of passive obedience to burn it, but I did obey. I congratulate you upon the happy issue to which the Lord has brought your affairs. I see that his good Spirit and good providence have been, and are with you. I doubt not but your union with Miss Barham will be a mutual blessing, and on your part, heightened by being connected with such a family. I could enlarge upon this head, if *my* letter likewise was to be burnt as soon as you have read it. I look upon the friendship the Lord has given me there, as one of my prime privileges; and I hope I shall always be thankful that it proved a means of introducing you into it.

I congratulate you likewise upon your accession to Beckenham, not because it is a good living, in a genteel neighbourhood, and a fine country, but because I believe the Lord sends you there for fulfilling the desires He has given you of being useful to souls. Church preferment, in any other view, is dreadful; and I would as soon congratulate a man upon seeing a millstone tied about his neck, to sink him into the depths of the sea, as upon his obtaining what is called a good living, except I thought him determined to spend and be spent in the cause of the gospel. A parish is an awful millstone indeed to those who see nothing valuable in the flock but the fleece. But the Lord has impressed your heart with a sense of the glory and importance of his truth, and the worth of souls, and animated your zeal by the most powerful motive, the knowledge of his constraining love. Your case is extraordinary. Perhaps, when you review in your mind the circle of your former gay acquaintance, you may say, with Job's servant, "I only am escaped alive." The rest are either removed into an eternal state, or are still hurrying down the stream of dissipation, and living without God in the world. Yet there was a time when there seemed no more probability on your side than on their's, that you should obtain mercy and be called to the honour of preaching the glorious gospel. You are setting out with every possible advantage; in early life, with a cheerful flow of spirits, affluent circumstances, and now, to crown all, the Lord gives you the very choice of your heart as a partner; one who, besides deserving and meeting your affection, will, I am persuaded, be a real help-meet to you in your spiritual walk. How much is here to be thankful for!

I trust the Lord has given you, and will maintain in

you a right spirit, so as not to rest in his gifts, but to hold them in connexion with the love and favour of the Giver. It is a low time with us, when the greatest assemblage of earthly blessings can seem to satisfy us without a real communion with him. His grace is sufficient for you; but, undoubtedly such a scene of prosperity as seems to lie before you, is full of snares, and calls for a double effort of watchfulness and prayer. Your situation will fix many eyes upon you, and Satan will doubtless watch you, and examine every corner of the hedge around you, to see if he can find a gap by which to enter. We have but few rich gospel ministers; but it is too evident that he has found a way to damp the zeal and hurt the spirits of some of those few, who for a time acted nobly, and seemed to walk out of the reach of the allurements of the world. I am not jealous of you; I feel a comfortable persuasion that the Lord has taken a fast hold of your heart, and given you a fast hold of his almighty arm. Yet I believe you will not be displeased with me for dropping a hint of this kind, and at this time.

You have heard of the trial with which the Lord has been pleased to visit us: it still continues, though considerably alleviated. It is tempered with many mercies, and I hope He disposes us in a measure to submission. I trust it will be for good.* My dear friend, you are now coming into my school, where you will learn, as occasions offer, to feel more in the person of another

---

* Under date, December 5, Mr. Newton thus writes in his *Diary* of the illness of Mrs. Newton, the trial here referred to. "We are still in the furnace, but I hope Thou, my gracious Lord, art near as a refiner of silver. I hope this affliction has quickened me to prayer, and will be sanctified to us both. Oh, speak to my heart and calm all its tumults, and make it submissive and quiet at thy foot. I praise Thee for moderating our trial. Though not removed it is tolerable, and sweetened with many mercies."

than in your own. But be not discouraged; the Lord only afflicts for our good. It is necessary that our sharpest trials should sometimes spring from our dearest comforts, else we should be in danger of forgetting ourselves, and setting up our rest here. In such a world, and with such hearts as we have, we shall often need something to prevent our cleaving to the dust, to quicken us to prayer, and to make us feel that our dependence for one hour's peace is upon the Lord alone. I am ready to think I have known as much of the good and happiness which this world can afford, as most people who live in it. I never saw the person with whom I wished to exchange in temporals. And for many years past I have thought my trials have been light and few, compared with what many, or most of the Lord's people have endured. And yet, though in the main possessed of my own wishes, when I look back upon the twenty-seven years past, I am ready to style them, with Jacob, few and evil; and to give the sum total of their contents in Solomon's words,—All is vanity. If I take these years to pieces, I see a great part of them was filled up with sins, sorrows, and inquietudes. The pleasures too are gone, and have no more real existence than the baseless fabric of a dream. The shadows of the evening will soon begin to come over us; and if our lives are prolonged, a thousand pains and infirmities, from which the Lord has in a remarkable measure exempted us hitherto, will probably overtake us; and at last we must feel the parting pang. *Sic transit gloria mundi.** Sin has so envenomed the soil of this earth, that the amaranth will not grow upon it. But we are hastening to a better world, and bright unclouded skies, where our sun will go down no more, and all tears shall be wiped from our eyes. I am, etc.

* So passes away the glory of the world.

To the Rev. William Rose.

Letter III.—Growing old—Thankful for the continuance of many mercies—Looking to the future.

My dear Friend,—I am aiming to leave off wishing, and indeed I see but little in this poor world worth wishing for, if a wish could procure it. Yet it would have gratified me, if I could have seen you when you called, because I love you.

Our times for meeting at Beckenham do not coincide. I have not been from home yet this year. But I am now, if the Lord permit, and my curate, who has been ill and is mending, is able to take my place, upon the eve of a journey to Southampton.

I have been engaged for more than two months to Paul's Cray, but have not yet found opportunity to go, nor am I sure that I shall be able. But if I can I must. It is a call of duty to confirm the word and to strengthen the hands of dear Mr. Simons, by preaching to his people. But I am so taken up that I can seldom command a day or two to follow my inclination of visiting my friends. My visits are chiefly confined to the sick and the sorrowful.

The sands in my glass begin to number. I am within three weeks of my seventy-second year, and though my health is remarkably good, I think never better, yet I have reason to expect some change, and perhaps a sudden removal every day. Much of my time has run to waste. It ought to be my chief care to redeem and improve the little uncertain remainder, and to account every hour a talent. Indeed I have lived long enough for myself.

I have seen an end to all perfection this world can afford. For in my own judgment and in my own way, I have been as happy as the possession of my own desires could make me. *I have been*, but it is all now past like the remembrance of a dream when we awake. On the other hand I have as little reason as any one to be weary of living, for my situation is in all points comfortable. My wants are all supplied. My dear Miss Catlett is the best substitute for her dear mamma that the nature of the case will admit. I have many kind friends, domestic peace, affectionate and faithful servants. And I bless the Lord I have a large attentive peaceful thinking auditory. We have cheering tokens of the Lord's gracious presence in our assemblies, many exemplary individuals amongst them : more than a few have, I hope, been awakened, and the good work seems to be still going forward.

As I have reason to hope the Lord makes me acceptable and useful I would be thankful that my life is prolonged, especially as my old age is not burdened with sickness or pain, nor are my faculties sensibly impaired. In short since the memorable year '90 my situation has been remarkably tranquil, and I have scarcely met with anything that deserves the name of a trial. Considering what I was in Africa and what the Lord has done for me since, my case seems an unique one in the annals of the church.

How I have run on about self! but it is to you, and I believe you will bear with me. One line has drawn out another insensibly. I may now say with the apostle, " The time of my departure is at hand." I trust I can also say with him, " I know whom I have believed," etc. May I be enabled to add likewise at the close of life, " I have fought the good fight, I have finished my course, I have kept the faith," and live with my eye fixed upon that crown of righteousness which the Lord has promised to all that love his appearance. I daily anticipate the solemnity of a dying hour. The transition for all that I have seen and loved here into an unseen, untried, unchangeable state will be very serious and important. But I am encouraged to hope that when I pass through the dark valley He will be with me. Then I need fear no evil. Everything short of this appears to me *now* lighter than vanity.

Though we seldom meet, I give you full credit for the continuance of our old friendship. It is still warm and flourishing on my side. Give my best love and Miss Catlett's to Mrs. Rose and Miss Rose. May the Lord bless you and yours and me and mine with the best blessings.

I am your affectionate and obliged,
JOHN NEWTON.

July 14, 1796.

The Rev. William Bull.

MR. BULL became pastor of the Independent church at Newport Pagnell about the same time that Mr. Newton came to Olney. (The two places were but five miles apart.) The acquaintance between these friends did not commence till some time after this. No sooner, however, did they come really to know each other than this acquaintance speedily ripened into a very intimate, and, as it proved, a life-long friendship. In his *Diary*, at this time, Mr. Newton speaks again and again of the high esteem in which his friend was held. Thus he says: "I find few or any with whom I can converse with equal advantage, whose manner of thinking is so deep and solid." Again: "He has just called and spent an hour with me. I could sit silent half a day to listen to him, and am almost unwilling to speak a word for fear of preventing him." Once more: "I admire Mr. Bull; so humble, so spiritual, so judicious and so savoury . . . I think he will be my most profitable companion in these parts."

The intercourse between Mr. Newton and Mr. Bull, as may be well supposed, was very frequent, so long as the former resided at Olney; and when he removed to London there was abundant opportunity for its renewal, as Mr. Bull was in the habit, for many years, of preaching for several sabbaths at the Tabernacle and at Tottenham Court and Surrey Chapels. The flame of their affection burnt brightly to the last; for, as Mr. Newton writes in 1800, when to write had become a task, "If two needles are properly touched by a magnet, they will retain their sympathy for a long time. But if two hearts are truly united to the Heavenly Magnet, their mutual attraction will be permanent in time and to eternity. Blessed be the Lord for a good hope, that it is thus between you and me. I could not love you better if I saw or heard from you every day."

Mr. Bull was pastor of the church at Newport for fifty years; a church which he was enabled, by the blessing of God, to raise from a very low condition to a state of great prosperity. For a considerable portion of this time he also presided over a theological institution, in the formation of which Mr. Newton took a very active part, and the special design of which was to train suitable young men of evangelical sentiments for the Christian ministry, without regard to denominational distinctions.*

Mr. Bull was educated for the ministry under the Rev. Dr. Ashworth, at Daventry. He was a man of great natural endowments and of much culture, possessed of fervent piety, and very popular and useful as a preacher. He counted many great and good men amongst his friends, both in and out of the Established Church. The poet Cowper was of the number, and thus he writes of him to Mr. Unwin: "You are not acquainted with him; perhaps it is well you are not. You would regret, still more than you do, that there are so many miles interposed between us. He spends part of the day with us to-morrow. A Dissenter, but a liberal one; a man of letters and genius, master of a fine imagination, or rather not master of it; an imagination which, when he finds himself in the company he loves and can confide in, runs away with him into such fields of speculation as amuse and enliven every other imagination that has the happiness to be of the party. At other times he has a tender and delicate sort of melancholy in his disposition, not less agreeable in its way . . . . He can be lively without levity, and pensive without dejection. Such a man is Mr. Bull. But he smokes tobacco. Nothing is perfect: "*Nihil est ab omni parte beatum.*"

The letters which follow are selected out of one hundred and twenty-nine in the Editor's possession, and which he ventures to think, from the perfect sympathy existing between these friends, will be found as characteristic and interesting as any contained in the present volume.

* See *Newton's Life*, by the Rev. Josiah Bull, M.A., p. 257, etc.

To the Rev. WILLIAM BULL.

LETTER I.—Presence of the Lord: its blessed effects—His own state of mind—Occupations.

DEAR AND REVEREND SIR,—I call you *dear* because I love you; and I shall continue to style you *reverend* as long as you dignify me with that title. It is, indeed, a pretty sounding epithet, and forms a striking contrast in the usual application. The inhabitants of the moon (if there be any) have, perhaps, no idea how many reverend, right reverend, and most reverend sinners we have in England. And yet you *are* reverend, and I revere you, because I believe the Lord liveth in you, and has chosen you to be a temple of his presence, and an instrument of his grace.

I hope the two sermons you preached in London were made useful to others; and the medicines you took there were useful to yourself. I am glad to hear you are safe at home, and something better. Cheerful spring is approaching; then, I hope, the barometer of your spirits will rise. But the presence of the Lord can bring a pleasanter spring than April, and even in the depth of winter. That heathenish, fulsome compliment of Horace to Augustus is a beautiful prayer in the mouth of a Christian, and has sometimes touched my heart, as if I had found it in the Bible.

> Lucem redde, tuæ, dux bone, patriæ;
> Instar veris enim vultus ubi tuus
> Affulsit populo, gratior it dies
>   Et soles melius nitent.*

---

* Come then, auspicious Prince, and bring
   To thy long gloomy country, Light,
For in thy countenance the Spring
   Shines forth to cheer thy people's sight.
Then hasten thy return, for thou away
Nor lustre has the sun, nor joy the day.—*Francis.*

Time has been when I could say, and did say, something like this, in my own way:

> How tedious and tasteless the hours
>   When Jesus no longer I see!
> Sweet prospects, sweet birds, and sweet flowers
>   Have lost all their sweetness with me.
>
> The Midsummer sun shines but dim;
>   The fields strive in vain to look gay;
> But, when I am happy in him,
>   December's as pleasant as May.

At present it is January with me, both within and without. The outward sun shines and looks pleasant, but his beams are faint, and too feeble to dissolve the frost. So it is in my heart. I have many bright and pleasant beams of truth in my view, but cold predominates in my frost-bound spirit, and they have but little power to warm me. I could tell a stranger something about Jesus that would perhaps astonish him: such a glorious person, such wonderful love, such humiliation, such a death. And then, what He is now in himself, and what He is to his people. What a Sun! what a Shield! what a Root! what a Life! what a Friend! My tongue can run on upon these subjects sometimes; and could my heart keep pace with it, I should be the happiest fellow in the country. Stupid creature, to know these things so well, and yet be no more affected with them! Indeed, I have reason to be upon ill terms with myself. It is strange that pride should ever find any thing in my experience to feed upon; but this completes my character for folly, vileness, and inconsistence, that I am not only poor but proud; and, though I am convinced I am a very wretch, as nothing before the Lord, I am prone to go forth among my fellow-creatures as though I were wise and good.

You wonder what I am doing, and well you may. I am

sure you would, if you lived with me. Too much of my time passes in busy idleness, too much in waking dreams. I aim at something, but hindrances from within and without make it difficult for me to accomplish anything. I dare not say I am absolutely idle, or that I wilfully waste my time; but I have seldom one hour free from interruption. Letters come that must be answered, visitants that must be received, business that must be attended to. I have a good many sheep and lambs to look after, sick and afflicted souls dear to the Lord; and therefore, whatever stands still, these must not be neglected. Amongst these various avocations night comes before I am ready for noon, and the week closes when, according to the state of my business, it should not be more than Tuesday. O precious irrecoverable time! Oh that I had more wisdom in redeeming and improving thee! Pray for me that the Lord may teach me to serve him better.

Mrs. Newton has been one week confined to her chamber through illness, but is pretty well again. We abound in mercies and causes for gratitude; but what a shame and pity to make such poor returns to the Author of them! I long to come to Newport to see you, but I believe I must wait for that pleasure till the days are a little longer. In the meantime you will be as welcome to us here, if you will trot over, as a new guinea to a miser's pocket.

I am, very affectionately, yours,
JOHN NEWTON.

P.S.—Send or bring me some notes on Job xiv. 14.

January 27, 1778.

To the Rev. William Bull.

Letter II.—Duty and benefit of exercising charity and patience—Expressions of regard—A speckled bird.

My dear Friend,—You see I readily accept your proposal of exchanging another threepenny letter. As we are so soon to meet, I have nothing very important to communicate, and many things occur which might demand my time. I have no other plea to offer either to you or myself, for writing again, but because I love you.

I pity the unknown considerable minister with whom you smoked your morning pipe. But we must take men and things as we find them. And when we fall in company with those from whom we can get little other good, it is likely we shall at least find occasion for the exercise of patience and charity towards them, and of thankfulness to him who made us to differ; and these are good things, though perhaps the occasion may not be pleasant. Indeed a Christian, if in a right spirit, is always in his Lord's school, and may learn either a new lesson or how to practise an old one, by every thing he sees or hears, provided he does not wilfully tread upon forbidden ground. If he were constrained to spend a day with the poor creatures in the common side of Newgate, though he could not talk with them of what God has done for his soul, he might be more sensible of his mercy, by the contrast he would observe around him. He might rejoice for himself, and mourn over them, and thus perhaps get as much benefit as from the best sermon he ever heard.

It is necessary, all things taken together, to have connexion more or less with narrow-minded people. If they are, notwithstanding their prejudices, civil to us, they have a right to some civility from us. We may love them, though we cannot admire them, and pick something good from them, notwithstanding we see much to blame. It is perhaps the highest triumph we can obtain over bigotry, when we are able to bear with bigots themselves, for they are a sort of troublesome folk, whom Mr. Self is often very forward to exclude from the comprehensive candour and tenderness which he professes to exercise towards those who differ from him.

I do not wish you to live in London, for my own sake as well as yours; but, if the Lord should so appoint, I believe He can make you easy there, and enable me to make a tolerable shift without you. Yet I certainly should miss you; for, excepting a friend about twelve miles off,* I have no person in this neighbourhood with whom my heart so thoroughly unites in spirituals, though there are many whom I love. But conversation with most Christians is something like going to court, when, except you are dressed exactly according to a prescribed standard, you will either not be admitted or must expect to be heartily stared at. But you and I can meet and converse *sans contrainte*, in an undress, without fear of offending, or being counted offenders for a word out of place, and not exactly in the pink of the mode.

I know not how it is, I think my sentiments and experience are as orthodox and Calvinistical as need be, and yet I am a sort of speckled bird among my Calvinist brethren. I am a mighty good churchman, but pass amongst such as a Dissenter in principle. On the other hand, the Dissenters (many of them, I mean) think me defective, either in understanding or in conscience, by staying where I am; while there is a middle party called Methodists, but neither do

* J. Foster Barham, Esq., of Bedford.

my dimensions exactly fit with them. I am somehow disqualified for claiming a full brotherhood with any party; but there are a few among all parties who bear with me, and love me, and with this I must be content at present. But so far as they love the Lord Jesus Christ, I desire, and by his grace I determine (with or without their leave) to love them all. Party walls, though stronger than the walls of Babylon, must come down in the general ruin, when the earth and all its works shall be burned up, if no sooner. The Lord helped me through another of his golden privileged days. He enabled me to speak, I hope, a little to the purpose. I wish I could feel more of the truths I propose to others. But He has wise reasons for keeping me short. He will do what is best for us all.

Mrs. Newton has had a whole week of tolerable health; help me to praise him. We join in love.

I am sincerely yours,

JOHN NEWTON.

July 13.

To the REV. WILLIAM BULL.

LETTER III.—Forgetfulness — A pleasant visit — Requesting his friend's prayers.

DEAR MR. BULL,—What a calf am I! You mentioned preaching here to-morrow, and I had not wit enough to say, be sure you dine with us. My heart positively meant it, though my head (which is often wool-gathering) missed the nick of telling you so. I committed the fault, and you must pay the penny.

Is it ever right to look a gift horse in the mouth? If you think it will bear, please to tell Mr. Barton (another business my wise head forgot) that his half-guinea looked well, but when weighed in the balances was found too light, sad emblem, I fear, of the case of too many professors.

We arrived safe and well at home. No rain when we walked; though it marched before us and threatened our rear. It was a hot evening, and we seemed fatigued, so that we had not much pretty chat. We all agreed in the judgment we formed of our visit, that it had been very pleasant, our friends very kind, and that we ought to go to bed very thankful.

When you are with the King, and are getting good for yourself, speak a word for me and mine. I have reason to think you see him oftener, and have nearer access to him than myself. Indeed, I am unworthy to look at him, or to speak to him at all, much more that He should speak tenderly to me; yet I am not wholly without his notice. He supplies all my wants, and I live under his protection. My enemies see his royal arms over my door and dare not enter. Were I detached from him for a moment, in that moment they would make an end of me.

Love to Mr. and Mrs. Bull, Mr. and Mrs. Barton, and all in your house.

I am, as I ought to be, your affectionate and obliged,

JOHN NEWTON.

My birthday, August 4, 1778.

To the REV. WILLIAM BULL.

LETTER IV.—An invitation.

Bucks to wit.

You are hereby required and enjoined to appear personally at our episcopal seat in Olney, on the present

Wednesday, 19th August, to dine with the Rev. Henry Venn,* and with us. And hereof you are not to fail.

Given at our den—*die supra dicto.*

JOHN NEWTON.

To the Rev. William Bull.

Read *to-morrow*: You receive it Tuesday night.

To the REV. WILLIAM BULL.

LETTER V.—A troublesome lodger.†

MY DEAR FRIEND, . . . We are still favoured with many mercies. My dear is tolerably well. Mary Woolnoth, my other dear, seems pretty well likewise, and has a good deal of company on levee days. I have many pleasant and kind connections; but I have a troublesome inmate, a lodger, who assumes as if the house were his own, and is a perpetual incumbrance, and spoils all. He has long been noted for his evil ways; but though generally known, is not easily avoided. He lodged with one Saul of Tarsus long before I was born, and made him groan and cry out lustily. Time was when I thought I would shut the door, to keep him out of my house, but my precaution came too late; he was already within; and to turn him out by head and shoulders is beyond my power; nay, I cannot interdict him from any one single apartment. If I think of retiring into the closest corner, he is there before me. We often meet and jostle and snarl at each other; but sometimes (would you believe it?) I lose all my suspicion, and am disposed to treat him as an inti-

---

* Then rector of Yelling.

† In reply to this letter Mr. Bull says: "Self, naughty self is fully as troublesome at my house as at yours."

mate friend. This inconsistency of mine I believe greatly encourages him, for I verily believe he would be ashamed and afraid to be seen by me, if I always kept him at a proper distance. However, we both lay such a strong claim to the same dwelling, that I believe the only way of settling the dispute will be (which the Landlord himself has spoken of) to pull down the house over our heads. There seems something disagreeable in this mode of proceeding; but from what I have read in an old book, I form a hope that when things come to this crisis, I shall escape, and my enemy will be crushed in the ruins.

Love to Mrs. Bull, and the little Bull, from my dear, and from your most affectionate, if not your most humble friend,

JOHN NEWTON.

HOXTON: *June* 7, 1783.

To the REV. WILLIAM BULL.

LETTER VI.—An accident at Norwich—Providence of God.

MY DEAR FRIEND,—Methought I saw them fall,* poor Mr. Foster first, then Mr. Bull upon him. He had the

---

* Mr. Bull had been invited by Mr. Thornton to visit him at Yarmouth. The Rev. Henry Foster and some other clergymen were of the party. These good men were continually engaged in preaching. Mr. Foster drove Mr. Bull to Norwich, where they spent the Sunday. The next day they went on to Martham to see the Rev. Mr. Bowman. On Tuesday they returned to Norwich, and to quote Mr. Bull's words on the occasion, in a letter to his wife: "Mr. Foster drove me in a one-horse chaise, and in coming through the streets he managed to overturn the chaise as completely as ever you were overset in your life. He laid himself in the channel, me upon him, and the chaise on us both. But He who manages all things for the best so ordered it that we neither of us received any hurt. We ought to be very thankful; and so the people told us who stood by." Such are the particulars of the incident referred to by Mr. Newton.

best of it. How soft he fell, like Downy Doctor upon a downy bed! Then the chaise upon both; so they lay well packed.

> Like two round nuts close squeezed in one strait shell.

When I found that these two valuable bodies of divinity had only a little dirt upon their binding, and had received no harm, I could not help smiling to observe how they looked upon themselves, upon each other, and upon the chaise, when they were safely upon their legs again. I was reminded of the old adage, *ne sutor ultra crepidam.** To preach the gospel acceptably to thousands is one thing; to drive a one-horse chaise through the streets evenly, so as not to spill the contents is quite another thing, and requires very different gifts and talents.

But, seriously, I would be very thankful that neither of you were hurt. Such catastrophes, as this may properly be called, have often been attended with dislocated or broken bones, a fractured skull, or instant death, so frail is man. Often when he thinks himself safe, and is dreaming of his own importance, as if he were a necessary part in the complicated movements of Divine Providence, he falls like grass before the scythe; not by the hand of a giant, nor the fangs of a tiger: the veriest trifle is sufficient to destroy him. How many loose stones do we see in the road! It seems no great matter where they lie; yet any one of them, by changing the direction of a wheel, is sufficient to confound all the plans of this mighty creature. One throws him down, he falls with his head upon another: in that very moment all his thoughts perish. But the Lord gave his angels charge over you and brother Foster; therefore you fell unhurt, and are still alive to praise and

---

* Let not the shoemaker go beyond his last.

serve him. I see so much of the uncertainty of life, and how little I can either foresee or prevent what the next moment may bring forth, that I should be a very great coward, afraid not only of riding in a chaise, but of walking across a room, if I were not in some degree enabled to confide in the Lord's protection.

I am at Southampton, or near it. I have been at Lymington and Portsmouth. I am going to-day to Salisbury, to-morrow to Bath; and shall be the next day at Bristol, if the Lord permit. In the course of next week we hope to return to beloved home. We have had a merciful excursion hitherto. Health, safety, kind friends, good accommodation, opportunities of hearing and preaching the good gospel, fresh air and salt water have agreed well with me. My dear has been tolerable; and Betsy, who was rather poorly before we set out, looks like a country girl again. But I am still a poor creature, and know not whether my causes for thankfulness or shame are most abundant. It is well that I am permitted to look to Him who lived and died for sinners. . . .

Yours indeed,
JOHN NEWTON.

September 5, 1786.

To the REV. WILLIAM BULL.

LETTER VII.—Comfort in the loss of friends—Special reference to the death of Mrs. Newton.

MON CHER TAUREAU, . . . I have often thought that though I loved my friends well while living, and wished them to live as long as possible, yet if the Lord saw fit to remove them, and I had hope that they died in the faith, I could pretty well make up my own loss, by considering to whom they were gone, and how they were employed, when I could see them no more. Thus the removal of Mr. Barham, Mr. Thornton, and others, though dear to my heart, cost me little more than a sigh on my own account. I thought, now they are safe and happy; now neither sin, sorrow, nor Satan, can touch them. They are escaped from the turbulent, tempestuous sea of this world, and are entered into the haven of eternal rest. These, and such kinds of considerations, soon and perfectly reconciled me to part with them for a time, expecting, before very long, to receive them again for ever.

But when my foreboding mind has anticipated the possibility of surviving my dear Mary, the question, How I could bear it? how I could ever expect to see another cheerful hour? involved a difficulty which could only be solved by referring it to the mighty power of God, of him that raised the dead. I did indeed hope that He would grant me grace to be silently submissive to his will; but that I should be able to watch hours by her bedside for her last breath; that I should think, write, and speak of her with so much composure after she was gone, that I should sleep soundly in the room, in the very bed, where she suffered so much and so long, that I should still prefer my home to any other house, and still retain a relish for all my remaining comforts, was more than I knew how to hope or to conceive.

At length, the trial which I most dreaded came upon me. Suspense was long; sensations were keen. My right hand was not chopped off at a stroke, I would be thankful, however, that it was not. It was sawn off by slow degrees; it was an operation of weeks and months; almost every following week more painful than the preceding. But did I sink? did I despond? did I refuse my food? did sleep forsake my eyes? was I so troubled in mind or weakened in body that I could not speak? Far, far from it. The Lord strengthened me, and I was strong. No part of my public service was interrupted; and perhaps, I never preached with more energy than at that period. It was the Lord's doing, and it was marvellous in my own eyes, and in the eyes of my friends. Indeed, some who knew me not said it was overdone, and charged me with a want of feeling. Indeed, I felt as much as I could well bear, but not too much; and to this hour I only stand because I am upheld. Were I left a little to myself, there is enough in my heart still to make me very wretched under a sense of my loss. . . .

Believe me to be your affectionate and obliged friend and brother,

JOHN NEWTON.

December 10, 1791.

To the REV. WILLIAM BULL.

LETTER VIII.—*His friendship unbroken—Requests his friend's prayers in his old age.*

MY DEAR OLD FRIEND,—Though the flame of our affection is not much supported by the fuel of frequent letters and converse, I trust it still burns brightly, for it is fed from a secret invisible and inexhaustible source. If two needles are properly touched by a magnet, they will retain their sympathy for a long time. But if two hearts are truly united to the Heavenly Magnet, their mutual attraction will be permanent in time and to eternity. Blessed be the Lord for a good hope, that it is thus between you and me. I could not love you better if I saw you or heard from you every day.

Dear Miss Catlett and I, and all the dear family we are with, consisting of about twenty people, are well. We lie down and rise up, go out and come in, in peace and safety. What a wonderful mercy in such a world as this, when so many are suffering and falling around us, and we, though upon the same field of battle, remain unhurt.

But the almanack tells me that if I live till Monday next, I shall enter my seventy-sixth year. I believe you will pray for me on that day. My eyes, ears, and legs likewise admonish me that I grow older. My writing days seem almost over; I cannot well see to write; but I make an effort to send you one letter more, which may probably be the last you will receive.

I have requested your prayers; shall I tell you what to ask for? You need not pray for my sudden removal, for I have as little reason as most people to be weary of life; and, through mercy, I feel at present quite willing to live my appointed time. Nor need you pray for my long continuance here, for I see little except my profession and ministry worth living for another day. But pray that I may be enabled to leave the time and manner of my dismission entirely in the Lord's hands; that if He sees fit to summon me suddenly, I may be willing to go without delay; and that if He is pleased to lay me aside, I may be as willing to retire and wait his time.

Pray likewise for me that no gross imprudence or misconduct may stain the latter part of my life, but that I may be enabled to exemplify in myself what I have laboured to inculcate upon others from the pulpit. I have observed in some good men and good ministers improprieties in their latter days, which I have been willing to ascribe rather to the infirmities of old age than to a defect in real grace. I pray daily to be preserved from these, and I request your assistance. I have known good men in advanced life garrulous, peevish, dogmatic, self-important, with some symptoms of jealousy, and perhaps envy, towards those who are upon the increase while they feel themselves decreasing. Do, my friend, pray earnestly that it may not be so with me, but that I may retire, if laid aside, like a thankful guest from a plentiful table, and may rejoice to see others coming forward to serve the Lord (I hope better and more successfully) when I can serve him no longer. May I never forget that the Lord brought me from Africa, where I was the servant, the scorn, and the pity of slaves; what He has done for me since, and what a long and highly favoured day I have had since He was pleased to put me into the ministry. Such likewise shall be my desire and prayer for you, if you should be spared to old age; for as yet I consider you rather as a youngish man.

Give our love to Mrs. Bull, brother Thomas, and all who are dear to you; to dear Mr. and Mrs. Neale, who I suppose are either returned or near it. I long to hear of or from them. Love to Miss Neale, Mrs. Tippin, and more than I can name, who come often to No. 8. I shall expect to hear from you likewise.

The Lord bless you and yours, in body, soul, and spirit. Amen!

I am your affectionate and obliged,
JOHN NEWTON.

SOUTHAMPTON: *August* 1, 1800.

To the Rev. William Bull.

LETTER IX.—Still able to preach—Miss Catlett's illness.

My dear Friend,—If my eyes will give me leave, I must thank you, however briefly, for your very kind letter of the 3rd. As my anniversary was on a Wednesday, I preached about Mr. Self, from the case of the demoniac in Mark v., which so nearly resembled my own, and particularly from verses 18, 19.

I am now two days in my seventy-eighth year. My health and strength are remarkable for my age; but I feel some symptoms of declining years. The day of opportunity wears away, and the night is approaching when no man can work. But while the Lord enables me to preach, and the people are attentive and willing to hear me in my poor broken way, I ought to be willing to live to the age of Methuselah, if I might but promote his glory, and be any way useful to my hearers. I am bought with a price, *ergo*, I am not my own. I wish to say from my heart, Lord, grant that the short uncertain remnant of my time may not discredit my profession, by pride or any evil tempers; and that when the summons shall come, it shall find me ready and waiting. To this purpose I have been permitted and encouraged to pray for many years past, and our God is a hearer of prayer.

My dear child* joins with me in love to you and yours, and in thanks for your kind prayers and wishes on our joint behalf. I have much to be thankful for on her account. The Lord has done great things for us, and I am waiting and praying for complete relief. But, however He may

* Miss Catlett. See Letter VII. to the Rev. J. Coffin.

dispose of us while here, I am sure that He does all things well, and that his choice for us will be eventually better than anything we can choose for ourselves. If there is any alteration since you saw her, I think it is for the better, and I am not without hope that a full deliverance is gradually approaching; but I trust we are both under the direction of Infinite wisdom, goodness, and power, and there I would leave all and say (Oh that I may say it from my heart!), Not my will, but Thine be done.

Now my eyes bid me hasten to a close. The Lord bless you in your person, family, and ministry, and return you sevenfold into your own bosom all that you have desired and prayed for us.

I am your very affectionate,
JOHN NEWTON.

August 5, 1802.

Love to Mrs. Bull. Brother Thomas Bull made us a very kind and acceptable visit yesterday, an hour and a half long.

The Rev. William Barlass.

MR. BARLASS was a minister of the Secession Church of Scotland, and about the year 1777, while still a student, he commenced a correspondence with Mr. Newton. He was led to write to him, as he says, with many apologies, in his first letter, from the deep interest awakened in his mind by the perusal of Mr. Newton's books, and also from a desire to seek the advice of one of whom he had conceived so high an opinion, in the difficulties which agitated his mind when about to enter the ministry.

Mr. Newton seems to have been much interested in his correspondent, and in the course of seven years wrote frequently to him. Mr. Barlass entered the ministry, and was settled at Whitehill, about thirty-six miles from Aberdeen. He is said to have been a zealous, faithful, and popular preacher, a good divine and scholar, mild and unassuming in his manners, and possessed of ardent piety.

A long-continued and severe malady led Mr. Barlass to give up the ministry and to emigrate to America. Here, being probably physically incapable of preaching, he engaged in teaching the young, and subsequently went into the book trade. In this latter occupation it was his especial object to introduce into his adopted country the most valuable books in divinity and in the learned languages, at a time when there was a great destitution of such works in New York.

Mr. Barlass died early in the year 1817.

To the Rev. William Barlass.

LETTER I.—Satan's temptations—Humiliating thoughts from his former condition.

MY DEAR SIR, . . . I could write a long note indeed, upon what I first meet with, your very great mistake in considering me as a very great man. If we could have a personal interview, I think you would be presently undeceived. Your mistake, however, has done me good. A whole quire of invective from an enemy could hardly have given me so keen a sense of shame. The Scripture assures us that our hearts by nature, like coin from the same mint, are all alike. And I hear my fellow-Christians complain of evils similar to what I feel, and they have the same right with myself to be believed. Otherwise I seem to have reason to conclude there cannot be one upon earth who knows the Lord, so inconsistent, so evil, as myself. . . .

What you say of Gurnal reminds me to put another book in your way (I think the author was a countryman of yours)—*Gilpin on Temptation.* I think the perusal of it would throw light upon some of your inquiries. I have only room for a few brief hints. They that go down to the sea in ships, and do their business in great waters, experience hardships, and likewise see wonders, which people who live on shore have no idea of. Many of the Lord's people are comparatively landsmen; others are mariners, and are called to conflict a great part of their lives with storms and raging billows. I believe much of the variety of this kind is constitutional. We are at a loss to conceive of the invisible world, and the invisible agents belonging to it; but we live in the midst of them. But it seems to me that people of very delicate nerves, and those who are subject to what we call low spirits, are more accessible to this invisible agency than others. I am rather but a landsman myself, and know but just enough of some of Satan's devices to qualify me to lisp about them. And I account it a mercy the Lord, in compassion to my weakness, has encouraged me to pray, "Lead us not into temptation." Satan's power, I apprehend, is chiefly upon the imagination. His temptations may be considered under two heads—the terrible and the plausible. By the former he fights against our peace; by the latter he endeavours to ensnare us in our judgment or conduct. The former are the most distressing; the latter not the least dangerous. The former are often the lot of humble, tender-conscienced Christians; in the latter he has most success when we are careless and self-dependent. By the former he shows his rage and power as a roaring lion; by the latter his subtlety and address as a serpent or angel of light. His attacks in the former way are so vehement, as when he fills the mind with dark and horrible thoughts, blasphemies and suggestions, at which even fallen nature shudders and recoils (which is the case with many), that his interference is plainly to be felt. In the latter, his motions are so insinuating, and so connatural to the man of sin within us, that they cannot be easily distinguished from the workings of our own thoughts. I suppose that when Ananias attempted to deceive Peter, he was little aware that Satan had filled his heart, and helped him to the lie. But Satan has a near and intimate connection with the man of sin,—the heart while unrenewed is his workshop, Ephes. ii. 2. And it is the same with believers, so far as they are unrenewed. Therefore, I believe he is never nearer to us, or more busy with us, than at sometimes, when we are least apprehensive of him. We have no clear ideas of the agency of spirits, nor is it necessary. The Scripture says little to satisfy our curiosity; but tells us plainly that he is always watching us, and desiring to sift us as wheat. I believe we give him no more than his due, when we charge him with having a hand in all our sins. I believe he cuts us all out abundance of work. But the other kind of temptations, in which people are rather passive, though they often think themselves compliant, it is not appointed for all believers to feel, at least, not frequently, or in a violent degree.

A fine general representation of them we have in that part of the *Pilgrim's Progress* which describes Christian's passage through the Valley of the Shadow of Death. Bunyan had been an exercised mariner in these deep waters, and he writes like one. As tempted souls go through the most distress, so they usually have the most affecting and striking discoveries of the wisdom, power, and glory of the Lord, and acquire a sympathy for afflicted minds, and a skill in dealing with them which cannot easily be obtained by reading books. Something of this skill may be acquired from a careful observation of others, but experience is the best school. This lesson, is, however, so painful to flesh and blood, that we may be thankful if the Lord permits us to pass it over. I have had some little experience of these things; but my situation in Olney, amongst a poor afflicted people, who, from a confined and sedentary employment (lace-making), are mostly afflicted with low spirits and nervous disorders, has made me something of a theorist in the business, and I know not but I could write a volume upon it. But no words can adequately express the dreadful tempests some of God's dear children sustain. They pass through fire and floods; but He is with them, and therefore the floods

cannot drown them, nor the flame destroy them. I doubt
not but the severest part of Job's trials were of this kind.
. . . . Oh! if my heart were not still vile beyond expression, the commendation of the whole universe could have no other effect than to cover me with
blushes and confusion. Ah, dear sir! what would you
have thought of me had you seen me when I lived at the
Plantains? The sight of me would have been offensive
to your eyes, and my speech would have struck you with
horror. Miserable and despicable in every view; pinched
with want, and the common mark of scorn and insult,
my whole wretched amusement and pleasure seemed to
lie in blaspheming the name and person of Jesus, and in
feeding my imagination with schemes of wickedness which
I had not opportunity to perpetrate. The Lord has since
given me a name and a place among his children; favoured
me with the friendship and love of many of his most
honoured and excellent people upon earth. And I have
reason to thank him, likewise, that He has given me a habitual recollection of those past dreadful scenes; so that
there is seldom a day of my life in which my thoughts are
not led back to my former state of estrangement from him,
and that pre-eminence of wretchedness into which my sins
plunged me. I hope He has often sanctified this review, to
abate in some measure the force of the temptations I have
been since exposed to,—to think myself something. If He
gives me liberty in preaching, or enables me to write a
letter to please a fellow worm, should it not suffice to keep
me from being elated to remember that I am the same
person who once delighted to treat him as an impostor, to
rank him with, or upon the comparison below, *Mohammed?*
or to think that some of my unhappy companions (as I have
reason to fear) perished in their sins, who had just cause

to charge the ruin of their souls to my account? For Satan himself, had he been upon earth in a bodily shape, could hardly have been more industrious in tempting to infidelity and profligacy than I was. . . .

I am, dear Sir, your affectionate friend and servant,

OLNEY, BUCKS: *July* 10, 1778. JOHN NEWTON.

To the REV. W. BARLASS.

LETTER II.—His own experience—False zeal—Uncertainty of earthly good.

March 21.

MY DEAR FRIEND, . . . I begin my letter with a memorable date; it is the anniversary of my great deliverance, when the Lord sent from on high, and saved me from sinking in the great waters. I have lived thirty-five years since, alas! to too little purpose. What multiplied proofs have I had in this space of a nature deeply depraved! What multiplied proofs and instances have I likewise had of the Lord's goodness to a chief sinner! I have seen many changes of situation since the year 1734, when I left off the seafaring life; but my path from that time has been, upon the whole, comparatively smooth, and every principal change and turn in life has been apparently for the better. He has honoured me with some usefulness; and since my removal to London my sphere of service has been greatly enlarged, and very comfortable, only the effects of indwelling sin are a constant and humbling abatement. Ah! how seldom am I, in my study, what perhaps I appear to others to be when in the pulpit. Indeed, my friend, the lamentable inconsistencies I feel, now I know the Lord, ought to affect and abase me more than all the shocking abominations of my state of ignorance; for then I knew not what I did. But now light and experience, and acknowledgments, and repeated surrenders, aggravate the evils which are interwoven with my frame. But, by grace, I am what I am: it is of grace that my poor story is not much worse. The Lord is my keeper, therefore I am still preserved. I have not made shipwreck of my profession. He has not taken his word out of my mouth. It is still, I trust, the great desire and aim of my life to serve him; his work is still pleasant; and I find no sensible abatement either of bodily or mental powers; and He is still pleased to bear witness to the word of his grace from my unworthy lips. Blessed be God for Jesus Christ. In him I find peace in the midst of conflict, and power in the midst of extreme weakness. . . .

[After speaking of the zeal of a friend of his correspondent, Mr. Newton proceeds:—]

I wish I had more zeal myself, if I could regulate it and fix it to its proper objects. Oh! there are subjects and causes almost sufficient to make a stone speak. If I had a due sense of what is implied in the words sin and grace, of what passed at Golgotha, and of the states in the unseen world, surely I could not be the cold dull creature I now am! But when zeal spends itself about the less essential matters of forms and names, about points in which the wisest and the best have always differed, I would, if I could, lull it fast asleep. I there think it preposterous and hurtful, mistimed and misemployed; like the industry of a man who should be busied and engrossed in painting and adorning his house, when the house itself was on fire. Let the safety of the building be first consulted. Is it not strange, that when we profess to receive the New Testament as our rule, and to form our plans upon it, some of the plainest and most obvious precepts should be so generally overlooked? How plain is that in Rom. xv. 7. Now, how does Christ receive us? Does He wait till we are all exactly of a mind? Does He confine his regards, his grace, his presence, within the walls of a party? Is He the God of the Presbyterians, or the Independents only? Do not some amongst you, and some amongst us, know with equal certainty that He has received them? Do not they, and do not we, know what it is to taste that He is gracious? Does He not smile upon your ordinances and upon ours? Are not the fruits of true faith the same on both sides of the Tweed, and in every corner of the land? And shall zeal presume to come in with its "ifs" and its "buts," and to build up walls of separation between those who are joined to the Lord by one Spirit, in direct contradiction to the tenor of the whole of Rom. xiv., and think it has a right to despise and censure, to judge and condemn, when it is expressly forbidden to interfere? See Rom. xiv. 3, 4, 10, 13. The Lord, by his apostle, says, "Let every one be persuaded in his own mind." And how dares zeal say otherwise? Yet many true believers are so much under the spirit of self and prejudice, that they verily mean to do the Lord service by substituting their own commands in the room of his. And they see no harm in saying, You must think and act as I do, subscribe my paper, and worship in my way; or else, though I hope the Lord has received you, I think it my duty to keep my distance from you. This assuming, dictating spirit, appears to me to be Popery, though amongst us in a Protestant form; indeed the root and source whence most of the Popish abominations have sprung. It is pretty much the same to me, whether the Scriptures are locked up from me or not, if I must read them with another person's eyes. I think we have all an equal right to judge for ourselves, and that we are no more bound to follow implicitly the *sic volumus, sic jubemus,* or the *sic arbitramur** of a bench of bishops, or a board of Independents, or a General Assem-

---

* "So we will," "so we command," "so we ordain."

bly, than of a conclave of cardinals. . . . We expected Mrs. Cunningham in April, and hoped she would live with us. But now we expect to hear of her death every day; for the last letters afford us no hope of her recovery. We were united, not only by the ties of a natural relation, but by a long and endeared friendship, and a participation in the same faith. We had proposed much pleasure in the thought of living together a few years upon earth; and still we may hope to meet and live together in a better world, where disappointment and separation shall not be known. Surely the Lord's design, by these dispensations, is to bring us more and more into the frame of the psalmist, when he said, "My soul, wait thou *only* upon God; for my expectation is from him." Cisterns must be broken, but the fountain of living waters is always full and always flowing. Gourds must wither, but the tree of life has shade and fruit sufficient for us all, and at all times. Creatures must die, but the Lord liveth. Creatures are like candles; while they burn they waste, and when they are extinguished, those who depend upon them are covered with darkness. But the Lord is a Sun to his people, and his bright beams can well supply the want of the candle-light of creature comforts. In this world we must be often sorrowing; but we have cause likewise for rejoicing evermore. . . .

Mrs. Newton joins me in love. We wish your physicians or friends would send you to London, for there are few persons whom we love without having seen them, whom we should be more heartily glad to see than Mr. Barlass. Remember us at the throne of grace, and let us hear from you when you can.

I am sincerely and affectionately yours,
JOHN NEWTON.

HOXTON: *March* 27, 1783.

Miss Jane Flower,

AFTERWARDS MRS. DAWSON.

THE following letters show in what esteem Mrs. Dawson was held by Mr. Newton, and indirectly exhibit some of the more prominent features of character by which she was distinguished.

Mrs. Dawson was the daughter of Mr. George Flower; a London merchant, and for many years deacon of the church at White Row, Spitalfields. Her elder sister was married to the Rev. J. Clayton of the Weighhouse Chapel. Mrs. Dawson was educated at Northampton by Mrs. Trinder, whose school had at that time attained a deserved eminence. Many ladies afterwards known in the religious world, received their first serious impressions under Mrs. Trinder's judicious training. Mr. Newton was a frequent visitor at the house, and his addresses to the young people were greatly appreciated by them. It was probably here that he first became acquainted with Miss Flower.

In 1782, Miss Flower was united in marriage to John Dawson, Esq. of Aldcliffe Hall, Lancaster—a union which was somewhat suddenly terminated in May 1804, Mrs. Dawson surviving till December 1826.

We are informed that the subject of our notice was possessed of great intelligence and conversational powers, was remarkable for amiability and the cultivation of every Christian grace, and was honoured and beloved by a large circle of friends like-minded with herself.

To Miss Flower.

LETTER I.—How to overcome the snares of the world.

October 3, 1778.

MY DEAR MISS FLOWER,—You would have me tell you what are the best means to be used by a young person, to prevent the world, with all its opening and ensnaring scenes, from drawing the heart aside from God. It is an important question; but I apprehend your own heart will tell you, that you are already possessed of all the information concerning it which you can well expect from me. I could only attempt to answer it from the Bible, which lies open to you likewise. If your heart is like mine, it must confess, that when it turns aside from God, it is seldom through ignorance of the proper means or motives which should have kept us near him, but rather from an evil principle within, which prevails against our better judgment, and renders us unfaithful to light already received.

I could offer you rules, cautions, and advices in abundance; for I find it comparatively easy to preach to others. But if you should further ask me, how you shall effectually reduce them to practice, I feel that I am so deficient, and so much at a loss in this matter *myself*, that I know not well what to say to *you*. Yet something must be said.

In the first place, then, I would observe, that though it be our bounden duty, and the highest privilege we can propose to ourselves, to have our hearts kept close to the Lord, yet we must not expect it absolutely or perfectly, much less all at once: we shall keep close to him, in proportion as we are solidly convinced of the infinite disparity between him and the things which would presume to stand in competition with him, and the folly, as well as ingratitude, of departing from him. But these points are only to be learned by experience, and by smarting under a series of painful disappointments in our expectations from creatures. Our judgments may be quickly satisfied that his favour is better than life, while yet it is in the power of a mere trifle to turn us aside. The Lord permits us to feel our weakness, that we may be sensible of it; for though we are ready in words to confess that we are weak, we do not so properly know it, till that secret, though unallowed dependence we have upon some strength in ourselves, is brought to the trial, and fails us. To be humble, and like a little child, afraid of taking a step alone, and so conscious of snares and dangers around us, as to cry to him continually to hold us up that we may be safe, is the sure, the infallible, the only secret of walking closely with him.

But how shall we attain this humble frame of spirit? It must be, as I said, from a real and sensible conviction of our weakness and vileness, which we cannot learn (at least I have not been able to learn it) merely from books or preachers. The providence of God concurs with his Holy Spirit in his merciful design of making us acquainted with ourselves. It is indeed a great mercy to be preserved from such declensions as might fall under the notice of our fellow-creatures; but when *they* can observe nothing of consequence to object to us, things may be far from right with us in the sight of him who judges not only actions, but the thoughts and first motions of the heart. And indeed could we for a season so cleave to God as to find little or nothing in ourselves to be ashamed of, we are such poor creatures, that we should presently grow vain and self-sufficient, and expose ourselves to the greatest danger of falling.

There are, however, means to be observed on our part; and though you know them, I will repeat the principal, because you desire me. The first is prayer; and here, above all things, we should pray for humility. It may be called both the guard of all other graces, and the soil in which they grow. The second, attention to the Scripture. Your question is directly answered in Psal. cxix. 9. The precepts are our rule and delight, the promises our strength and encouragement: the good recorded of the saints is proposed for our encouragement; their miscarriages are as landmarks set up to warn us of the rocks and shoals which lie in the way of our passage. The study of the whole scheme of gospel salvation, respecting the person, life, doctrine, death, and glory of our Redeemer, is appointed to form our souls to a spiritual and divine taste; and so far as this prevails and grows in us, the trifles that would draw us from the Lord will lose their influence, and appear divested of the glare with which they strike the senses, mere vanity and nothing. The third grand means is consideration or recollection; a careful regard to those temptations and snares, to which, from our tempers, situations, or connexions, we are more immediately exposed, and by which we have been formerly hindered. It may be well in the morning, ere we leave our chambers, to forecast, as far as we are able, the probable circumstances of the day before us. Yet the observance of this, as well as of every rule that can be offered, may dwindle into a mere form. However, I trust the Lord, who has given you a desire to live to him, will be your guard and teacher. There is none teacheth like him.

I am, etc.

To Miss Flower.

LETTER II.—King Alphonso's folly—Happiness of the married state—Sketch of sermon—A believer's complaints—How to treat them.

MY DEAR MISS JENNY,—Your letter came last night, and I begin my answer this morning. It is well to be you, as they say at Olney. But I write in such haste, for fear I should not be able to write at all while you are abroad;

for I hope, by this time, you are beginning to be homesick, and that you will make haste back. The *Goode* people*
you are with (to whom present our love), are now old-married folks. They are sufficient company for each other,—the Adam and Eve,—and may be safely left together. Therefore, make haste, take a peep at Northampton, and set your face homewards before floods, and storms, and snows make the country and the road quite unpleasant.

I hope, however, that while you continue abroad you will be happy and easy. How could you tantalize me with mentioning cottages and hills peeping between them? Cottages, hills, woods, birds and brooks, are words which always set my imagination on its tip-toes till sober judgment interposes and commands it to sit down again. Even admitting that Potters Pury far exceeds Windsor or Clifton, and were it June instead of November, neither the place nor the company should tempt me to wish myself *there* when the Lord appoints me to be *here*. Now, I am getting into the right track; so farewell jocularity, except I should meet thee again towards the bottom of the letter.

It is reported of a king of Spain, or rather of Portugal, that he presumed to say that if God had consulted him at the creation about the dispositions and motions of the planets, he would have contrived them better than they are. I suppose the poor man took the schemes and dreams of the astronomers of his day to be a just representation of the system. It sounds, however, like a blasphemous speech in our ears. We take it for granted that the Sun, the Moon, Jupiter, and the rest are exactly where they should be, and move just as they ought. But if we are content the Lord should manage the heavenly bodies

---

* The Rev. J. Goode and Mrs. Goode of Potters Pury. Mr. Goode was afterwards minister of the Independent church at White Row, London.

without our assistance, we are ready enough to advise him how He should dispose of our insignificant selves. We think we could point at twenty things in our situation which might be mended; and that we should serve him much better than we do if we were but at liberty to choose where and how we would be thus placed. Thus we can gravely censure the vanity and folly of King Alphonso, without being aware that the thoughts *we* sometimes indulge are no less arrogant than his, and that we might with as much reason offer to assist him in the government of the universe as in the direction of our own paltry concerns. I hope, however, as we grow older we shall grow wiser, and be more satisfied, that whether we are placed in town or country, whether we are sick or well, the present circumstances for the present time must be the best, because of his appointment.

We were very glad to hear that you had all a good journey. The vanity of human life and all its prospects has been sometimes confirmed by grievous disasters happening on a bridal day. Tell your friends I both congratulate and condole them. They will, I hope, by this marriage experience many comforts which they would have missed. They certainly will experience some inquietudes which they might have avoided, if they had been *wedded* to a single life. But if they can come near the golden medium, love each other very well and not too well, I think they will, on the whole, be better off than the solitary folks. I think to a feeling mind there is no temporal pleasure equal to the pleasure of friendship; and no friendship to be compared with that between man and wife, when their union is sanctified by grace and the Lord's blessing.

You heard the close of Jacob before you left town. I

have since entered upon Deut. xxxiii. 26–29. We have had two slices from this dish; and if you do not stay very long you may come in for a share before it is all gone. The first sermon was from ver. 26; the second from the first clause of ver. 27—The eternal God is thy refuge. If you wish to know what I said, ask Mr. Goode to preach from it, and it is very likely he will point out to you my leading ideas. It is a plain text, and I think you may preach to yourself from it, without asking either him or me what it means. However, as you do not read Hebrew, I will tell you that the word rendered refuge signifies more generally a habitation; or, as we say, a home. The eternal God is the church's dwelling place, and, consequently, the dwelling place of every believer. This dwelling place I considered in two respects: First,—A hiding place; and this likewise two-fold,—a sanctuary from guilt and punishment, and a castle or place of security from enemies. Second.—A resting place, where provision is made for every want, and such satisfaction is enjoyed as the world cannot afford. I leave you to guess out the rest. When you have finished your sermon you may observe that a believer, like a snail, go where he will, has his house with him and is always at home, because he dwells in God. I expect to close the subject of the Transfiguration next Sunday evening. What will be my next subject as yet I know not; but hope the Lord will show me in due time.

As to your complaints, you may diversify them as much as you please, but the apostle has said all that you mean in one short expression, "When I would do good, evil is present with me." I presume you cannot expect to be better, or better off than he was. The most pleasant and profitable course we can take is to be thankful. Let us praise the Lord that we know our disease and know our physician; that He has undertaken our case, and will, consequently, perfect it. But let us pray for patience and submission to be willing to wait his time, and to take things in his way. The plain English of half our complaints is that we don't like the cross. We would have victory without conflicts, and the crown without fighting for it. And while we lament many of the evils, we are apt to overlook or make light of the chief of all, which is the impatient workings of self, which would have everything its own way. We are, we must be, sinners while we remain here; but if we are sinners believing in the name of Jesus we may rejoice and sing. We *must* fight, we *may* be wounded, but we cannot be overcome. We may complain to the Lord; but when we write or speak to our fellow Christians, we should encourage each other and say, Let us love, and sing, and wonder.

I have had the rheumatism in my face, then in my back, then in my sides. I believe if I had kept a curate I should have been very bad; but necessity having no law I went forth to preach, and the pulpit cured me once and again.

When have I written so long a letter, especially in one day? If it pleases you, I am glad. If a single line, by the Lord's blessing, administers comfort or benefit, I shall be more glad. I compare my letter writing to fishing. A fisherman knows not what sort or size of fish he shall catch when he puts down the hook; but he knows as well as I can tell what sort of a letter I shall write when I take up the pen. I would send you turbot or tench if I could catch them; but if not, such as I can get rather than send none.

And now with our joint love to you and your friends,

and wishing you a good night, and much of the Lord's presence by night and by day,

I remain, your affectionate and obliged.

JOHN NEWTON.

HOXTON: *October 9.*

To MISS FLOWER.

LETTER III.—Regret at their separation, yet present with one another in spirit.

MY DEAR MISS FLOWER,—I thank you for your packet, and I thank the Lord for your friendship. It was He who formed it, and it shall be maintained by him. Neither absence nor distance shall affect it. It shall flourish amongst the amaranths, the incorruptibles and immortals of a better world. Hoping, believing and praying that the Lord will graciously make Mr. Dawson and you very happy together, and that his providence is leading you to a situation in which He has already designed to make you a blessing to many, I shall resign you with as good a grace as I can. It will give me a pleasing pain, a sorrowful sort of joy, and a great satisfaction mingled with a few grains of regret to join your hands, and then to say "Farewell." The pain I shall endeavour to keep to myself, and only wear the livery of pleasure and joy on the occasion. Do not suspect me of insensibility if I wear the best side outwards. But I have a request to make, or rather a demand. This approaching closing piece of service with which you propose to honour me is, must, and shall be its own reward. I will not be paid for it. And if, after this declaration of mine, the least word, look, or hint were to pass to alter this, my determination, I will not say I shall be offended; that would be too harsh; but I should be grieved, pinched, and hurt exceedingly. I will no more pocket any money on this occasion than I will pocket a red-hot heater.

If I now lived at Olney, I would promise to be a tolerable correspondent; but you know how I am circumstanced here, and, therefore, if I should be tardy, you will impute it to the right cause, or to any cause but the want of affection. However, if the old proverb stands good, "That where there is a will there is a way," I am ready to flatter myself I shall behave tolerably well on that head. As to advice, I do not think that you will need any; but to read the Bible and ply the throne of grace, and even this to you is not needful. The wisdom from above which is necessary and sufficient to guide you in every branch of your department, is to be had for asking. You will ask it, and consequently will have it. Every day will bring with it its own duties and comforts, and in one degree or another its own trials; and together with these it will bring you new supports and new instructions. I have reason to be thankful if I have been in any way serviceable to you. What I am in myself you know better than most others, by the recollection of what you have taken the trouble to read. However, with all my follies I am capable of esteeming and returning your friendship, and you may be assured in a few words, which my heart easily dictates, that there is hardly a person whose removal from London I could more sensibly feel than yours. However, we shall not be properly separated. Spirits need not be much affected by local distance. The throne of grace is the central point where those who are united to the Lord have one common home, and may meet daily. I shall sometimes think of you when you are not just thinking of me. I shall sometimes be in your thoughts when you are not in mine; but very often our thoughts will meet and join at the same instant. I have very little expectation of paying you a visit in Lancaster; but my mind will often be there, and thus we shall go on in our respective paths of duty, till He whose we are and whom we serve, shall say, Come up hither. Then we shall part to meet no more, and so shall we ever be with the Lord. May the God of all grace make you happy in yourselves, and in each other, and in all your connections. This will often be the prayer of your very affectionate and obliged

Friend and servant,

JOHN NEWTON.

To MRS. DAWSON.

LETTER IV.—Desire for her spiritual welfare—Lot's wife—Renewed expressions of friendship.

August 30, 1782.

MY DEAR MADAM,—Amid a variety of business I had nearly forgotten how easily I might send you a letter by Mr. Clayton.* I fear the notice is too short for me to write much; but will do my best, and will also lend you a couple of franks,† which I hope you will repay me as soon as you can, and with large interest. Your letter gave us pleasure, and I thank you for it. I do not wonder you were serious and thoughtful on your wedding day. I was so on mine. Indeed, I was so on yours. That may well be called an important hour which will have some influence upon every future hour of life. It may be compared to a gate admitting us into a road, from which, when we have once entered, there is no retreat. You will at times be

---

* The Rev. John Clayton of the Weigh House, London.

† A reference to the privilege then enjoyed by members of Parliament of sending letters free of postage, upon attaching their names to the direction. These franks were often given to their friends.

exposed to some exercises of which you had no idea in the single state; and I would observe that to be at all points and in every way happy in this world, is what we must not expect. It is polluted and cannot be our rest. The present condition of things exposes us to changes; and the remaining depravity of our hearts renders them necessary to us. But I hope you will always feel cause for thankfulness for comparative happiness, and that you will always be surrounded with a thousand blessings and comforts, of which many people are destitute, and will thereby be excited to praise him, who makes a difference between you and them. Above all, I hope you will obtain growing views of the Lord's wisdom, goodness, and faithfulness, and be enabled simply and heartily to prefer his management for you, to any choice you could possibly make for yourself. If we were perfectly united to his holy will we should be continually pleased; for all things take place according to his wise and holy will, and not a sparrow falls to the ground without him. That is best for us which is best for our souls, which is most suited to preserve us in a spirit of prayer and dependence, to keep our hearts awake to the vanity of earthly things, and to raise them upwards to a better world. I know the Lord has given you an enlarged idea of the proper temper and spirit to which the gospel is designed to form us. You have, I believe, an ambition to live to him, to serve him with your all, and to thirst for a conformity to his image in humility, spirituality, and benevolence. It is He who wrought in you thus to will, and He will work in you to do likewise according to his good pleasure. You are not altogether ignorant of Satan's devices, but now your situation is changed, he will probably change his methods of attack; but if the Lord keeps you sensible of your own weakness, if you look to him for strength and grace, you will not fear. You will discover and avoid every snare, and new conflicts shall ensure you new victories. To his gracious care I commend you, and doubt not but He will surely do you good.

Next Sunday evening, if the Lord pleases, we are to try to gain some instruction by looking at Lot's wife in the shape of a pillar of salt. Were you to ask me what I shall say about it, I could only tell you, in general, that it is a sad thing for those who have begun to make a profession to look back to the world they have seemed to forsake. There are too many such statues, stiffened with a lifeless form of godliness, who are dead, though they have a name to live.

I did not doubt, from Mr. Burder's[*] general character, that you would like him. I trust he will still grow upon you as you become more acquainted with him. I shall rejoice to hear that the Lord so blesses the ordinances to you, that you find not the least regret on that account for leaving London. Though you did not outwardly belong to my fold, yet I presumed to consider myself as a sort of co-pastor with Mr. Trotman,[†] as far as you were concerned. This part of my connection with you I cheerfully resign to Mr. Burder; but my place in your friendship I cannot consent to give up to any one. You will always be very near and dear to my heart. Your mother obliged us this afternoon with a ride to Highgate, and we had your nephew, Master John,[‡] with us. He is a very entertaining companion, and does me the honour to pay a particular attention to

---

[*] The Rev. George Burder, then minister at Lancaster, afterwards at Coventry, and finally at Fetter Lane, London. He was secretary to the London Missionary Society, and author of *Village Sermons*, etc.

[†] The Rev. Nathaniel Trotman, pastor of the church at White Row London.

[‡] Afterwards the Rev. John Clayton of the Poultry Chapel, London.

me. I have taken a place to go to Hastings to spend a few days with Mr. Thornton, who is there. I shall then have another interview with my old acquaintance, the sea; but I must converse with it at a distance, for Mrs. Newton will not allow me to go upon it. After the Lord has preserved me so often across the wide ocean, she is not willing to trust me to sail a few hours. You may think her wrong, but you will blame her very gently now you are yourself a wife; but perhaps you will soon learn to think Mr. Dawson is most safe when he is in your sight. Let me now add my love (the best thing I have to send him), and which Mrs. Newton sends to you both. May the Lord bless you abundantly, in yourselves and to each other, and when you are near the throne of grace, remember,

Your very affectionate friend,
JOHN NEWTON.

To MRS. DAWSON.

LETTER V.—On compliance with the practices of the world.

August 6, 1783.

MY DEAR MADAM,—[After a reference to the fact mentioned by Mrs. Dawson, that she had been invited to go to the theatre, and some strictures on the inconsistency of professors indulging in such entertainments, Mr. Newton proceeds as follows]: We cannot too much cultivate that spirit of love which disposes us to believe and hope the best we can of others. The Lord has favoured you with this disposition, and taught you to be a strict critic over your own conduct, and to make all favourable allowances for your neighbours. This is right. But our tenderness should not teach us to deviate from the standard of his word. There we read that the desires of the flesh, and of the eyes, and of the pride of life, constitute that spirit of the world which stands in direct opposition to his grace. And we may depend upon it that they who do not perceive this opposition, as with a glance of the eye, are some way or other defective in their views of the gospel. That religion which does not engage the whole heart for the Lord can be little better than a name. The comforts of the gospel neither require nor admit such poor assistance as worldly amusements offer. The new nature and the old have each their respective, proper food, suited to their different appetites and relish; and what is nourishing to one is death to the other.

The best that I can say of professors that hanker after the world is, that if they are not entirely dead, they are at least lamentably sick. It indicates a distempered constitution, and till they are debarred such trash, they will not recover their natural appetite. I must thus judge of gospel hearers, who are to be seen at one time sitting under the ordinances, and at others mixing with that world, at their plays, assemblies, or other diversions: either they never had a savour of divine things, or they have lost it. And to join with them in their follies, far from being the way to gain them, is the direct way to harden them, and to deceive them. And they are much more likely to draw us into the same spirit, than we are to reclaim them to a better conduct. "Let your moderation be known to all men." How much is that poor word, "moderation" misunderstood and abused. It is very different from that lukewarmness and indifference which many excuse and justify by the term. In popular language we speak of white as a colour; but philosophers tell us that white is properly no colour itself, but is formed by a union and combination of all the coloured rays of light. The union of two or three or more of them will form a compound of colours; but if they are all blended and reflected together, the effect will be a perfect white. Thus, moderation is not a grace distinct from others, or designed to correct any grace which would be extreme, or too strong without it; but it is the result, the united effect of all the graces of the Spirit—zeal, love, faithfulness, meekness, tenderness, humility, and the rest. All contribute to produce it. And the reason why instances of true moderation are so rare, is that there are few who have their zeal balanced by proportionate knowledge, or their gentleness stimulated by a due regard to the honour of God or the importance of truth. In the character of our Saviour as man we see all these Divine rays, in their vivid brightness perfectly combined and concentrated, and therefore He is a perfect example of true moderation. But, oh! how unlike is the character of many who bear his name and talk of moderation to this! They are neither enthusiasts nor profligates. They hope they mean well, and they hope that others mean as well as they. Such is their idea of moderation.

. . .

Your sincere and affectionate friend and servant,
JOHN NEWTON.

To Mrs. Dawson.

LETTER VI.—Knowledge of our hearts—What may be learnt from children—Deprivation of ordinances.

October 31, 1788.

MY DEAR MADAM,—Your letter found me at Weston, which you may remember is a mile and a half from Olney, and where Mr. Cowper and Mrs. Unwin now reside. Our head quarters were with those dear friends for a little more than three weeks; whence I made almost daily excursions amongst my old friends. We made one digression to Northampton and Creaton. We found Mrs. Unwin well, and Mr. Cowper rather getting forward in his gradual manner. He is cheerful in company, but the ground of his inward distress is not yet wholly removed.

Now I must take your epistle in paragraphs. If my letters afford you either profit or pleasure I am fully repaid, and I would write you many more if I could, but you wrong my affection if you estimate what I would do, by what is actually in my power to perform. I have not much to add on the subject of the ignorant poor. I can easily believe your difficulties and obstacles on this head are many and great, and have no reason to doubt your willingness to improve any opportunities that might offer. Be not discouraged. Perhaps you may find an opening where you least expected. While we remain upon earth we are in the Lord's school, and a principal lesson we have to learn is a knowledge of ourselves, and this can only be attained by a painful experience. Books, sermons, letters cannot teach it, nor can the observations we make on other people lead us far beyond the theory. To have some tolerable ideas of the human heart in general is one thing, to know our own hearts is quite a different thing. The deceitfulness of the heart which we allow in words, enables it to disguise, conceal, and cover its own emotions, so that the supposed sense we have of its deceitfulness is often the very thing that deceives us. We say that the sea is deceitful, and with reason. It sometimes looks so smooth and glossy that no one who has not tried it would think it dangerous; but this is only in a calm. A small breeze will ruffle it, and in a storm it roars and rages. But the heart is more deceitful than the sea. It will swell and rage when there seems no wind to put it in motion or to awaken any suspicion. If I feel impatience and discontent under the pressure of great troubles I am apt to blame the tempest for all the commotion and to excuse my own heart which tells me it would behave better in circumstances more favourable. But when the state of affairs is quite placid, when I have no trial worth mentioning, when I see myself surrounded with comforts, so that being judge in my own case I am forced to confess that I have a highly favoured lot, and can think of no person on earth with whom I would wish to change, if even these trifles, light as air, are sufficient to discompose me, and a word or a look not to my mind makes me for the time insensible to all my undeserved mercies, then I find my heart is deceitful indeed. It can raise itself into foam and fury, without being able to assign any tolerable cause for the uproar. But still the heart must be excused and will attempt to throw the blame upon the animal spirits, upon the nerves, or upon anything rather than charge the evil to its own pride and ingratitude. I wish we were better, but it is of importance to know (so far as we are able to bear it) how bad we really are. For they will most prize the physician, and most readily comply with his prescription, who are most sensible of the malignity of their disease.

I join with you in praising the Lord for his goodness. I understand the little stranger is to be called Jane, a name to which I am a little partial for the sake of some who bear it. If she is spared to you, I trust your best endeavours to teach her the good ways of the Lord will not be wanting, and you will find that while a child and even an infant she will be a teacher to you. You will be often reminded of that text, "Like as a father (or a mother) pitieth a child, so the Lord pitieth them that fear Him." And when you are forced to overrule the inclinations of the child whom you love and wish to gratify, when she cries because she cannot have what you know would be hurtful to her, and when a regard to her health constrains you to give her some salutary pains, you will be led to notice the true cause of many of your disappointments and trials. Should you see her sometimes misconstrue your tenderness, and think you unkind, notwithstanding a thousand daily proofs of your love and care, because you cannot comply with her wishes in every point, you will see in her too much of my picture, and something of your own. On the other hand the pleasure you will find in her affection and obedience, the readiness with which you will forgive her faults when she is sensible of them, and how much more you are disposed to caress her than to frown upon her, these feelings will lead your thoughts to our heavenly Father, who delights in our prosperity, does not willingly afflict us, nor permit us to be in heaviness without a need be for it. Thus while we are in the Lord's school, as I hinted, and desire to be taught by him, we may be always learning, even though we should not be favoured with public preaching of the gospel. An attention to the Bible will enable us to derive profitable instruction from children, servants, friends, enemies, comforts and crosses, from all we see, hear, or meet with in the daily course of life. I think it cannot be well with us if we do not set a high value upon gospel ordinances. They are designed and adapted to feed and refresh our souls. Yet we may in some circumstances over-rate them. They are not so indispensably necessary but that we may feel and grow and thrive without them, provided the want of them is not owing to our neglect or indolence or to their being providentially out of our reach. They may in that case be well supplied by a stedfast application to the word of grace and the throne of grace. My friend Mrs. Gardiner has been confined to her drawing-room and chamber these five years. For so long a time she has not been able to set a foot down a single stair, nor does she ever expect it. Yet I think a more lively, cheerful, exemplary Christian than she, is scarcely to be found in London. And since it is the will of God to confine her, she seems to have no more desire to go out of the door than out of her chamber window. The God of ordinances is, at all times and in all places, near to those who love and seek him, and He is all-sufficient to make up and to make good whatever they seem to want. So I found it during the last two or three years that I was at sea. I had not then so much light and knowledge as I have been favoured with since, but I had a certain fervour of spirit in communion with God upon the vast ocean, at a distance from the public means, without the help of a Christian friend, (yea, though I was engaged ignorantly in the wretched slave-trade,) which I should be glad to feel at present. . . .

My best wishes attend you and Mr. Dawson and Miss Jane.

I am, your sincere and
Affectionate friend and servant,
John Newton.

Mrs. Hannah More.

THERE are few, if any, of our readers who are ignorant of the history of this distinguished and most useful woman; who have not become acquainted with the remarkable story of the talents and accomplishments which at an early period of life introduced Miss More into the highest circles of the literary and fashionable world, of her religious enlightenment, and of her energetic and devoted labours, in connexion with her sisters, in the establishment of schools in the darkest neighbourhoods around her and over a wide extent of country, and of the great success, notwithstanding bitter opposition, which followed these efforts, and finally of her tracts and other writings which achieved so extraordinary a popularity: truly a wonderful instance of the blessed fruits of talents sanctified and consecrated to the service of God.

Mr. Newton's acquaintance with Mrs. More commenced in 1787. She had read *Cardiphonia*. Struck with its truths, and the manner in which they were presented she sought to know its author, and an interesting correspondence was the result. In the autumn of 1791 Mr. Newton visited Cowslip Green, the residence of Mrs. More, when, as he tells us in his journal, he preached on the Sunday at Shipham to the children of Mrs. More's Sunday school. "It was a pleasing sight: the whole congregation were attentive, and I was favoured with liberty." He officiated again in the afternoon at Wrington, and in the evening had a parlour preaching.

In reference to this visit Mrs. More wrote soon after:—
"I assure you your kind wishes and affectionate remembrance of the mountains of Mendip, and of the little hermitage at the foot of it, are returned with great sincerity. Your pipe still maintains its station in the black-currant tree, and that hand would be deemed very presumptuous and disrespectful which should presume to displace it. For my own part, the pipe of Tityrus, though

in my youthful days I liked it passing well, would now not be deemed a more valuable relic. And even the little sick maid Lizzy, who gratefully remembers the spiritual comfort you administered to her, often cries out, 'Oh dear! I hope nobody will break Mr. Newton's pipe.' . . . Patty and I remember you as we are trotting over the hills. She desires her affectionate regards, as do all the rest. . . . Adieu, my dear sir. May the remainder of your peregrinations be prosperous. Pray remember that no one stands more in need of your prayers than your most obliged and faithful,

"H. MORE."

Some lines were written by Mr. Newton in Mrs. More's album on occasion of this visit to Cowslip Green.

To Mrs. Hannah More.

LETTER I.—Love of rural scenery; but other sights more attractive—Spiritual blessings to be obtained only from Christ, to whom we must come as sinners—The perception of spiritual things gradual.

1787.

MY DEAR MADAM,—It is high time to thank you for your favour of the first of November. Indeed I have been thinking so for two or three weeks past; and perhaps it is well for you that my engagements will not permit me to write when I please.

Your hermitage! My imagination went to work at that, and presently built one, I will not say positively as pretty as yours, but very pretty. It stood (indeed without a foundation) upon a southern declivity, fronting an inland prospect, with an infant river, that is a brook, running between. Little thought was spent upon the house, but if I could describe the garden, the sequestered walks, and the beautiful colours with which the soil, the shrubs, and the thickets were painted, I think you would like the spot. But I awoke, and behold, it was a dream. My dear friend William Cowper has hardly a stronger enthusiasm for rural scenery than myself; and my favourite turn was amply indulged during the sixteen years I lived at Olney. The noises which surround me in my present situation of carriages and carts and London cries, is a strong contrast to the sound of falling waters, and the notes of thrushes and nightingales. But London, noisy and dirty as it is, is my post, and if not directly my choice, has a much more powerful recommendation: it was chosen for me by the wisdom and goodness of him, whose I trust I am, and whom it is my desire to serve; and therefore I am well satisfied with it; and, if this busy imagination (always on the wing) would go to sleep, I would not awaken her to build me hermitages: I want none.

The prospect of a numerous and attentive congregation, with which I am favoured from the pulpit, exceeds all that the mountains and lakes of Westmoreland can afford; and their singing, when their eyes tell me their voices come from the heart, is more melodious in my ear than the sweetest music of the woods. But were I not a servant, who has neither right nor reason to wish for himself, yet has the noblest wish he is capable of forming gratified,— I say, were it not for my public services, and I were compelled to choose for myself, I would wish to live near your hermitage, that I might sometimes have the pleasure of conversing with you, and admiring your flowers and garden, provided I could likewise at proper seasons hear from others that joyful sound which is now the business, the happiness, and the honour of my life to proclaim myself.

What you are pleased to say, my dear madam, of the

state of your mind I understand perfectly well. I praise God on your behalf, and I hope I shall earnestly pray for you. I have stood upon that ground myself, and I see what you yet want to set you quite at ease; and, though I cannot give it you, I trust that He who has already taught you what to desire, will in his own best time do everything for you, and in you, which is necessary to make you as happy as is compatible with the present state of infirmity and warfare. But He must be waited on and waited for to do this; and for your encouragement it is written, as in golden letters, over the gate of his mercy, "Ask, and ye shall receive; knock, and it shall be opened to you." We are apt to wonder that, when what we accounted hindrances are removed, and the things which we conceived would be great advantages are put within our power, there is a secret something in the way which proves itself to be independent of all external changes, because it is not affected by them. The disorder we complain of is internal, and in allusion to our Lord's words on another occasion, I may say, it is not that which surrounds us, it is not anything in our outward situation (provided it be not actually unlawful) that can prevent or even retard our advances in religion: we are defiled and impeded by that which is within. So far as our hearts are right, all places and circumstances, which his wise and good providence allots us, are nearly equal. Such hindrances will prove helps, such losses gains; and crosses will ripen into comforts. But, till we are so far apprized of the nature of our disease, as to put ourselves into the hands of the great and only Physician, we shall find, like the woman in Luke viii. 43, that every other effort for relief will leave us as it found us.

Our first thought, when we begin to be displeased with

ourselves, and sensible that we have been wrong, is to attempt to reform, to be sorry for what is amiss, and to endeavour to amend. It seems reasonable to ask, What can we do more? But while we think we can do so much as this we do not fully understand the design of the gospel. This gracious message from the God who knows our frame, speaks home to our case. It treats us as sinners, as those who have already broken the original law of our nature, in departing from God our Creator, Supreme Lawgiver and Benefactor, and in having lived to ourselves, instead of devoting all our time, talents, and influence to his glory. As sinners, the first things we need are pardon, reconciliation, and a principle of life and conduct entirely new. Till then we can have no more success or comfort from our endeavours than a man who should attempt to walk while his ankle was dislocated. The bone must be reduced before he can take a single step with safety, or attempt it without increasing his pain. For these purposes we are directed to Jesus Christ, as the wounded Israelites were to look at the brazen serpent (John iii. 14, 15). When we understand what the Scripture teaches of the person, love, and offices of Christ, the necessity and final causes of his humiliation unto death, and feel our own need of such a Saviour, we then know him to be the light, the sun of the world and of the soul, the source of all spiritual light, life, comfort and influence; having access to God by him, and receiving out of his fulness grace for grace.

Our perception of these things is for a time faint and indistinct like the peep of dawn; but the dawning light though faint is the sure harbinger of approaching day (Prov. iv. 18). The full-grown oak that overtops the wood, spreads its branches wide, and has struck its roots to a proportionable depth and extent into the soil, springs from a little acorn. Its daily growth, had it been daily watched from its appearance above ground, would have been imperceptible, yet it was always upon the increase. It has known a variety of seasons. It has sustained many a storm, but in time it attained to maturity, and now is likely to stand for ages. The beginnings of spiritual life are small likewise in the true Christian. He likewise passes through a succession of various dispensations, but he advances, though silently and slowly, yet surely, and will stand for ever.

At the same time it must be admitted that the Christian life is a warfare. Much within us and much without us must be resisted. In such a world as this, and with such a nature as ours, there will be a call for habitual self-denial. We must learn to cease from depending upon our own wisdom, power, and goodness, and from self-complacence and self-seeking, that we may rely on him whose wisdom and power are infinite.

Commending you to his care and blessing,

I remain, my dear madam, with great sincerity,

Your affectionate and obliged servant,

JOHN NEWTON.

To Mrs. Hannah More.

LETTER II.—Idolatrous love of his wife—Creature love and divine love.

I HAVE begun to levy prayers and praises on my dear friends, and I was about applying to you for your quota of the contribution, when your letter came. You will observe that I ask not only for prayers but also for praises on my behalf. I could begin every letter with the words of David, "Oh magnify the Lord with me, and let us exalt his name together." Great has been his goodness. I am a wonder to many and to myself. You perhaps know, madam, from what you have read of mine, and possibly from what you have seen in me, that my attachment to my dearest was great, yea excessive, yea idolatrous. It was so when it began. I think no writer of romances ever imagined more than I realized. She was to me precisely (how can I write it?) in the place of God. By degrees He who has the only right to my heart, and who alone can fill it, was pleased to make me sensible of his just claim, and my idol was brought some steps lower down. Yet still I fear there was somewhat of the golden calf in my love, from the moment that we joined our hands to the moment of separation.

[After a relation of the particulars of Mrs. Newton's death, and of the wonderful manner in which Divine support was afforded him, he proceeds:]

Now, my dear madam, I have done. I shall trouble you with no more in this strain. . . .

The blessed God is an infinite object, and our obligations to him as creatures, and especially as redeemed sinners, are immense. And therefore those who know him and truly love him will always be sensible that their love, when in the most lively exercise, is very disproportionate to what it ought to be, and that their warmest returns of gratitude and service fall far short of what they owe him for his goodness. They who think they love him enough certainly do not love him aright, and a jealousy lest our love should not be cordial, effectual, and entire, is rather a favourable sign than otherwise, and is not peculiar to you, but is experienced at times by all who have spiritual life. We seem to want some other word by which to denote our supreme regard to God than that which expresses our affection to creatures. When we speak of loving him, it must be in a different sense. Creature-love is a passion, divine love is a principle. It arises from an apprehension of his adorable perfections, especially as they are displayed in the great work of redemption, without which it is impossible for a sinner to love him. Much of his wisdom, power, and goodness are discernable in the works of creation and in his providential government, but the only proper, adequate, and full-orbed exhibition of his glorious character suited to promote our comfort and sanctification is in the person of Christ Jesus and him crucified. We must go to the foot of the cross to understand what the Scripture declares of his holiness, justice, and truth, and the wonderful method by which they are brought to harmonize with the designs of his grace and mercy in the salvation of sinners. There is a sensibility of feeling and creature-love which is no proper standard of our love to God. This, depending much upon constitution and the state of the animal spirits, is different in different persons, and in the same persons at different times. It is variable as the weather, and indeed is often affected by the weather and a thousand local circumstances, no more in our power than the clouds that fly over our heads. It is no uncommon thing to judge more favourably of ourselves on this point on a bright summer's day, and while contemplating a beautiful prospect, than in the gloom of winter or the hurry of Cheapside. The high affection of some people may be compared to a summer's brook after a hasty rain, which is full and noisy for a little time but soon becomes dry. But true divine love is like a river which always runs, though not always with equal depth and flow, and never ceases till it finds the ocean.

The best evidences are,—admiration of his way of saving sinners,—humble dependence on his care,—desire of communion with him in his instituted means of grace,—submission to the will of his providence,—and obedience to the dictation of his precepts. To keep his commandments, and to keep them as his commandments, from a sense of his authority and goodness is the best, the most unsuspicious test of our love to him. If we wish to love him more, or to be more satisfied that our love is genuine, we must not love the world nor be greatly solicitous of saving appearances in it. We must not be ashamed of the cross, nor think it strange or hard that the spirit which crucified our Saviour should show itself unfavourable to us, if we have courage to avow our attachment to him. These are hard sayings to us for a time; and for want of a more early compliance with them, we perhaps long walk like a man with a thorn in his foot. Every step we take is slow, difficult and painful. How often have I in the morning surrendered myself to God, and before the day has closed have been ashamed or afraid that people should suspect that I thought of him! It is no wonder that such treasonable hesitation should often hinder my comfort. But He is gracious. He gradually convinces us of our folly, humbles us for it, and strengthens us against it. Whenever He has made us thoroughly willing, we may depend upon him to make us able and successful, yet in such a way that our whole life will always be a warfare, and we shall always have cause for humiliation and shame. . . .

To Mrs. Hannah More.

LETTER III.—Case of the poet Cowper—Lessons to be learnt from it—Reference to his own circumstances.

May 24, 1800.

My dear Madam,—Glad should I be to have another peep at you, but all is uncertain; and if the precept, "Boast not thyself of to-morrow," is a proper admonition to all persons, at all times, it certainly does not become me, at the age of seventy-five, to look so far forward as to the end of a whole month.* Well! my times are in the Lord's hands, and should we not meet on earth, I trust we shall meet before the throne, where neither sin nor sorrow shall be able to distress us. Here we are sometimes called to sow in tears, but the harvest will be one of everlasting and uninterrupted joys. Oh, this blessed hope softens the trials of life, and will gild the gloomy valley.

My most dear and intimate friend, William Cowper, has obtained a release from all his distresses. I preached a funeral sermon for him on the 11th inst. from Eccles. ii. 2, 3. Why was he, who both by talents and disposition seemed qualified, if it were possible, to reform the age in which he lived, harassed by distresses and despair, so that the bush which Moses saw all in flames was a fit emblem of his case?

The Lord's thoughts and ways are so much above ours, that it becomes us rather to lie in the dust in adoration and silence than to inquire presumptuously into the grounds of his proceedings; yet I think we may draw some lessons from his sufferings. I wish to learn from them thankful-

---

* This visit was never accomplished.

ness for the health and peace with which I have been favoured, and caution not to depend upon whatever gifts, abilities or usefulness, past comforts or experiences, have been afforded me. In all these respects, my friend was, during a part of his life, greatly my superior. He lived (though not without short conflicts), in point of comfort and conduct, far above the common standard, for about ten years; and for twenty-seven years afterwards he knew not one peaceful day. May it remind me likewise of the precarious tenure by which we hold all our desirables. A slight alteration in the nervous system may make us a burden and a terror to ourselves and our friends. It may likewise reconcile us to lighter troubles, when we see what the Lord's most favoured and honoured servants are appointed to endure. But we are sure that He is rich enough, and that eternity is long enough to make them abundant amends for whatever his infinite wisdom may see meet to call them to, for promoting his glory in the end; for this bush, though so long in the flames, was not consumed, because the Lord was there. The last twelve hours of his life he lay still, and took no notice, but so long as he could speak, there was no proof that his derangement was either removed or abated. He was, however, free from his great terrors. There was no sign either of joy or sorrow when near his departure. What a glorious surprise* must it be to find himself released from all his chains in a moment, and in the presence of the Lord whom he loved, and whom he served! for the apostle says, "When absent from the body, present with

---

* There is a remarkable statement in Dr. Johnson's letter to Mr. Newton on occasion of Mr. Cowper's death. Of his appearance after that event his relative says, "The expression with which his countenance had settled was that of calmness and composure mingled, as it were, with holy surprise."

the Lord." There is no intermediate state. How little does he think now of all that he suffered while here!

This is a disinterested letter. It neither requires nor expects an answer from you. When I wrote last I was desirous of possessing one more token of your kindness. You have gratified me and I ask no farther. Probably this will likewise be my last to you. My health is remarkably good, but eyes, ears, and recollection fail. I aim to adopt the words of Dr. Watts, and sometimes I think I can:—

> The breaches cheerfully foretell
> The house will shortly fall.

Yet as I am still able to preach and am still heard with acceptance, I have no reason to wish to be gone. Pray for me, my dear ladies, that I may work while it is called to-day, and that when the night cometh I may retire like a thankful guest from an abundant table. My case is almost as singular as "Jonah's." He was the only one delivered after having been entombed in the belly of a fish, and I, perhaps, the only one ever brought from bondage and misery in Africa to preach "Jesus Christ and him crucified." In early life I knew much of the evil of the world, but I brought it all upon myself. During the last half century I have been favoured with as much of the good which such a world as this can afford, as perhaps any person in it. I have had internal conflicts, abatements, bereavements, and sharp trials; but I think upon the whole I have been as happy in temporals as the present state of mortality will admit. Even now I can think of nothing with a serious wish, beyond what I have, if a wish could procure it. But all the past is like the remembrance of a dream, gone beyond recall. The present is precarious, and will soon be past likewise. But, oh! the future! Blessed be He who brought immortality to light by the gospel. I need not say to myself or to my dear friends who are in the Lord *Quo nunc abibis in loco ?** We know where they are and how employed. There I trust my dear Mary is waiting for me, and in the Lord's own time I hope to join with her and all the redeemed in praising the Lamb, once upon the cross, now upon the throne of glory.

How apt is self to occupy too much of my paper, when I am writing to those I love! Excuse a fault that flows from a sincere regard, which cannot be confined by forms. I love you, I love Miss Patty, I love you all. If I were a poet I should think more frequently of the five sisters and Cowslip Green, than of the nine muses and Parnassus. The Lord bless you all separately and jointly, with all the blessings pertaining to life and godliness.

I am, my dear madam,
Your very affectionate and much obliged,
JOHN NEWTON.

To Mrs. Hannah More.

LETTER IV.—Suffering for righteousness' sake—The providence of God in the events of the times.

1801.

MY DEAR MADAM,—"Blessed are ye when men revile you and persecute you, and speak all manner of evil against you falsely," and, "for my name's sake." When I consider whose words these are, I am more disposed to congratulate than to condole with you on the unjust and hard treatment you have met with. Yet I do feel for you. These things are not joyous, but grievous at the

* Whither will ye now go?

time.* It is afterwards that they yield the peaceable fruits of righteousness. Cheer up my dear friend. Tarry thou the Lord's leisure. Be strong, and He shall comfort thy heart. Depend upon it all shall turn out to the furtherance of that gospel for which you are engaged. (See Ps. xxxvii. 4, 5, 6, and Rev. iii. 7—13). That whole message belongs to you, and I trust you will live to see it fulfilled. When Sennacherib insulted Hezekiah, and blasphemed the God of Israel, the king said, "Answer him not. I will put the cause into the Lord's hands, and He will plead for us better than we could for ourselves." So the event proved in the issue. I have little doubt but the stir that has been made will conduce to your vindication and honour. But if not the Lord will honour and own you before the assembled world in the great day of his appearance. In the meantime let us pray for and pity those who know not what they do. A word from him can open the eyes of the blind, and soften the heart of stone.

The new year we have begun is likely to prove very eventful. The eye of sense starts at the prospect, but faith sees a hand guiding in the darkest cloud, and reports that "the Lord reigns be the earth never so unquiet." He is carrying on his great designs in a way worthy of himself, and with an especial regard to his church. To manifest his glory in the salvation of all who believe in the Son of his love, and that his character in the combination of

---

* The self-denying efforts of Mrs. Hannah More and her sisters in establishing schools in their neighbourhood after being prosecuted for some time, and with great success, were assailed with the most bitter opposition. They were abused month by month in the *Anti-Jacobin Review*, and in other publications. The most shameful and groundless charges were brought against them. But they committed their way to the Lord. The trial passed away, and as Mr. Newton says, "It turned out for the furtherance of the Gospel."

his infinite wisdom, power, holiness, justice, sovereignty, mercy, grace, and truth, might be fully exhibited to the universe, was, I believe, the great purpose for which the earth was formed. (Prov. viii. 23, 31.)

He does and will overrule all the designs of men for the furtherance and accomplishment of his holy plan. Not only his friends but his enemies contribute to it. The wrath of man, so far as it is permitted to act, shall praise him, and the remainder of their wrath, whatever they mean more than is subservient to his purpose, He will restrain. Moses and Joshua were his willing servants, but Sennacherib and Nebuchadnezzar were equally his servants, though they regarded him not. They acted under his secret commission, and could do no more than He appointed them. It is the same now with Bonaparte. When I heard of his unexpected escape from Syria, and his arrival in France, I instantly concluded that the Lord had some important business for him to do. And when he has done his work, he will be laid aside, as many have been employed in services (not so fit for the godly) have been before him. We, perhaps, have been tempted almost to wish that some persons had not been born, or had been taken away before they had opportunity of doing so much mischief, but what the Lord said to Pharaoh will apply to all like-minded, "For this very cause have I raised thee up." Pharaoh's oppression of Israel prepared the way for their deliverance, and issued in his final overthrow. He permits his people to be brought low that his interposition in their behalf may become the more signal, and more glorious.

When I consider all second causes and instruments as mere saws and hammers in the workman's hands, and that they can neither give us pleasure nor pain, but as our Lord and Saviour is pleased to employ them, I feel a degree of peace and composure. I have been long aiming to learn this lesson, but I am a slow scholar, and when I hope I have made an attainment one day, perhaps the very next, I have to learn it over again. Appearances make me anxious, and I forget the report of faith. But though we believe not, yet He abideth faithful. I am, at least in my deliberate judgment, firmly assured that He has done, still does, and will do, all things well. How little can we judge of this great drama by a single scene! But when we see the catastrophe, how shall we love and praise and wonder!

Dear Miss Catlett was lately visited by a fever with some alarming symptoms, but our great Physician heard prayer. He soon rebuked the fever, and it left her. She was abroad again within the week. Help us with your prayers and praises. We both love you and all your sisters. We still remember the kindness and pleasures of Cowslip Green.* May the Lord bless you all with that wisdom which cometh from above, and with that peace which the world can neither give nor take away.

The old man of seventy-six is still favoured with perfect health, and can still preach as loud, as long, and as often as formerly. He is still heard with acceptance and has cause to hope the Lord owns his ministry. "Oh to grace how great a debtor," is the poor African blasphemer and profligate.

I am, my dear madam,
Your very affectionate and much obliged,
JOHN NEWTON.

* Visited by Mr. Newton in 1792.

The Rev. John Campbell.

MR. CAMPBELL coming to London in 1790 on account of the state of his health, obtained an introduction to Mr. Newton. That visit seems at once to have awakened a feeling of mutual interest in each of these good men. From that time for the next thirteen years, indeed so long as Mr. Newton was able to write, many letters passed between them. Mr. Campbell saw Mr. Newton on several occasions during the last months of his life, and has left on record some important notes of these visits.

Mr. Campbell's history is a striking illustration of the power of Christian principle and of the success of zealous and untiring efforts in doing good. It may not, therefore, be without interest briefly to note some of its leading events. Mr. Campbell was born in Edinburgh in 1766. In early life he was left an orphan; but the relations to whose care he was entrusted trained him in the fear of God, and he appears, when quite young, to have come under the influence of religious truth. He was soon convinced that religion consisted in something more than the care of his own soul, and that he was bound to seek the good of others as well as his own. Accordingly he betook himself to various efforts of usefulness, manifesting therein not only a singular degree of zeal but also much Christian prudence. Thus he originated a tract society in Edinburgh, some few years before the institution of the Religious Tract Society of London. Thoroughly sympathizing with the efforts of Messrs. Haldane and their coadjutors in endeavouring to arouse the people of Scotland to a more anxious concern for the things of religion, Mr. Campbell took an active part in that great work. He established sabbath evening schools in his native city. He sought to promote the welfare of the most abandoned and unhappy class of society and with others established The Magdalen in Edinburgh, and at the same time he preached regularly to the prisoners in the Bridewell of the city. All this time Mr. Campbell was in business. This he now gave up, and put himself under the direction of the Rev. Greville Ewing of Glasgow, with a view to the regular ministry.

After a time the providence of God directed Mr. Campbell's steps to London, and he became pastor of the Congregational church at Kingsland. He took a deep interest in the subject of missions to the heathen, and on two occasions went to South Africa to visit the stations of the London Missionary Society in that part of the world, and subsequently travelled through most of the counties of England to plead the cause of that Society.

The death of this excellent man was like his life, characterized by great humility and simple dependence on the Saviour, and while regarding himself but as an unprofitable servant, he was full of hope and joy in the prospect of the blessedness awaiting him. Mr. Campbell may justly be said to have been a benefactor to his race. His earnestness, his practical wisdom, his deep sense of responsibility for the talents entrusted to him are worthy of all imitation. In a word he was an eminently good and holy man. As a writer, especially of books for the young, he was remarkably useful; and his ministerial labours were blessed to the conversion of many souls.

To the Rev. John Campbell.

LETTER I.—Intellect and heart—Fuller on the Calvinistic and Socinian systems.

LONDON: *August* 1, 1794.

DEAR SIR, . . . In preferring a warm heart to a clear head you certainly judge by the rule of Scripture. The Lord looketh to the *heart*, not to the stature, the address, the intellect, the rank or wealth of a person. These are to the man no more than the trappings to a horse which is the same animal whether laden with panniers, or dressed in a fine caparison. So at the theatre people do not admire an actor merely for the character he sustains, but for the manner in which he performs it. All flesh is grass, and all the goodliness thereof like the flowers of the field. The mass of mankind may be compared to grass, and those who are distinguished by intellectual or external accomplishments of any kind to the flowers which look more gaudy and are perhaps a little taller than the grass, but when the mower comes the scythe finds no difference. Both fall by the same stroke, and wither with equal speed. Indeed I believe the most lively grace and the most solid comfort are known among the Lord's poor and undistinguished people. Every outward advantage has a tendency to nourish the pride of the human heart, and requires a proportionable knowledge of the deceitful self and the evil of sin to counterbalance them. It is no less difficult to have great abilities than great riches without trusting in them. And believers who are remarkably sensible and clever are frequently teased with whims and vagaries of thought which do not trouble plain people. If I were qualified to search out the best Christian in the kingdom, I should not expect to find him either in a professor's chair or in a pulpit. I should give the palm to that person who had the lowest thoughts of himself, and the most admiring and cordial thoughts of the Saviour. And perhaps this person may be some bedridden old man or woman, or a pauper in a parish workhouse. But our regard to the Lord is not to be measured by our sensible feelings, by what we can say or write, but rather by the simplicity of our dependence, and the uniform tenor of our obedience to his will.

. . . I know not if I mentioned Mr. Fuller's book, *The Tendency of the Calvinistic and Socinian Doctrines compared as to Morals,* but I suppose you must have seen it. I think it the most complete unanswerable refutation of the Socinian scheme, and the best book of controversy I ever saw. The great learned doctors dodged Dr. Priestly about his Greek and Latin to little purpose. It was reserved to Mr. Fuller to cut off this great Goliath's head. I think there is none of the party hardy enough to attempt to answer it.

On Monday next, if I live, I shall enter my seventieth year. The time of my dismission cannot be very distant. Pray for me that whenever it comes it may find me waiting, willing, and ready; that my decline of life (if I am not called away suddenly) may be honourable and consistent with my profession; that I may live as becometh a saint, and die as becometh a sinner, with no other plea or hope, but that Jesus lived and died, and rose and reigns to save to the uttermost those that put their trust in him.

I commend you to the Lord. May He guide, guard, and bless you, and make you a blessing to all your connections.

Your affectionate friend and servant,

JOHN NEWTON.

To the REV. JOHN CAMPBELL.

LETTER II.—Interest in the work of God—Our sufficiency of him—Dreams—Holiness of men and angels—Dying experiences.

LONDON: *November* 26, 1794.

DEAR SIR, . . . I do not wonder that Moses should have been willing to wait a little longer for heaven, to have seen Israel established in Canaan, though he was sure it would be after his decease. God has in mercy so constituted the human frame as to produce an engagement of heart in necessary affairs, so that we are not only *employed* in his service, but *interested* in what He appoints us to do. Because it is *his* concern it becomes *our own*. This wonderfully sweetens labour and likewise keeps up that attention and exertion, which are necessary for our doing things as well as we can. Perhaps you have seen parents who seemed very willing to go to heaven (if it were the Lord's time) and yet not unwilling to live a little longer to see a dear child comfortably settled, before they went. Surely the object of Moses's desire was as noble and important as anything that we propose on earth now. Moses loved Israel, and longed to see them settled; but when the Lord forbade it, he cheerfully acquiesced.

Abraham was, as you observe, a great man; yet he was but a man. We may admire his faith and obedience, for the Bible commends them, and holds him forth to us as a pattern. Yet he had no more inherent or properly his own than you or I. When left a little to himself, this great believer stooped to equivocation and falsehood to save his life, when it was in reality in no danger. Let us learn a lesson from him in this case likewise, not to presume upon our past experience, upon the grace or comfort of yesterday, as though these would warrant our standing to-morrow. We cannot see by the light of yesterday, nor subsist long upon yesterday's food. We need continual supplies, help every moment. Therefore let us not be high-minded, but fear. So long as we feel our weakness, and lean upon an almighty arm we are safe, but no longer.

. . . I have known more instances than one of dreams resembling Miss Tooley's, and they are worth recording when verified by the event, but this is not always the case. Dreams are to me a sufficient proof, first, That we are surrounded by invisible agents, and liable to impressions from them when our senses are asleep, and perhaps when they are indisposed by nervous disorders, but not when we are in perfect health or distinctly awake. N.B. It is a great mercy that some of these agents are under a restraint, or we should be scared by dreams and terrified by visions every night. Second, I infer from dreams that there is a power belonging to the mind adapted to the unseen state, and which, though dormant when we are awake, is active in sleep. Then we seem to perceive by *intuition*. We are engaged in scenes we had no consciousness of before, and yet we know all that is going forward, take a part in the business, and are engaged in and interested as if we were quite at home. This appears very wonderful to me. I think we know very little of our own powers at present. Third, Though some dreams are important, perhaps monitory, perhaps prophetical, as I believe that mentioned in my narrative was, yet there is so much uncertainty in their general character, that we should be cautious of laying much stress upon them at the time. I had once a young lady a month at my house, who had the singular faculty of dreaming that she heard a sermon every night, and she usually told us the text, the heads, and much of the discourse at breakfast. The preacher was sometimes one whom she knew, and sometimes an utter stranger. But when she married she lost her gift, and, poor thing! she has since met with many things she never dreamed of.

. . . The holiness of sinners and angels which you seem to compare differs, not only in degree, but also in kind. A hare or a greyhound can run swiftly, but they cannot fly like an eagle. Had they been made to fly they would have had wings. We hope to be as the angels before long, but at present in our compound state of spirit and matter, the distinction between us and them is no less real than between birds and beasts. The holiness of a sinner consists chiefly of low thoughts of self, and high thoughts of the Saviour. These will always be in proportion. The lower we appear to ourselves, the more highly we shall esteem him. The more his glory strikes us, the more we shall sink in our own eyes. Could you find the man who has most of these properties, you would find the most holy man upon earth. And as we advance in these we shall in the same degree attain to everything else that properly belongs to holiness. Why are we liable to anger, pride, positiveness, and other evil tempers but because we think too highly of ourselves and suppose we are not treated as we ought to be? Why are we so apt to be captivated by the gewgaws of the world, but because we are so faintly impressed with a real sense of the excellence of Jesus? We say indeed that his loving-kindness is better than life, but if we really and fully thought so, hard things would be easy, and bitter sweet, and there would be no room for impatience or discontent in our hearts. But alas! all within us, and all around us is defective and polluted.

The death of Mr. Y— and of many others who are daily removed are encouragements to us to trust the Lord when our call shall come. They who are born of God belong to his heavenly kingdom. They who are not belong, at least for the present, to the kingdom of the wicked one. Neither the one nor the other, while in the body, can have a full perception of what awaits them, but at the approach of death the respective scenes begin to open,

> The soul's dark cottage tatter'd and decay'd
> Lets in new light through chinks.

It is not necessary to suppose that the believer on his dying bed is, strictly speaking, *better* than the believers who are around him listening with admiration to his words; but now he stands upon the threshold of glory he sees more, and therefore he can say more than he did formerly.* And often the impenitent sinner before his departure has such discoveries as terrify not only himself, but all who are about him; but what passes within the curtains seldom transpires abroad. We observe that Christians who walk uprightly and humbly, generally express the same feelings when they come to die; or rather they give intimations of views and feelings which they find no words to express. . . .

I am, your affectionate friend,

JOHN NEWTON.

To the REV. JOHN CAMPBELL.

LETTER III.—Special manifestations of God to the soul—Toleration and Romanism.

LONDON: *February* 23, 1795.

MY DEAR SIR, . . . I congratulate you on the visit the Lord favoured you with. Such favours call for a double guard of watchfulness and prayer. The pickpockets are busy about our bank when the dividends are paying, and sometimes they who have received a good sum of money have been deprived of it before they returned home, but

---

* Mr. Campbell says in reference to this case that Mr. Y. was converted under the ministry of Mr. Whitefield, and that he lived a humble, consistent Christian to the age of fourscore. In health he said but little on the subject of religion; but, though towards the end of life his faculties were greatly impaired, in his last illness he thought himself in heaven, and spoke much to the honour of God, and to the comfort and joy of those around him.

they seldom attempt to rob a poor man. Thus, Satan, the arch-thief, lets a poor formal professor pass unmolested; but if he sees one whom the Lord has enriched, he watches him with a malicious eye, and longs to spoil him of his treasure. It seems he once formed a plan to rob Paul himself upon such an occasion, 2 Cor. xii. But the Lord constrained him to send a messenger of his own to defeat his own design, and to put Paul on his guard. Messengers from Satan and thorns in the flesh are *gifts* and mercies if they preserve us from being exalted above measure. For there is that in our nature which can extract poison even from gracious manifestations and spiritual comforts. A man who has his dividend in his pocket buttons up close, avoids a crowd, and looks and moves as if he thought every person he meets might be a thief. Let us imitate them. May the Lord's voice to Peter sound frequently in our ears, " Satan has desired to have you that he may sift you as wheat." But if we are enabled to walk humbly and circumspectly we shall walk safely.

The slips and falls (some very great) of the most eminent servants of God, are recorded for our admonition. Abraham, Lot, Noah, Aaron, David, Solomon, and Hezekiah, were not *novices*; but men who had known much of his goodness, and their greatest faults were usually committed just after some signal deliverance, or after some singular manifestation, or after they had been honoured by the performance of some important service. Lord, what is man? and what are we? Let us not be high minded, but fear.

Such extraordinary views of Divine things are very desirable, provided we can safely bear them, of which He who knows our frame is the proper judge. They have not been a part of my experience; though, I hope, I likewise rest upon the simple truth, but it is as it *lies in the book*. What I read I am enabled to believe, so far as to venture my soul and my all upon it. And I trust it has some general effect upon my temper, aims, and expectations; but not often much more at one time than another. My walk is chiefly upon even ground. I am seldom greatly elevated or greatly depressed. I would be thankful for that word of Our Lord to Thomas, "Blessed are they who have not seen and yet have believed." For, indeed, in the way of sensible impression I have seen but very little.

. . . I think the Roman Catholics in Ireland were long treated much like Israel in Egypt. I do not consider their toleration as any way connected with religion, and as a political measure I highly approve it, upon this principle, that I am glad of liberty to worship God according to my light, and therefore am willing that others should have the same liberty. Toleration, if considered as a matter of favour, is an insult upon conscience, and an intrusion upon the prerogative of the Lord of conscience. I should be glad of a toleration to eat, if I might not eat without it, yet I should think it hard if I could not breakfast or dine without the leave of Parliament.

Popery has always showed a persecuting spirit; and, therefore, when the Protestants got power on their side, as they were unwilling to run the risk of being again called to the honour of suffering for the gospel's sake, and equally unable to trust in the providence of God, they entrenched themselves within a bulwark of cruel, unchristian penal laws. The Jewish nation was a theocracy, and idolatry was not only a sin against God, but a crime against the state, and therefore punishable with death. Protestants avail themselves of this precedent, call the papists idolators, and then you may treat them as you please. Tear away their children from them; hinder them from worshipping God at all. Let any rebellious profligate son claim his father's estate; if he will but renounce popery, he need not have any religion: he may be an atheist provided he promises not to be a papist. Oppress them as much as you can, and still, if you do not murder them, you may admire your own mercy. I abhor the treatment of the presbyterians in Scotland in Charles the Second's time; and I do not think much better of the severities against the papists in Ireland.

I do not wonder at the contempt the Lord poured upon the well-meant but mistaken zeal of the Protestant Association of the year 1780. Can the gospel of Christ authorize such things? Are these the fruits of love? Is it thus we would do as we wish to be done by? Surely the Son of man came not to destroy men's lives but to save them.

Thus much for the present. I commend you to the care and blessing of the Lord, and with Miss Catlett's respects, I subscribe myself

Your affectionate friend and servant,
J. N.

To the Rev. John Campbell.

LETTER IV.—Calvinism and Arminianism—Secret prayer.

LONDON: *April* 17, 1795.

DEAR SIR, . . . A *Calvinist* professes that a man can receive nothing except it be given him from heaven. If so, we need not wonder that others who are not favoured like us cannot see with our eyes. However, if a man be born again, I am content he should call himself an Arminian; and if he be not born again, his Calvinism will do him but little good. Religion, my friend, is not a system of sentiments, it is a new nature, a new life; and they who have it are under Divine teaching, and will in due time learn all the Lord sees it needful for them to know. Some of my frequent hearers, whom I rank amongst the best of them, would start at the word Calvinist, which, therefore, they never hear from me; nor the words election and predestination, unless they lie in my text, and then I explain them in an experimental way, and they receive the truths intended as a young child does milk. They will not allow themselves to be Calvinists; but they are humble, spiritual, peaceful; they love the Lord and his people; they overcome the world; they are satisfied with me, and I with them.

Some people have a sharp eye, others are near sighted; but both sorts love the light, and can see by it to walk and work, though good eyes have the advantage in viewing an extensive prospect. It is thus in spirituals. Yet if the heart be upright, we usually grow wiser by years and experience. Thus some who set out as Arminians, in the Lord's time become Calvinists; and many who were once speculative and positive are ripened by age, and become less assuming and dogmatical, learn to bear and forbear; and though they have not changed their sentiments, are strongly suspected by some, because they can love even an Arminian. . . . I think I could match you and overmatch you on the head of coldness and wanderings in secret prayer. But in prayer I am to confess my sins and depravity, which I could not honestly do, unless I felt them. Nor do I expect to be much better than Paul was, who found that when he would do good evil was present with him. Further, if the Lord favours me with some liberty before men, it may be a great mercy that he leaves me to feel in private how little I can do without him. Otherwise pride will tempt me to consider that as my own which experience now assures me I only receive, and am dependent entirely upon him for, without whom I can do nothing. You will meet with the sum of all your complaints in the *Olney Hymns*, Book i. No. 119, which was written long before I heard of you. As face answereth to face in a glass, so the heart of man to man. Your guinea and mine bear the same impression, because they come out of the same mint. When we feelingly say, " O, wretched man that I am!" we may still cheerfully add, "I thank God, through Jesus Christ, my Lord." There is a difference in us, according as the Lord is pleased to afford or suspend his power. But in ourselves, we are no better at one time than another; for there *dwelleth* in us no good thing. The eye can see when there is light; but it has no light in itself. . . .

With my love to all who love the Saviour in Edinburgh, Leith, and elsewhere, as they come in your way; and my prayers for your and their best welfare,

I remain, your affectionate and obliged,

J. N.

To the REV. JOHN CAMPBELL.

LETTER V.—Itinerant labours in Scotland—Prosperity at St. Mary's—Personal experience.

LONDON: *October* 14, 1797.

MY DEAR SIR,—I thank you for your letter, dated Sept. 8th. It gave great pleasure, not only to me, but to my friends at Southampton. Give my love to Messrs. Haldane and Aikman,* and tell them that I rejoice in their zeal, their acceptance, and their success. Why should not the Orkneys and the Highland Islands deserve attention as much as the islands in the South Sea. I hope gospel zeal will in due time sail northwards to Shetland, and westward to St. Kilda, and all the intermediate islands. . . .

May your schools prosper! The Lord make you like the tree in Psalm i. I congratulate you and myself on what some may call latitudinarianism in Scotland. May we not say with the apostle, "Grace be with all that love the Lord Jesus Christ in sincerity?" I think this is a latitudinarian prayer. I hope many agree in loving him who sadly disagree about trifles. Such is the weakness and wickedness of the heart, even in good men. There is a great and old established house, which does much business, and causes no small disturbance in the world and in the church. The *firm* is Satan, Self, and Co. Till this powerful, extensive partnership be dissolved, we cannot expect perfect peace and union among all believers. It

---

* It would be irrelevant in this place to speak of the great work effected in Scotland by those excellent and devoted men, the Messrs. Haldane. A circumstance in reference to Mr. Aikman must, however, be mentioned as having more immediate relation to Mr. Newton and his writings. The editor may repeat the following words from his *Life of Newton*. Mr. Aikman's acquaintance with Mr. Newton, as in so many other cases, was through the writings of the latter. But the circumstances were peculiar, and we give them as related to us, more than thirty years ago, by Mr. Aikman himself. Conversing with him about Newton, Cowper, and Bull, the good old man told us, with deep feeling, how great were his obligations to the author of *Cardiphonia*. "I was returning," he said, "to Jamaica, where I was engaged upon one of the plantations, and wishing to take out some books for the use of the people there, amongst others I selected was Newton's *Cardiphonia*. Its title struck me, and I supposed it was a novel." He went on to say: "Looking over the books on the voyage I took up this, and soon found it something very different from what I had thought; and *that book* was, in God's providence, the means of my conversion." Mr. Aikman was, for many years, a useful and much esteemed Congregational minister in Edinburgh. See *Life*, p. 324.

will be a joyful day when its credit shall totally fail. Such a day we are warranted to hope for.

. . . We returned from Southampton in peace and safety, the 14th of September, after ten weeks' absence. I have a nice curate, Mr. Gunn. I know not whether his report is heard in Scotland. I have reason to hope that the Lord owns both his labours and mine. The church is crammed, the hearers are attentive; we often hear of new inquirers, especially young people, and I know of no gross miscarriages among those who profess the gospel. Last time we had more than three hundred communicants. We are situated, as it were, upon an island. The storms of controversy and dissension which make such havoc upon that great continent,—the religious world, are not permitted to reach our peaceful shore. We know but little of them, and that little only by report. I may truly say (oh, that I could say it with due thankfulness) the lines are fallen to me in a pleasant place.

As to myself, I am in statu quo. I am a year older than when I went to Southampton last summer; in other respects I am much the same. Though I have been remarkably exempted from trials since the year 1790, I am a poor creature still. My best is defective and defiled, and needs pardon before it can hope for acceptance; but through mercy my hope is built, not upon frames and feelings, but upon the atonement and mediation of Jesus. When I am called home, I trust I shall leave all my abominations behind me, as my dear friend Cowper says in his hymn.—

To the Rev. John Campbell.

Letter VI.—Evil of pride—Religion and politics.

London: *March* 4, 1800.

My dear Friend, . . . Though the eye of our judgment and the end we propose be simple and disinterested, self, unless watched as narrowly as a cat watches a mouse, will interpose. Self loves to be very busy and very useful, and who can blame him? But if an ounce of grace, so to speak, will suffice to carry us on in active life, it may require a pound to keep us quiet and submissive by the fireside. The Lord stands not in need of sinful man, nor will He ever want instruments to carry on his work. They are happy whom He honours to be his servants in the gospel, provided they give themselves up to him without reserve, depend upon him, and lie low in the dust before him. The Lord abhors pride and self-importance. The seeds of these evils are in the hearts of his own children; but rather than suffer that which He hates to remain in those He loves, He will in mercy pound them as in a mortar, to beat it out of them, or to prevent its growth.

The account of your highland tour is pleasant and interesting. I hear of no such sudden general awakenings in our kingdom; but I hope the gospel does spread, though more gradually and silently, especially in the Establishment. Several very promising young men are ordained in the course of the year, and the number of serious students in both the universities seems to be still increasing. But I fear the savour of the good ointment is in some places injured, and its efficacy in a measure obstructed by the dead fly of *politics*. . . .

You see how large a letter I have written to you with mine own hand. Through mercy, dear Miss Catlett and old seventy-five are both as well as when you left us. The Lord bless you and your friends, and me and mine. Let us meet often at the throne of grace, and rejoice in the hope of meeting before long in a better world.

I am your affectionate and obliged,

J. N.

The Rev. James Coffin and Mrs. Coffin.

IN the preface to a volume of sixty-eight letters, from which the following are taken, addressed by Mr. Newton to Mr. Coffin, the interesting circumstances under which the correspondence originated are thus referred to. Both Mr. and Mrs. Coffin were first awakened to a sense of the importance of vital religion by the perusal of some of Mr. Newton's works. Under much religious concern, though personally unknown to the author of these volumes, they were led at once to seek counsel from him, stating, without reserve, the new position in which they found themselves. This communication led to a correspondence and a friendship which lasted till Mr. Newton's death.

It is justly said, that the following letters show, that in his instructions to a younger clergyman becoming desirous to preach Christ and him crucified, in his administrations of comfort to those who were unnecessarily cast down, and in his advice upon the duties and relations of the domestic circle, the writer gave equal evidence that he was taught of God, and was watchfully anxious that "his children should walk in the truth." And yet further, that these letters will appear the more important, as containing Mr. Newton's matured thoughts and experience, and may therefore be said to put the seal of his faith and approbation, in what he had so long taught and preached.

Mr. Coffin, who held the living of Linkinhorne, in Cornwall, was a faithful and affectionate preacher of the gospel, and an instrument of good to many.

To the REV. JAMES COFFIN.

LETTER I.—False humility—Flight of time.

MY DEAR SIR, ... Now I have found your letter. I have no doubt you think others better than yourself:

thus far you are conformed to the Scripture rule, Phil. ii. 3. You should not therefore be displeased with yourself on that account. I shall not contradict you. But some of those you deem so were planted in the Lord's garden many years before you. Why then should you complain that you are not so tall, nor your branches so wide, nor your root so deep, in two years' growth, as others who have been growing twenty or thirty years? Should a little sapling, just springing up from an acorn ask, Why am not I as large as the stoutest oak in the wood? you would know how to answer it. I want you to teach Mrs. Coffin a lesson; but you must first learn it yourself. Do not let Satan impose a false humility upon you. Depend upon it there is more of self and self-righteousness in these complaints, than we are usually aware of. It is better to be thankful for what you have received than impatient because you have no more. If you can make yourself better, do it by all means; but if you cannot, wait simply the Lord's time, at the Lord's feet. If your heart is upright, you have only to attend to the means and precepts of grace. The Lord must do the rest, and He will, otherwise it can never be done. Try to be thankful; it is both a *utile* and a *dulce*.* You cannot be too humble, or think too little of yourself; but these views need not break your peace. You are to be strong, and to rejoice, not in yourself, but in Jesus Christ the Lord, and in the power of his might. One view of the brazen serpent will do you more good than poring over your own wounds for a month.

. . . We sensibly miss dear Mrs. Gardiner; but this is a changeable state. Meeting always implies parting in this world; but they that meet above shall part no more. Let us look upward and forward. Time, which is

* Both useful and pleasant.

short in itself, passes swiftly away. Like passengers in a coach, whether we sleep or wake, we are lessening our distance from home every minute. Our coach will not stop, or make a moment's delay, till it brings us to our journey's end; and the hills and dales we have already travelled over, are out of sight and gone. The trials of yesterday are no more to us now, than those of the antediluvians. And tomorrow shall be as to-day; when once past it will return no more. Oh, for more faith! which is the evidence of things not seen. The vail of flesh and blood, and unbelief, conceal them from us; but they are not distant. I believe we now live in the midst of them. Ere long these vails will be removed; we shall awake from the dream of life, and be satisfied by his likeness. With Miss Catlett's and Miss Gardiner's love, and the respects of your friends below stairs,

I remain,
My dear sir,
Your affectionate friend and brother.
JOHN NEWTON.

July 24, 1793.

To Mrs. Coffin.

Letter II.—Simple faith.

MY DEAR MADAM, . . . If you will persist in putting the cart before the horse, how can you get forward? If you were better you would believe; but you must believe first or you cannot be better. Surely you know that Christ did not come into the world to save the righteous, but sinners. The only question then is, Are you a sinner? If you are not, the Gospel can do you no good; but if you are a sinner, and feel your need of mercy, Jesus says, "Come unto me, and I will give you rest." He does not invite you, to raise your desires, and then to disappoint them. I doubt not but if you thought *I* could save, you would depend upon my good will. He both can, and He has promised He will; but He will not allow you the honour of contributing to save yourself. When you desist from the attempt, you will find peace. I feel for your family afflictions; but the submission the Lord gives you both to his will makes me amends. I can perceive that He is with you, whether you perceive it or not. I have heard of a cockney (a mere Londoner), who, on going first into the country, which was to him a new world, when the people he was with admired the beauty of an adjacent wood, wished them to show it to him. They pointed to it; but he said, I cannot see it, there are so many trees in the way. Apply this story to yourselves. The best evidences of a work of grace are the very things which prevent you from perceiving what the Lord has already done for you. You have much cause for praise, none for complaint. May the great Physician heal your minds, and your children's bodies. Put all into his hands. Has He not said, "I will surely do you good?" Believe his word, and you shall prosper. . . . I believe much of your complaint is constitutional. . . . Think a little, and pray as much as you possibly can: avoid musing by yourself, and reasoning. This is Satan's sure ground; and we give him great advantage if we venture to meet him upon it. Keep to the sword of the Spirit, the good word of God; if you resist him with this, he will flee from you; all other weapons are to him as straw and rotten wood. I enclose you a book which I think suits your case; but after all, the Lord keeps the key of comfort in his own hand. Your help must come from him : though it tarry, wait for it. If you meet with those who say they are exempted from conflicts, you may take it for granted they do not know their own hearts. St. Paul does not talk so ; he says, " Without were fightings, and within were fears." And he speaks of the warfare between flesh and spirit, as the common experience of all believers, Galatians v. 17. . . .

JOHN NEWTON.

December 28, 1793.

To the REV. J. COFFIN.

LETTER III.—Advice about accepting another living.

MY DEAR SIR,—I am not sorry that you must give your final determination before you can hear from me. How could I undertake to send you shoes from London unless I exactly knew the size of your foot? Or how can I pretend to advise in the case before you, unless I was perfectly acquainted with every circumstance? I am willing to take it for granted that you meant in this instance to do what is right, and that you sincerely sought the Lord's direction. We seldom go wrong when we desire his guidance ; and, if, when our intentions are upright, we are permitted to make a mistake, He will overrule it for our good. But when our peace of mind, or our characters are nearly concerned, if we lean not to our own understanding, we may rely on him to direct our paths ; for He has promised that He will do so. If, therefore, you have accepted the new offer, I shall hope that the Lord is calling you to a place, where it will please him to bless you and make you useful. On the other hand, if upon mature deliberation,

you resolve to remain where you are, I shall not be sorry.
I hardly think that the personal comfort either of you or
Mrs. Coffin would be increased by an exchange; though
the thought of personal ease ought to give way to the
Lord's service, if He does indeed require you to remove.
You know the *whole* of your present situation; of the other
you can as yet know nothing. Your habits of life are
adapted to Linkinhorne; at the new living you would be
in a new world. Where you are, you have been led on so
gradually to preach the gospel, that your people are now
prepared, and know what they are to expect; in the other
place you would have all to begin over again. In short,
while you have any hesitation, whether or not it would be
right to go, I think the safest and surest side is to stay,
till you obtain satisfaction that it is his will that you
should arise and depart. I certainly dare not advise you
to retain your present living if you accept the other, unless
you could contrive to be in two places at once. To hold a
living for the sake of keeping the gospel in the place by a
curate is very plausible; but if the gospel is preserved
there, I think the present incumbent is the most proper
person to preserve it. I think our service is no less attached to our persons, than that of a sea captain; and I
question if any of them undertake to navigate two ships at
one time. Circumstances may excuse this. Cecil had two
small livings at Lewes; but the place was so unfavourable
to his health that he could not live there. He holds them
still; but he has the archbishop's express permission to put
in a curate, and the archbishop knows that so far from
drawing a single shilling from a benefice which he does not
personally serve, he is yearly out of pocket by his preferment. Pluralities are the great opprobrium of our church;
and the earnestness with which they are sought and seized

by those whose care is not for the flock but the fleece, should make faithful ministers very cautious how they countenance such mercenaries by their example. You would find it very difficult to procure two or three curates to your mind. I believe it would not be in my power to recommend *one* to you; and unless they are right men in their views, and agreeable to you in their dispositions, you would have a heavy burden. In short, from my opinion of your leading motives, I shall hope that if you determine to go, you have done well; but if you are resolved to stay, I shall think you have done better. Your people will love you more, when they know that a bait was thrown in your way to draw you from them, and that you refused to bite at it. A providential opening as it is called, is sometimes but another name for temptation, that is, a trial how far we can reduce our theory to practice. As ministers we preach against the love of money. The Lord permits an occasion to be presented, to show that we are disinterested, and that we love our charge too well to desert it for what the world calls an advantage. And though the world may call a man a fool for refusing such advantages, I believe they will secretly respect both him and his profession the better for it. Such an opportunity Mr. Foster had, by declining the living of C—, though it was left him by will, and worth 600*l.* per annum. But the opportunity of approving himself in the sight of the church and the world, was worth much more.

Poor Miss Jean!* If I were quite sure that I knew what I ask, I would pray earnestly for her recovery. I think I may warrantably pray that either she may be restored to health, and spared long to your comfort, or that the Lord may give you to see such a gracious change in her, that

* Mr. Coffin's daughter.

you may be as willing to resign her as I was to part with my dear Eliza Cunningham. Give my love to her, and assure her that she is often upon my mind. My leg is better; the good Lord preserve us from falls and strains, and broken bones, in a spiritual sense. I commend you and yours to his care and blessing.

I am always,
Your affectionate friend and brother,
JOHN NEWTON.

April 5, 1791.

To MR. *and* MRS. COFFIN.

LETTER IV.—Strong and weak faith—Witness of the Spirit.

DEAR AND HONOURED SIR,—So you begin, and therefore so will I. Let us both be honoured, or neither . . . I am glad to find Dr. H—— comes forward in the Magazine. The instance he gives of weak faith is, as he observes, by no means singular. The stoutest believer in the kingdom would find himself as weak, if the Lord were to suspend his influence. I should not say that man who followed and served the Lord, walked honourably in his profession, and overcame the world for a course of many years, was a person of weak faith because he met with conflicts, and was kept short of comfort in his last illness. Faith, perhaps, is never stronger than when it is most tried. Job's faith was not weak when he said, in defiance of all dark appearances, "*Though He slay me, yet will I trust in him.*" Yet, to be sure, faith may be said to be weak, when it cannot depend simply upon the work and promise of the Saviour, without expecting some extraordinary manifestations to confirm its warrant; but this weakness we are all liable to. When we are lively and comfortable in our frames, that is, when we see or feel, then we believe. But though such comfortable manifestations are very desirable, they are not the scriptural evidences of faith, which may be true and even strong without them. The object of faith is Christ; as living, dying, rising, reigning, interceding for sinners. The warrant to believe is the word of God. "This is my beloved Son, hear him:" "Him that cometh to me, I will in *no wise* cast out:" "He is able to save to the uttermost," etc. The proper act of faith is to receive these testimonies, and to cast ourselves on the Saviour, without regarding anything in ourselves but a consciousness that we are unworthy, helpless sinners, and that we are willing and desirous to be saved in this way of God's appointment. The best evidences that we believe are a broken spirit, obedience to the Lord's precepts, submission to his will, and love to his cause and people. Our frames and sensible feelings are like the weather, changeable, and equally out of our power. I should think the doctor's friend was affected by low spirits, or what we call nervous disorders; and these, I well know, are sufficient to hide comfort from us; yea, in many cases, to plunge a strong believer into a state of despair for a season. Thus it is with my dear friend Cowper, who has been miserable, and, to his own apprehension, forsaken of God for many years; though for many years before he was a burning and a shining light, full of alacrity in the Lord's service, and rejoicing in the sunshine of his presence. But in the midst of all these changes, the foundation of God standeth sure. . . .

Now, madam, I come to your part. You write about sickness and death, and fear and unbelief, all sorrowful subjects; but they are familiar to thousands whom you never saw. Such is the lot of mortality, such the nature of the Christian warfare. You ask, When shall I say, My

God? I answer, you will never have better warrant to say so than at present. You will say it, whenever you can trust in his word as much as you would in mine. But we cannot shake off our natural unbelief by any effort of our own. Wait and pray with patience, and He will enable you in due time to call him *yours*. You think if you could do this you should not be alarmed though the mountains were cast into the midst of the sea; but you are mistaken. They whom you think strong in the faith are no less apt to be moved by trifles, if left a little to themselves, than you are. They have nothing inherent, and are only strong as the Lord strengthens them. . . . You see the Lord can work in the darkest places, and by unlooked-for means. He knows how and where to find his lost sheep; and when they begin to seek *him*, they may be sure that He has been beforehand with them, and has sought and found them first. . . .

What you complain of in yourself, comprises the best marks of grace I can offer. A sense of unworthiness and weakness, joined with a hope in the Saviour, constitutes the character of a Christian in this world. But you want the witness of the Spirit; what do you mean by this? Is it a whisper or a voice from heaven, to encourage you to believe that you may venture to hope that the promises of God are true, that He means what He says, and is able to make his word good? Your eyes are opened; you are weary of sin; you love the way of salvation yourself, and love to point it out to others; you are devoted to God, to his cause and people. It was not so with you once. Either you have somewhere stolen these blessings, or you have received them from the Holy Spirit. While you are slow to believe what the Lord has absolutely promised, you are expecting and hankering after what He has not promised.

What He has done for you amounts to the best witness of the Spirit. But there is a spice of legality in you: you want to have something that you might admire in *yourself*; but you will get more solid comfort by looking to Jesus and admiring *him*. Try to be thankful; be as much humbled as you please, but do not expect to be an angel while you are in the body. If you had no feeling of sin in you, why should you confess yourself to be a sinner? Depend upon it, if you walk closely with God forty years, you will at the end of that time have a much lower opinion of yourself than you have now. So Job, at the end of his trials, could say more emphatically than ever, "Behold, I am vile;" and we are sure the latter end of Job was better than his beginning, though that likewise was good.

. . .

I am your affectionate,
JOHN NEWTON.

May 7, 1795.

To Mrs. Coffin.

LETTER V.—Benefits of change—Earthly blessings God's gifts—Arguments against discouragement.

MY DEAR MADAM, . . . I wish you to come, not only from the pleasure I hope for from your company, but upon your own account, for two reasons. First, I hope the change of air and exercise will do your spirits good. Sometimes when nervous people come to me, distressed about their souls, and think *that* is their only complaint, I surprise them by asking if they have no friend in Cornwall, or in the north of Scotland, whom they could visit; for I thought a ride to the Land's End, or John o'Groat's House, might do them more good than all the counsel I could give them. Now if a trip from us to you might be salutary to weak nerves, why not a ride from you to us? Secondly, you would not only breathe a different air, but you would see new faces; you would talk with new people; you would meet with new cases; which, though new to you at first, you would find to be very much like your own. You would likewise have plenty and variety of preaching, which is not amiss for a stranger, and for a season; though I am afraid this over-plenty gives many who live in London a spiritual surfeit. By one or other of these means, or all taken together, I hope, with the Lord's blessing, you would return to Linkinhorne improved in health and spirits, and thereby stronger in faith, and more comfortable than when you set out. . . .

If I had no other food than horse-beans or acorns, it would be better than I deserve; and yet the Lord is pleased to send me many good things in the course of the year. I say, the Lord; for though I thank you for the turkey, I would consider it as his gift likewise. Whatever kindness we show to one another, it is only as his instruments: disposition and ability are both from him. The snow on the tops of mountains is at times very generous, and pours abundance of waters into the valleys; but it is only while the sun shines upon it. When the sun is withdrawn, the snow becomes selfish and niggardly at once, and will not afford another drop: a fit emblem, I think, of how much, or rather how little, may be expected from creatures, further than as they are under his influence. I wish you not to compare yourself with H———, or any one else, but judge by the sure word of God. You see but the *outside* of others, but they have all an *inside* as well as you. A hypocrite seldom suspects himself. I corresponded with H—— through the whole of his dark time, as he calls it, and had as good an opinion of him then as I have now. He has been an honourable professor for many years, and was looked up to by others, when his frame was at the lowest. My good friend, be willing that the Lord should carry on his work in his own way, and do not prescribe to him how He shall deal with you. Only hold fast by the promise, and it will bring you through. I earnestly advise you not to wish for more trouble and disquietude than you have. If the Lord should grant your wish, you would soon be at your wit's end. I doubt not but your conscience bears you witness as to your motives and aims. Be thankful for this. Obedience is the best test of sincerity: feelings are various, transient, and often deceitful; but a broken humble spirit, and an upright walk, evidence the finger of God: other things may be, and are, often counterfeited.

I wish you joy of Miss Jean; for though early impressions are not always, or perhaps often, abiding, they are pleasing and comfortable ones. Many blossoms fall from the tree; but when there are no blossoms we can expect no fruit. The Lord usually knocks again and again at the door, before He enters and takes full possession. Let us pray and hope. May the Lord enclose not only Jean but your whole family, so that there shall not be a hoof left behind. May great grace be with us all.

I am your very affectionate,
JOHN NEWTON.

February 2, 1796.

To Mr. and Mrs. Coffin.

LETTER VI.—On serving God in the ordinary duties of life—Doing what we can.

MY DEAR FRIENDS,—It did indeed give us pleasure to see a testimony of the Lord's goodness to Mrs. Coffin under her own hand. May little David be taught of the Lord, from his early years, to use the sword of the Spirit, the shield of faith, and the sling of prayer, that he may conquer all the lions, bears, and Goliaths which infest this wilderness world. . . .

I wish Mrs. Coffin to consider that a simple desire to please God, to walk by the rule of his word, and to do all to his glory, like the feigned philosopher's stone, turns all to gold, consecrates the actions of common life, and makes everything that belongs to our situation and duty in civil and domestic life a part of our religion. . . . It is an unpleasant mistake to think all the time as lost which is not spent in reading, or hearing sermons, or prayer. These are properly called *means* of grace; they should be attended to in their proper season; but the *fruits* of grace are to appear in our common daily course of conduct. It would be wrong to neglect the house of God: it would be equally wrong to neglect the prudent management of her own house. It is chiefly as a mother and a mistress of a family that she can let her light shine to his praise. I would not have her think that she could serve the Lord better in any other station than in that in which his providence has placed her. I know that family cares are apt to encroach too much, but perhaps we should be worse off without them. The poet says:

> Life's cares are comforts, such by heaven designed :
> He that has none, must make them or be wretched.

At the best, if a contemplative life is more quiet, an active life is more honourable and useful. We have no right to live to ourselves. I do not think our Lord blamed Martha for providing a dinner for himself and his twelve apostles, but I suppose she was too solicitous to have things set off very nicely, and perhaps lost her temper. Methinks I see her breaking in upon him, with her face red with heat and passion, to huff her sister. This was her fault. Had she sent the dinner in quietly, and with a smiling face, I believe He would not have rebuked her for being busy in the kitchen, while He was talking in the parlour. We like to have our own will; but submission to his is the great point. Religion does not consist in doing great things, for which few of us have frequent opportunities, but in doing the little necessary things of daily occurrence with a cheerful spirit, *as to the Lord*. Servants in the apostles' time were slaves, they could have but little time at their own command; books were scarce, and few of them could read. The servants of heathen masters had doubtless much to suffer; yet the apostle expects these poor slaves would adorn the doctrine of God their Saviour, and follow his example in all things. He says, Art thou called, being a slave? Care not for it. If Christ has made you free, the trials of your slavery are scarcely worth your notice. The time is short. You that are now slaves shall soon be equal to angels. And at present you may hope for strength according to your day, and a peace passing understanding, such as the world can neither give nor take away. How much is our situation preferable to that of a slave! The Lord's mercies and favours to *us* are renewed every morning; only He appoints us a daily cross. Shall we not thankfully and patiently bear it for his sake, who bore a dreadful cross for us?

As it is not that which goeth into a man that defileth him, but that which cometh out, so our peace and spiritual progress depend not upon our outward circumstances, but the inward frame of our minds. If the heart be set right, submissive to the will of God, devoted to please him, and depending upon his faithful word, we may be happy in a prison; and otherwise we must be unhappy in a palace. I suppose Eden did not lose all its beauty and verdure the moment when Adam ate the forbidden fruit; but it was no longer Eden to him. He was changed, though the place remained the same: he had lost all relish for it. It matters not whether we live at Linkinhorne or in Coleman Street, so that we are where the Lord would have us to be, and simply yield ourselves to him.

The woman in Mark xiv. had done no very great thing; she had not built or endowed a church or an infirmary, but she had done *what she could*, and our Lord accepted it, not according to her *ability*, but according to her *intention*. He that gives a cup of cold water to a prophet, for the Lord's sake, if it be all he *can* do, shall receive a prophet's reward. The evils of the heart, of which you complain, are not peculiar to you, but common to all who are alive to God. We may be humbled for them, and abhor them, and we ought; but they are inseparable from our present state, and we can no more escape from them than from our skins. But if they are our cross, they shall not be our bane. We have an advocate with the Father, who knows our frame. His blood cleanseth from all sin. May the blessing of the Lord rest upon you and yours.

Very affectionately yours,
JOHN NEWTON.

May 25, 1797.

To Mr. and Mrs. Coffin.

LETTER VII.—Illness of Miss Catlett—Desire to glorify God by submission to his will.

MY DEAR FRIENDS,—Before you read further, I beg you not to be alarmed. I trust all is, and shall be, well. My trial did not spring out of the dust: it is the Lord's doing. He has promised all things shall work together for good; and, blessed be his name, He enables me to hope in his word. Since the removal of my late dear partner, I have had a long halcyon season: my path has been comparatively smooth till lately; but now I have a trial indeed. It is his pleasure to touch me in a tender point. Oh, for grace and strength according to my day! My dear Miss Catlett, my Eliza, who has been long, by the Lord's blessing, the staff and comfort of my old age, is at present laid aside. For a year she has been much troubled with an indigestion. . . . This has lately abated; but the disorder has had an awful effect upon her nervous system (which has always been weak), and, by the Lord's permission, has given Satan an open door to fill her imagination with the *Horribilia de Deo et terribilia de Fide*.* He persuades her that all her former religious profession was hypocrisy; that the Lord has now deserted her, cut her off, and set her up as a mark of his endless displeasure, etc., etc.; and though, a few weeks since, the Lord suddenly dispersed the gloom, and gave such a manifestation of his love and grace as, she said, she had never before experi-

---

* Horrible thoughts concerning God and his word.

enced, nor ever expected, she now says this likewise was delusion. It was indeed short, it lasted not a quarter of an hour; but it has given me much comfort. It was sudden and unlooked for, and showed me what the Lord can do in a moment. At present I think, so far as concerns herself and her own feelings, she is deranged, though, in other things, attentive and sensible. She is always under the immediate apprehension of death, which is very terrible in her state of despondency. I seldom leave her but she says I shall find her a corpse on my return. . . .

I think, if the Lord please, to take her to Reading next week. My friend Mr. Ring lives in a large house and garden, fine air and prospects: he is a medical man. I am willing to use the means; but I believe only the help of him who made heaven and earth, and who raises the dead, can effectually relieve us. I aim to commit her into his faithful hands, and I trust He will *help me* to abide by the surrender I have made, of myself and my all, to him; but I feel too often the workings of unbelief and self-will. I have often told my friends and hearers, when in affliction, that the post of trial is the post of honour. He now appoints me to practise my own lessons. I feel that without him I can do nothing; but may I not humbly hope that I shall do and suffer all things through Christ strengthening me? My life has been a series of wonders, mercies, supports and deliverances, in which I can myself (though I cannot prove it to others) perceive the hand of my Lord, no less clearly than in the miracles He wrought by Moses in Egypt, and at the Red Sea. If after all this I should murmur and distrust, I should imitate the worst part and the worst conduct of the Israelites. Yet this I certainly should do, were He to leave me to myself; but He has said, "My grace is sufficient for thee:" "I will never leave thee:"

"When you walk through floods and flames, I will be with thee;" and

> His every word of grace is strong
> As that which built the skies.

Therefore, though cast down, I am not destroyed. My chief desire on my own account is that I may honour him while in this fire; that I may not stain my character and profession, by impatience, despondence, or any wrong tempers. Then, I trust, this trial will promote his glory and the good of others. When they see that, though we are like the bush (Exodus iii.) we are not consumed, because the Lord is there, it may encourage them to bear their own burdens with submission and hope. Through mercy, when I am in the pulpit, I seem to leave all behind me for the season; and perhaps my trouble may occasion me to preach with more emphasis and earnestness than before. I hope, likewise, it has quickened my spirit in prayer. And who can say how much worse it was sent to preserve me from? Perhaps Satan was spreading a net for my feet, or preparing a spell to lull me to sleep upon the enchanted ground, and the Lord has in this way interposed to disappoint his malice. I cannot doubt but when, hereafter, we look back by a clearer light upon the way we have been led, we shall see cause to number our sharpest afflictions amongst our chief mercies.

My eyes are so dim that I write with difficulty, and cannot easily read my own writing, nor a letter from a friend unless written in a large hand, and with black ink. Now again I sensibly miss my dear secretary. She was indeed my *factotum*. The poor likewise will miss her greatly. To them she was an assiduous and benevolent friend. She delighted to follow her Lord in going about doing good. But all this He knows (Psalm cxlii. 3); yet

He permits, yea, *invites* me, to pour out my heart before him; and He is a God who heareth prayer.* . . .

I long to hear from Linkinhorne. I do not forget you; but we were a month at Walworth, and my attention and time were so divided between my feelings for her, and my calls for service in the City, that I could do little else. . . . May the Lord bless you in all things, and hear our mutual prayer at a throne of grace: yet a little while, and we hope to join our praises before a throne of glory. Worthy is the Lamb that was slain. The Lord bless you both, your children, and your child's child, and Mrs. Walker.

My respects and best wishes to Major Horndon; he has a place in my heart, though I only know him through you and Mr. Storry.

     I am,
      Your very affectionate,
       JOHN NEWTON.

May 8, 1801.

---

* Miss Catlett, the orphan child of Mrs. Newton's brother, Mr. George Catlett, had lived with her uncle and aunt from her early childhood. She was very dear to Mr. Newton, and latterly, as he says, "the staff and comfort of his old age." There is something very touching in the brief entries made in Mr. Newton's *Diary* during his stay at Reading (see *Life*, p. 348). Though Mr. Newton bore this trial in a truly Christian spirit, his sensitive nature was deeply affected by it. His friend, Mr. Bull, saw him about this time, and says, "He is almost overwhelmed with this most awful affliction. I never saw a man so cut up. He is almost broken-hearted." Miss Catlett grew worse, and it was found necessary to place her in Bethlehem Hospital. She was, however, gradually restored to health, and became all to Mr. Newton that she was before her illness.

Thomas Ring, Esq., M.D.

Dr. Ring, of Reading, was a man for many years greatly esteemed and beloved in the town of his residence. Not only was he highly appreciated for his professional ability, but was possessed of great intelligence, of a very genial temper, a heart ever alive to the necessities of others, and above all he was the subject of a deep and consistent piety.

Dr. Ring and his wife were in early life converts of the Hon. and Rev. W. B. Cadogan, and notwithstanding the reproach then attaching to the open profession of the gospel, they at once determined to take up their cross, and to cast in their lot with the people of God. We find an illustration of this in the first of the following letters from Mr. Newton, when a large company were invited to meet him at the house of Dr. Ring, to be present at a religious service; and it was but one of many such occasions. This excellent man lost no suitable opportunity of speaking to others, in his own circle, of their religious interests; nor was he unmindful of the physical and spiritual wants of the poor. It will be readily supposed that Dr. Ring took an interest in the religious and social interests of the town of Reading. We learn that he was the principal founder of the chapel in Castle Street; and it was mainly through his influence that, as St. Mary's chapel, it was afterwards licensed in connexion with the church of England,—a church to which Dr. Ring, was especially attached, though entertaining the most friendly feeling towards other Christian denominations. To his energy, also, it was mainly owing that the Royal Berkshire Hospital was erected. Nor were his interests limited to one particular locality. To all worthy objects he gave his willing aid; but he was especially interested in the efforts of the British and Foreign Bible Society, and of the London Missionary Society. Dr. Ring died in June, 1840, in his eightieth year, rejoicing in the hope of the gospel which he had adorned by his long and consistent life.

It was in the year 1793 that Mr. Newton was first introduced to Dr. and Mrs. Ring, by their mutual friend, Mr. Ambrose Serle. Mr. Newton was afterwards a frequent visitor at Reading, and it was on occasion of one of the religious services above referred to, that he is said to have spoken somewhat as follows, on the words, 1 Cor. xv. 10—" By the grace of God I am what I am." "1. I am not what I ought to be. Ah! how imperfect and deficient. 2. Not what I might be, considering my privileges and opportunities. 3. Not what I wish to be. God, who knows my heart, knows I wish to be like him. 4. I am not what I hope to be; ere long to drop this clay tabernacle, to be like him and see him as He is. 5. Not what I once was, a child of sin, and slave of the devil. Though not all these, not what I ought to be, not what I might be, not what I wish or hope to be, and not what I once was, I think I can truly say with the apostle, 'By the grace of God I am what I am.'"

To Dr. and Mrs. Ring.

LETTER I.—Recollections of the past—Sympathy with his friends in their devotedness to God, and in their religious advantages.

MY DEAR FRIENDS,—I can truly style you so, though upon a short acquaintance. I have reason to believe that the providence of God was signally concerned in leading me to Reading, and particularly to lodge under your hospitable roof. The time I was with you was a very pleasing part of a very pleasing excursion, and I wish to be thankful for it, both to the Lord and you.

I address my letter to you both, because the Lord has made you one not only in relation, but in affection and spirit. The remembrance of my past happiness in wedlock was never more sensibly revived than while I was with you, but I assure you it did not excite in me either pain or envy, but on the contrary, a very sincere pleasure. Oh! that I could see the like in every married pair. The object of my affection is removed, the time is past, but the bare recollection of what it once was, is worth much more than anything else that this poor world can afford. May the Lord maintain, yea, increase, your mutual regard, but may He likewise sanctify it, that you may avoid my sin and my suffering.

It ought to be a lasting source of humiliation to me to remember that my dearest earthly comfort so often proved the occasion of discovering the vileness and ingratitude of my heart in a more striking light than I should, perhaps, otherwise have known it. There is a danger in an over-attachment. It has cost me many a pang; yet, when I think of the apostle's charge, that "Husbands should love their wives as their own flesh, yea, as Christ loved the Church;" these strong expressions lead one to conclude that the danger is not in loving too much, but in loving improperly. When a wife gives her husband her whole heart, she has still room for all her friends and his; and should those friends be increased twenty-fold, still there is room for them all. But there is a peculiar kind of regard which is due to her husband only. If she allows herself to transfer this regard to any other man, though it went no further, it would be criminal. Thus, while we love the Lord supremely we may love our husbands, wives, and children, or friends, as much as we can. But all must be held in subordination and subserviency to what we owe to him, otherwise they will be idols, and we shall be idolaters; and the Lord will, in one way or other, let us know that He is a jealous God, and will not bear a rival. Above all, I congratulate you that the Lord has called you both out of the world, and given you the same views and desires of better things than can be possessed here. This is a mercy which some of his people have not. It often happens that of two in one house, the one is taken and the other left. Had this been your case, had you differed in the most important concerns, the more tenderly you loved each other, the more unhappy you must have been, but great is the privilege of walking together in the way to the kingdom.

Please to give my love to your forty friends, and mine, whom I had the pleasure of meeting in your drawing-room.* When you first spoke of inviting some friends to meet me, I thought they would be only to dinner or tea, and was not in the least aware of the public step you were going to take. I was a little apprehensive of the consequences, but by what I heard and saw, before and after, I am persuaded that it was not the effect of a transient warmth, but that you had deliberately counted the cost, and were willing to let it be known far and near that you had made up your minds, and were determined, by the grace of God, that, whatever others do, you and your house, so far as your influence can prevail, will serve the Lord. In this view I greatly rejoiced in the opportunity, and it pleased me highly to see a room consecrated to him, which, I suppose, has formerly been filled in a very different manner.

We were favoured with a safe and comfortable journey, and reached house about one o'clock. Our servants testified both by words and looks that they were glad to see us. It is a great comfort to be served by those who love us, and it is a comfort which many cannot procure. The Lord only can give it. He it is who maketh people of one mind in a house. A consistency of character, with a

* See the above notice of Dr. Ring.

prudent condescension and kindness to those placed under us are means which seldom fail of some good effect; but when a whole family are united by spiritual ties, and act as under the eye of the same common Master, when the parlour and kitchen are in unison, then domestic order, love, and peace make a family happy indeed.

I have ordered Mr. Robinson's books, and hope they will be with you before the week closes. They will be accompanied by two or three sermons, which I hope you will accept as a peppercorn acknowledgment of my love and thanks.

I hope we had a good sabbath. I preached in the morning from Matt. xiii. 16, 17. This sermon was intended to impress my dear people with a sense of the value of gospel ordinances. This is another privilege, my dear friends, with which the Lord has favoured you. He could keep your souls alive though you lived in the darkest spot, but the lines are fallen to you in a pleasant place, where you have every desirable help for promoting your spiritual progress. May his grace keep you humble and dependent! May you walk before him with a single eye! May you burn and shine and go on from strength to strength! You have great advantages for usefulness to others, and of being happy in each other and in yourselves. Trials will sometimes occur, and vanity will cleave (like the ivy to the oak) to all worldly enjoyments; but the Lord whom you know is all-sufficient, and his promises are sure. I commend you to his blessing. Believe me to be,

Your affectionate and obliged,
JOHN NEWTON.

6, COLEMAN STREET:
October 1, 1793.

To Mrs. Ring.

Letter II.—A tour—God's providence—Preparation for the future—Mr. Simeon—True use of life.

My dear Madam,—I often think with pleasure on the few days I passed with you and Mr. Ring at Reading, and of your kind visit to Coleman Street. As we cannot meet so often as we wish, a little communication must be kept up now and then by letter, though I hope we meet frequently at the throne of grace.

Our tour to Cambridge and its environs was very pleasant. We saw many friends, and I preached at several places. We travelled in safety, and found all well at home. At Bedford, indeed, by a false step, I strained my left knee, so that, for a time, I have had two lame legs, but I would not allow this the name of a trial when set against such a variety of favours and comforts. I can now walk pretty well again. My health is the same as when you saw me. Miss Catlett is likewise well. My servants all well, my friends kind, my spirits good, my cupboard not empty. What more of this world's good can I wish for? I was not nearer to Peterborough than at Great Stukeley, two miles from Huntingdon. I have some acquaintance with Dr. Madan,[*] the present bishop, and believe he loves the truth, and will countenance those who preach it. There is good doing at Cambridge. Mr. Simeon is much beloved and very useful. His conduct has almost suppressed the spirit of opposition which was once very fierce against him. Probably I shall see poor

---

[*] Dr. Spencer Madan, brother of the Rev. Martin Madan, chaplain of the Lock Hospital.

Heckfield * no more; but I am glad that I have seen it. I have a map of the house, gardens, woods, etc., and a long list of pleasing incidents while I was there, drawn or written in my mind. If I had not seen Heckfield I should not have known Mr. Ring, or you, nor should I have been so well acquainted with Mr. Serle and his family, now they are in town, as I hope to be, unless I had first visited them in the country. There is much of the hand of the Lord to be observed and acknowledged in the forming of our connexions. He often leads us by a way we know not.

I am almost six weeks in my seventieth year. It is time for me to think less of going about, and more of going home. I cannot now be far from my journey's end. May the good Lord help me, and you also, to praise him for what is past, and to trust him for what is to come. He appointed the hour of our birth; and the hour of our dismission is with him likewise: whether sooner or later, it will be just at the right time. If it finds us with our loins girt and our lamps burning, and if He who kindled them is pleased to supply us with fresh oil, neither the world, the flesh, nor the powers of darkness shall be able to extinguish them; otherwise they must go out of themselves, for we have no stock of our own. But we need not put an *if* on his faithfulness, provided we are sensible of our weakness, and wait upon him in those means by which He has promised to renew our strength.

Mr. Simeon preached for me last Wednesday from Rev. v. 11, 12, and 13th verses. He spoke of the company, the object of their worship, and their song, I was going to say, as if he had just come down from among them. I think he had a favoured peep within the veil, and there

* The residence of Ambrose Serle, Esq., author of *Horæ Solitariæ*, and *The Christian Remembrancer*.

was such a visible impression on his hearers as is not common. Why are we not aiming to realize that scene when we hope to join them soon, and likewise hope that amongst the thousands and myriads which encompass the throne, "day without night rejoicing," there are some who were intimately near and dear to us? While they were upon earth we sympathized with them in their sorrows, and why not sympathize with them now in their joys? Oh! could we but see them as I believe they see us, it would greatly weaken our sense both of the bitters and the sweets of this poor life; but perhaps it would totally unfit us for attending to the duties of our station. The weakness of our mental frame would not permit us to think of anything but what we saw. This seems to have been the apostle's case (2 Cor. xii.). While he saw invisibles and heard unutterables, he knew not whether he was in or out of the body. We are, therefore, at present to walk not by sight, but by faith. But there is much attainable even here which our unbelief keeps from us. It is comfortable to have a hope of heaven hereafter, but we should desire to have as much of heaven as possible while we are here, to resemble the angels who always do the will of the Lord, and behold his presence. What should we think valuable in this life but to live to him who died for us? We should consider what opportunities our situation, time, abilities, connexions, influence, and substance may afford us for promoting his service, and the good of our fellow-creatures; for verily we are debtors, and whatever is given is more properly entrusted to us, and we should employ them all as good stewards of his manifold blessings. We should aim at the honour and pleasure of being useful, that we may experience the truth of our Lord's aphorism: "It is more blessed to give than to receive." And if we obey with a single eye, and depend upon his grace with a single heart, He will surely favour us with a peace that passeth all understanding, which will keep our hearts and minds composed under all the changes we may pass through on our pilgrimage, and ere long we shall see him as He is, and be with him for ever.

Give our love to all our friends as they come in your way; and when you have distributed all you can for us, we have still abundance of love left for you and Mr. Ring. Let us often pray for each other, that the Lord may fulfil in us all the good pleasure of his goodness, and the work of faith with power.

I am, my dear friend,
Your affectionate and obliged,
JOHN NEWTON.

COLEMAN STREET:
September 16, 1794.

To Mrs. Ring.

LETTER III.—On the death of Mr. Cadogan.

COME, my dear madam, I think you have wept enough. I now write and entreat you to wipe away your tears. You have had a great wound, and you cannot but feel it; but it was not the wound of an enemy. I hope you are now aiming to say, "The will of the Lord be done." This afflictive dispensation did not spring out of the ground, nor happen by chance. It was the appointment of him whose wisdom and love are infinite. He could easily have prevented it, and undoubtedly would, if it was not his purpose to overrule it eventually for good. The removal of Mr. Benamor* was not so public and general a loss as

---

* Mr. Newton's curate, to whom he was much attached, and whom he had been instrumental in bringing forward.

yours, though it touched me very sensibly; but I was soon brought to acquiesce, and to adopt the psalmist's words, "I was dumb and opened not my mouth, because thou didst it."

Your beloved pastor* is gone a little before you. We expect and hope to follow him soon. It will be a joyful meeting when we shall part no more. In the mean time you will do well to consider that he neither did nor could do you any good but as an instrument, and that his Lord and Master who honoured him with acceptance and usefulness still lives, and the supply of the Spirit is still with him. What did the first disciples feel when their Master was not only taken from them, but crucified before their eyes? Yet He had said to them a little before, "It is expedient for you that I go away: the Comforter will come to you." Surely *that* Comforter, whose influence was more than a compensation for the want of the Saviour's visible presence, can fully repair our losses and heal our wounds. And He is as near to his people now, and as willing and able to help them as He was then. The fountain from which dear Mr. Cadogan obtained the water of life, which he communicated to his people, is still full and still flowing; and you are still welcome to come to him and drink. But we are prone to lean too hard upon the ministers by whom the Lord conveys his blessings to us, as if they were necessary. Perhaps to cure us of this mistake is one reason why He often unexpectedly takes them from us. I have been at Reading in spirit almost continually since I first heard the sad news. I was particularly with you on Sunday last. Methought I saw many tears shed and heard many sighs at St. Giles'. I did not blame you. Your loss is great. The first emotions of grief were unavoidable,

* The Hon. and Rev. W. B. Cadogan.

and He who knows our frame allows us that these things for the present are "not joyous but grievous." But neither shall I commend you if you indulge a continuance and excess of grief. Now the Lord has made known his will by the event our part is submission. I pray that you may be willing to be helped, and then I am sure He *will* help you. Say not, "What shall we do?" The Lord has many resources when ours seem wholly to fail. I remember when my friend, Mr. Talbot,* was removed, they who loved him too hastily thought the glory was departed from Reading. They knew not that his successor, whom they at first disliked, was appointed and sent to show them still greater things. I doubt not but every proper step will be taken to obtain a gospel minister. It is possible the Lord may send one who as yet knows not the gospel, to learn it from its gracious effects on Mr. Cadogan's people, and the same work may still be carried on by another hand. If He is pleased to keep them together in a spirit of union, love, and prayer I shall entertain great hopes. A patient waiting upon the Lord in prayer has often done wonders; for He is able to do more than we can ask or think.

Your affectionate and obliged,
JOHN NEWTON.

COLEMAN STREET :
    January 25, 1797.

    * The predecessor of Mr. Cadogan at St. Giles'.

The Hon. and Rev. W. B. Cadogan.

THE Honourable W. B. Cadogan was the second son of Lord Cadogan. Being designed for the church, he was educated at Oxford, where he obtained literary honours, and was not altogether unmindful of the important work before him. Upon the living of St. Giles' at Reading becoming vacant by the death of the Rev. W. Talbot, Mr. Cadogan was presented to it by the Chancellor, Lord Bathurst. Mr. Cadogan's views of religion were entirely different from those of his predecessor; and the people heard of his appointment with grief. Their hope, was, however, that he might be willing to retain the services of Mr. Hallward, Mr. Talbot's curate. But this he resolutely refused. Many left the church. Mrs. Talbot, however, considered it her duty to remain, hoping for a better state of things, and that she might encourage and help forward those to whom her husband's labours had been blessed. She opened her house for religious services, and invited clergymen like-minded with herself to conduct them. At the same time prayer was continually offered up under her roof for Mr. Cadogan's conversion. By all this he was greatly offended. Letters passed full of remonstrance and even reproach on Mr. Cadogan's part, but which Mrs. Talbot answered with meekness and wisdom. Mr. Cadogan was overcome, and ever afterwards confessed that Mrs. Talbot's letters and example were the principal means of leading him to the saving knowledge of Christ. And now the vicar of St. Giles', renouncing all hopes of preferment in the church for Christ's sake, preached those truths which heretofore he had so strenuously opposed. He became most diligent in doing good, and was so popular that multitudes flocked to hear him, and the esteem of his congregation almost bordered on veneration. He established Sunday schools, was exemplary in the performance of his pastoral duty, and benevolent beyond his means. In a word, he was mindful of the apostle's injunction to Archippus, he took heed to his ministry and fulfilled it. But in the midst of these labours, in the forty-sixth year of his age, he was seized with illness, and in a few days entered into the joy of his Lord.

To the Hon. and Rev. W. B. Cadogan.

LETTER I.—*Desire to visit him—God's wondrous grace in calling men to his service, and keeping them faithful in it.*

MY DEAR SIR,—Your kind reception of me would be sufficient, independently of my great regard for Mrs. Talbot, to make me rejoice in an opportunity of visiting you again. I thank you, however, for renewing your obliging invitation. I can honestly say inclination has not been wanting, and could I have transported myself with a wish you would have seen me again. There is no place where I could think of spending a few days with more pleasure than at Reading. But though I have several agreeable connections in the country, I am somehow precluded from them all; and, if I had time to visit one, and but one, I should perhaps be under a difficulty to determine to which I could give the preference without appearing ungrateful to the rest. There are reasons, perhaps, why I ought to give some preference to the people among whom I laboured so long at Olney. But I have not been able to see them this year, and I usually make them a sort of plea to excuse myself to other friends, who have a right to expect that I should not slight their kindness. Should I live to feel the warmth of summer suns again, I will watch the motion of the cloud and pillar of fire in hopes that they may lead me to Reading. Without some concurring circumstances to intimate that the Lord opens my way I cannot move with liberty.

I rejoice in the Lord's goodness to the town of Reading, and congratulate you that He has conferred on you an honour which I am persuaded you esteem far greater than any you can derive from family, the high honour of being his servant in the gospel. He has likewise given you a wisdom far superior to what bears that name among men, for he has made you "wise to win souls." There is a great diversity of cases amongst his people; but they all (and perhaps all equally) illustrate the power of his grace and the riches of his mercy. What a difference between your case and mine. I, though long a ringleader in blasphemy and wickedness, was spared, and though banished into the wilds of Africa, where I was the sport, yea the pity of slaves, I was, by a series of providences little less than miraculously recovered from that house of bondage, and at length appointed to preach the faith I had long laboured to destroy. Possibly the annals of the Church will not furnish an instance in all respects parallel. But your case is likewise singular. Your birth, early habits, connexions and prospects in life, and I suppose your character also, were such bars in the way of your happiness and usefulness, as nothing less than the power of God could break through. I suppose you are the only person in the kingdom so closely related to a noble family who is able or willing to preach the gospel of Christ, and to glory in the cross of our Lord. Thus that line, "Oh, to grace how great a debtor," is applicable to us both; and you, as well as I can declare, not merely from hearsay, but from experience, that the grace of our Lord Jesus Christ is exceeding abundant. In one respect I ought to be more affected with a sense of this grace than you can be on the same ground. I have been longer in the way than you. I cannot exactly ascertain when I saw so much of the gospel as to enable me to venture myself upon it for salvation, but I think it is more than thirty years since. Oh, sir, in the course of these years, what awful proofs I have had, and have given, of the deceitfulness and vileness of my heart. What wretched returns of my ingratitude and perverseness I have made for mercies received, is known only to him who has borne with me. Much of this dark part of my story I have forgotten, but I remember enough to fill me with shame. It is true that, as to my outward profession, I have been preserved from making any considerable blots, but this enhances the wonder and the mercy; for I am conscious to myself of hair-breadth escapes from such entanglements as might and would, without the Lord's interposition, have issued in final apostacy. And in this space of time, how many whom I had reason to esteem better than myself have I seen fall (some I fear to rise no more), while I am still left to speak of his mercy. I have seen enough to remind me of the difference of setting out, and holding out to the end, and to warn me that we can have no security from gifts, labours, services, or sufferings, from clear views, or past experiences; but that from first to last our only safety is in the power, compassion, and faithfulness of our great Redeemer.

That the Lord may daily add to your comfort and success, may make you as a well-watered garden in your own soul, and a never failing spring to convey the water of life to multitudes, is my sincere prayer.

An hour of leisure which I cannot always command, and the pleasure I feel in writing to you, have insensibly drawn me beyond the usual bounds of a first letter, but I shall enlarge no further than to offer my respects and Mrs. Newton's.

Your much obliged and affectionate servant,
JOHN NEWTON.

HOXTON: *November* 5, 1782.

To the Hon. and Rev. W. B. Cadogan.

Letter II.—Value of afflictions to a minister.

My dear Sir,—Now the road of correspondence is opened between us, how should I pester you with letters, were my leisure proportioned to my inclination; but the throng of engagements around me will, in a good measure, secure you from my importunity. . . .

It was with much concern that I heard of your illness. The importance and seasonableness of your visitation I could learn only from yourself. Every day almost I meet with occasions of admiring the wisdom, care and faithfulness of our Great Shepherd intimating and adjusting his dispensations exactly to our need and state. When the enemy is spreading a snare for our feet, when our deceitful hearts are beginning to start aside, when we have perhaps actually taken some steps in that path, which if persisted in might terminate in apostasy, Oh! then how gracious, how seasonable, how salutary are those tokens of love (called affliction in the language of mortals), which He sends to break the snare, to check our progress, and to recall our wandering feet into the path of duty and peace. How many turns of my life can I recollect of which, though at the time they were not joyous but grievous, I may now say, *Nisi periissem, periissem.*"* I rejoice to think that you were delivered before I knew your danger. Could I have known how it was with you my concern and anxiety would have been great. What the Lord appeared to have done for you and by you had given you a near place in my heart, and nothing appears to me so awful as a minister, who having given for a time proofs of a zeal for God and love for souls, afterwards declines and dies away

---

* Unless I had perished, I had perished.

from the good cause. Oh! my dear sir, ought we not, and by the grace of God shall we not think it vastly more desirable to be afflicted with all the afflictions of Job, to be stoned to death, or to be buried alive, rather than to be left to such a conduct as might stumble the weak and encourage the wicked? I may congratulate you upon your danger likewise, now it is happily over. Perhaps the Lord saw that such an experience was no more than needful to preserve you from other dangers to which your situation, talents, and services might expose you. Whatever we seem to be in the eyes of man, we are nothing in his sight further than we are humbled and abased in our own. It requires much discipline to keep pride down in us, even considered only as Christians, more as ministers, still more as ministers conspicuous for ability and usefulness; and, when the appendages of family and influence are added, the temptations to self-importance are still increased. Such persons will have many admirers, many friends, not a few flatterers, but perhaps very few such friends as will have the courage to give plain and faithful advice, especially as the rules which politeness and decorum (so called), have established, form a fence which is not easily broken through; but the Lord by leaving you a little to yourself, has provided you with something to reflect on, which I trust will be a sanctified means of keeping you less dependent upon yourself. There is none teacheth like him. Hereby likewise you will be more sensibly aware of the dangers and difficulties to which your hearers are liable. You will be better able both to warn them of the snares in their way, and to encourage and comfort them when they are desirous to return. Thus He speaks to all in what He said to Peter (Luke xxii.), "Simon Simon, Satan hath desired to have you that he may sift you as wheat, but I have prayed for thee that thy faith fail not." The doctrinal parts of our message are in some degree familiar to us, but that which gives a savour, fulness, energy, and variety to our ministrations is the result of many painful conflicts and exercises which we pass through in our private walk, combined with the proofs we receive, as we go along, of the Lord's compassion and mercies under all the perverseness and folly we are conscious of in ourselves. It is only in this school of experience that we can acquire the tongue of the learned and know how to speak a word in season to those that are weary. Thus by his wise arrangement, "Out of the eater cometh meat." He breaketh the heads of the leviathan in pieces, and teaches us to get food from them, and we are strengthened and established by the very plots our enemy formed to entangle and overthrow us. Well may we say, Who is a God like unto Thee?

The other night I buried the wife of a friend of mine. They were remarkably happy in each other, and she has left him with four children, the eldest under four years of age. He sensibly feels the loss, but has been wonderfully supported. He told me that he knows not if he was ever so comfortable in his soul as since her death, and that he is so perfectly satisfied with the Lord's wisdom and goodness in removing her, that were it possible by a single wish to restore her to her former place, he could not form it.

I have just left room for the seal of a tender of Mrs. Newton's respects, and to subscribe myself,

    Dear Sir,

      Your affectionate and much obliged,

          JOHN NEWTON.

HOXTON: *October* 22, 1782.

www.ingramcontent.com/pod-product-compliance
Lightning Source LLC
Chambersburg PA
CBHW022109290426
44112CB00008B/612